DARTNELL'S 30TH SALES FORCE COMPENSATION SURVEY

Dartnell is a publisher serving the world of business with books, manuals, newsletters and bulletins, and training materials for executives, managers, supervisors, salespeople, financial officers, personnel executives, and office employees. Dartnell also produces management and sales training videos and audiocassettes, publishes many useful business forms, and many of its materials and films are available in languages other than English. Dartnell, established in 1917, serves the world's business community. For details, catalogs, and product information, write to:

THE DARTNELL CORPORATION
4660 N Ravenswood Ave
Chicago, IL 60640-4595, U.S.A.
or phone (800) 621-5463 in U.S. and Canada

This publication is designed to provide accurate and authoritative information in regard to the subject matter covered. It is sold with the understanding that the publisher is not engaged in rendering legal, accounting, or other professional service. If legal advice or other expert assistance is required, the services of a competent professional person should be sought.

—From a Declaration of Principles jointly
adopted by a Committee of the American Bar
Association and a Committee of Publishers.

Copyright 1999
in the United States, Canada, and Britain by
THE DARTNELL CORPORATION

ISBN 0-85013-344-0

Library of Congress Catalog Card Number 98-73769

CONTENTS

LISTING OF FIGURES

ABOUT THE AUTHOR

Christen P. Heide, executive editor for sales and marketing publications at The Dartnell Corporation, is also the author of *Dartnell's 29th Sales Force Compensation Survey* (1996), *Dartnell's 28th Sales Force Compensation Survey* (1994), and *Dartnell's 27th Sales Force Compensation Survey* (1992). He is a respected speaker and writer on the topics of sales compensation and sales force management. His articles have

appeared in such publications as *Advertising Age* and *Marketing News*, and he is widely quoted in the business presss as a sales and marketing authority. Heide is an expert on contemporary issues in compensation and has been a featured sales compensation speaker at several national conferences. He is the editor of Dartnell's *Sales and Marketing Executive Report* and former editor of *Marketing Times*, the official publication of Sales and Marketing Executives International (SMEI). He is also a former board member of SME-Chicago.

THE DARTNELL CORPORATION

One of the world's leading producers and distributors of business information and training materials, Dartnell has been a recognized source for the best in sales training and information for more than seventy years. Sales managers have counted on the Dartnell Sales Force Compensation Survey for current, accurate data since 1929. Today, Dartnell offers books, manuals, newsletters, audiocassettes, and films and videos for diverse business audiences on a variety of important business topics.

ACKNOWLEDGMENTS

Many people contributed their time and effort to the 30th edition of this survey. The prompt, accurate completion of the survey questionnaires was the vital first step, and the author is grateful to the participants.

In addition, the author wishes to acknowledge the considerable data preparation work of Ron Metz and Annette Salapatek.

Also thanks to Hal Fahner, former Vice President of Corporate Marketing, Blue Cross & Blue Shield of Florida, for his insights on aligning the corporate business plan with the compensation plan; to William Atkinson, for his work in interviewing sales executives for the material in Section 14; and to Leo Witkoski, a sales management authority with Meenan Oil Company, Upper Darby, Pennsylvania, for his thoughts on using statistical analysis for increased sales success.

Additional thanks to the Dartnell team members who contributed their time and effort to this project: Biff Johnson, information systems manager; Megan Mulligan, production manager; Andrew Epstein, creative director, Amy Flammang, page formatting; Annie Chesney, survey coordination and tabulation of supplemental survey results; and Anne Garry, who checked final pages.

PART ONE — OVERVIEW

WELCOME TO OUR 30TH SURVEY EDITION!

You are about to embark on an adventure that will take you through all the nooks and crannies of what it takes to succeed in sales today. This 30th edition of *Dartnell's Sales Force Compensation Survey* puts a treasure trove of up-to-date, hard-to-find sales compensation and sales management information together in an easy-to-use, reader-friendly format. In these pages, you'll find a wealth of facts, figures, and commentary that will enable you to create a complete picture of today's professional salesperson.

This edition is also one of our most comprehensive to date: More than 650 companies employing a total of more than 55,000 salespeople participated in this survey. In addition, the results of supplemental data collection efforts help provide a detailed "snapshot" of what's really going on in the selling arena today.

WHAT'S THE SAME

This edition of the survey uses the same formats for data tables as used in the previous three editions, enabling you to compare our most recent findings with earlier data. As in the past, all charts contained are self-explanatory, allowing you to quickly pinpoint the data you need and put it to use in your programs. Thanks to heavy participation in this survey, we are again able to provide geographic breakouts for selected sections of the data.

Textual passages from the previous edition have been retained where the material has not changed over the last survey period. Throughout this edition, the text has been carefully reviewed and updated; however some text and hypothetical examples illustrating common compensation practices have been retained to maintain continuity between editions.

To make it easy for users of this survey to see exactly what kinds of companies are represented, we are again listing survey participants by 4-digit Standard Industrial Classification (SIC) codes. This listing can be found in Section 15.

WHAT'S NEW

This edition contains two new sections that will help you better understand compensation issues.

In Section 13, "Aligning Your Compensation Plan with Your Business Plan," we take a look at some of the basics of business planning and compensation plan design so you can get more out of your compensation plan. All too often, sales executives regard the sales compensation plan as an expense item to be justified instead of as a tool to increase profits. This section will show you how to turn your plan into a profit-producing machine.

In Section 14, "Trends in Sales Compensation: What Enlightened Companies Are Doing to Boost Performance," we present 12 case histories. These case histories examine the compensation plans of companies in a variety of industries to see how others have leveraged their plans to boost performance. These examples may well give you additional idea on how you can adjust your pay plan to make it even more effective.

We also have collected a wide variety of sample compensation plans to help you generate ideas for your own compensation plan. Often, seeing what others are doing can point us in the right direction. You can find these compensation plans at **http://www.dartnellcorp.com/sfcomp.html**

This edition also takes a look at what's going on in the field — what salespeople tell us about the important issues affecting them. These issues include:

- Whether technology is simplifying — or complicating — their work.
- Whether they are using the Internet — and, if so, how?
- If they think their sales compensation plan is fair.
- If they feel they are paid fairly, underpaid, or overpaid.
- Whether more compensation would make them more productive.
- How they respond when they see dishonesty in the field.
- The kinds of dishonesty they see in the business world.
- How they rank a variety of common nonfinancial incentives.

In the more than 70 years that Dartnell has tracked sales compensation and sales performance issues, our aim has always been to provide sales and marketing executives with an indispensable tool to improve the productivity of their sales forces as well as the bottom line of their companies. We think you will agree that this edition of *Dartnell's Sales Force Compensation Survey* delivers on this promise.

SURVEY METHODOLOGY

This survey report presents the results of *Dartnell's 30th Sales Force Compensation Survey*, collected from organizations through mailed questionnaires. The survey focuses on sales productivity, sales management, and sales compensation, and spans 10 levels of sales executives, managers, and representatives. In addition, we have collected information on incentive plan design practices, benefits, training, and expense practices.

SURVEY PARTICIPANTS

Our continuing efforts to broaden survey participation have led to increases in both the number and the average size of participating companies. The current survey data has been collected from more than 650 companies in more than 30 industries. (See Section 15 for a 4-digit Standard Industrial Classification [SIC] code listing of the various types of companies represented in this survey.)

Some companies had more than one sales force reporting and in those cases we counted each different sales force as an individual participant.

GROUPINGS OF PARTICIPANTS

Because sales issues are often significantly influenced by industry type, we have segmented the data by industry (SIC) code. However, we have found that many issues also tend to be driven by other broader groupings. Thus, in addition to industry groupings, we also have segmented much of the data by type of buyer (industry, consumers, retailers, and wholesalers/distributors/jobbers); by type of product or service sold (industrial, office, or consumer); and by organization size, as reflected by total annual sales volume. Data for an organization that sells to several buyer types (or that sells a combination of products and services) is reported under each type for that grouping, but only once in the overall survey results. We believe that these additional groupings will improve the usefulness of the survey results, especially for those industries with thin representation.

Often, a small amount of representative information is better than none at all. However, in order to ensure the confidentiality of the responses of any individual participant, we do not report data for any particular category with fewer than seven companies submitting information.

SURVEY POSITIONS

We asked survey participants to match positions in their sales forces to the 10 positions described in the questionnaire. Matches are based primarily on the positions' responsibilities, as well as on reporting relationships and frequently used titles. (Position descriptions can be found in Section 5 — "Content Summary" — and again in Section 15.)

ABOUT THE SURVEY DATA

The collection of data for this survey took place during the spring of 1998. Base salary data is effective as of January 1, 1998. Incentives which were earned in 1997 may have been paid in 1998.

COMPENSATION DATA

Participants were asked to report the average level of base salary, annual incentive, and total cash compensation for each survey position. For positions with more than one individual in the position, we asked each survey respondent for the third-quartile and highest levels as well. In general terms, the average, third-quartile, and highest figures reflect those compensation levels paid to the average, better, and best-performing salespeople in a sales force. (For an in-depth discussion of the terminology used in this survey, see Section 5 — "Content Summary.")

The following chart provides a breakout of responding companies:

	PERCENTAGE OF COMPANIES
COMPANY SIZE	
UNDER $5 MILLION	30.2%
$5MM–$25MM	36.9
$25MM–$50MM	10.8
$50MM–$100MM	8.6
$100MM–$250MM	5.7
$250MM–$500MM	2.4
$500MM–$1B	2.6
$1B–$2B	1.1
$2B–$5B	0.7
$5B OR MORE	1.0
PRODUCT OR SERVICE*	
CONSUMER PRODUCTS	32.0
CONSUMER SERVICES	32.0
INDUSTRIAL PRODUCTS	47.0
INDUSTRIAL SERVICES	36.1
OFFICE PRODUCTS	20.7
OFFICE SERVICES	26.6
COMBINED PRODUCTS	18.9
COMBINED SERVICES	20.2
TYPE OF BUYER*	
CONSUMERS	71.5
DISTRIBUTORS	33.4
INDUSTRY	36.9
RETAILERS	40.0
COMBINED	48.5
AREA OF DISTRIBUTION	
LOCAL	13.7
REGIONAL	27.6
NATIONAL	28.3
INTERNATIONAL	30.4

*TOTAL EQUALS MORE THAN 100% DUE TO MULTIPLE RESPONSES.

We are again providing geographic breakouts for selected portions of the data. (See Section 11.) Geographic breakouts of this data were made possible due to the large number of survey participants. Users of this survey are cautioned, however, that small "cuts" of the data can yield figures that are nonrepresentative and unreliable. Our level of response from some geographic regions was extremely small, and readers are urged to use this data with a large dose of good judgment. On the other hand, it is worth noting that data from geographic areas that are poorly represented nonetheless "makes sense" when compared with our national averages. The geographic data in this survey, then, is best used to indicate possible trends and relationships between other regions of the country.

The percentages of respondents from the nine selected geographic regions of the United States are as follows:

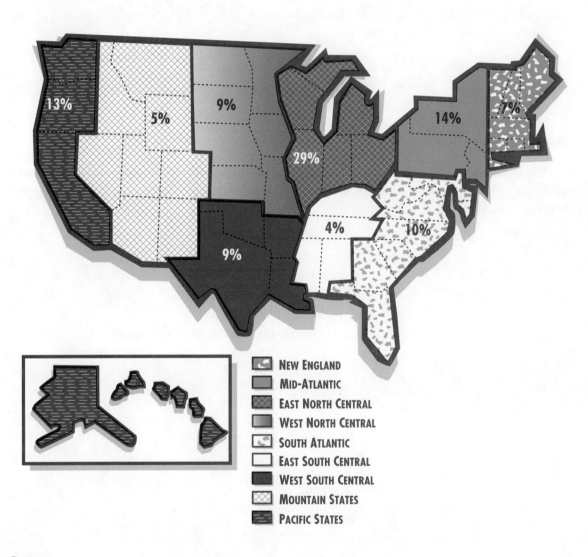

Legend:
- NEW ENGLAND
- MID-ATLANTIC
- EAST NORTH CENTRAL
- WEST NORTH CENTRAL
- SOUTH ATLANTIC
- EAST SOUTH CENTRAL
- WEST SOUTH CENTRAL
- MOUNTAIN STATES
- PACIFIC STATES

REGION

NEW ENGLAND	MID-ATLANTIC	EAST NORTH CENTRAL
CONNECTICUT	NEW JERSEY	ILLINOIS
MAINE	NEW YORK	INDIANA
MASSACHUSETTS	PENNSYLVANIA	MICHIGAN
NEW HAMPSHIRE		OHIO
RHODE ISLAND		WISCONSIN
VERMONT		

REGION

WEST NORTH CENTRAL	**SOUTH ATLANTIC**	**EAST SOUTH CENTRAL**
IOWA	DELAWARE	ALABAMA
KANSAS	FLORIDA	KENTUCKY
MINNESOTA	GEORGIA	MISSISSIPPI
MISSOURI	MARYLAND	TENNESSEE
NEBRASKA	NORTH CAROLINA	
NORTH DAKOTA	SOUTH CAROLINA	
SOUTH DAKOTA	VIRGINIA	
	WASHINGTON, D.C.	
	WEST VIRGINIA	

REGION

WEST SOUTH CENTRAL	**MOUNTAIN STATES**	**PACIFIC STATES**
ARKANSAS	ARIZONA	ALASKA
LOUISIANA	COLORADO	CALIFORNIA
OKLAHOMA	IDAHO	HAWAII
TEXAS	MONTANA	OREGON
	NEVADA	WASHINGTON
	NEW MEXICO	
	UTAH	
	WYOMING	

NOTE TO USERS OF THIS SURVEY

All users of the survey are invited to suggest improvements that will make future editions even more useful tools for assessing sales force effectiveness. Please direct your comments and observations to:

The Dartnell Corporation
4660 N. Ravenswood Ave.
Chicago, IL 60640–4595
Telephone: (800) 621-5463
Fax: (773) 561-4842
E-mail: cheide@dartnellcorp.com

How to Use This Survey

Although it might be tempting to just start thumbing through the charts and data tables presented in this survey, we suggest you read through this section as well as Section 4 ("Executive Summary") and Section 5 ("Content Summary") first. These sections provide a quick overview of our survey results and define the terminology used.

This survey consists of much more than compensation data; it holds a wealth of information on how seemingly disparate elements affect the dynamics of the day-to-day selling job. Readers who take the time to understand how this data interrelates will gain a much better understanding of how sales forces operate.

How the Data Tables Are Constructed

Following is a discussion of how the data tables are constructed. At the conclusion of that discussion is a typical example of how to apply the survey data to a common situation. We suggest you spend some time familiarizing yourself with the concepts and techniques involved in understanding the data before drawing conclusions from this data.

The data tables in this survey are self-explanatory; however, here are some guidelines you can use when analyzing compensation figures for your organization. Additional guidelines are presented in front of each series of compensation tables in the survey. (Also see Section 5 for a discussion of the terminology used in this survey.)

Compensation data for position levels covered in this survey is presented in a variety of ways to enable you to look at those separate segments of the data that are most pertinent to your own situation.

Figures 10 to 19

Figures 10 to 19 provide average total cash compensation by plan type and all plans used. If you are analyzing compensation paid on an all-incentive plan or all-salary plan, these tables provide a complete picture of total compensation paid. They additionally include data for salary and incentive compensation for those salespeople on a combination plan.

Bear in mind, however, that compensation data for combination plans on this series of tables includes figures that encompass our entire range of responses. In other words, for users of combination plans, these tables report data that includes *all levels of salespeople, regardless of ability, and all companies, regardless of whether they are average-paying or higher-paying companies*. Additional compensation tables provide further breakouts for those companies using a combination plan.

Figures 20 to 29

Figures 20 to 29 provide average total cash compensation figures for *average*, *better*, and *best* performers. Additionally, this data is reported for typical-paying (*"median"*) companies and higher-paying (*"third-quartile"*) companies. (See Section 5 for definitions of the previous italicized words and terms.) These tables provide average total cash compensation broken out by company size, product or service sold, type of buyer, and industry for average, better, and best performers in median and third-quartile ranges. Although these tables will give you total cash compensation figures, you will still need to break the total cash compensation figure into its base salary and incentive components. Figures 30 to 39 will help you determine base salary levels for combination plans.

FIGURES 30 TO 39

After you have determined total cash compensation for those positions paid on a combination plan, use Figures 30 to 39 to determine average base salaries. These figures are again broken out by company size, product or service sold, type of buyer, and industry for average, better, and best performers. The difference between average total cash compensation and average base salary is the average amount of incentive paid.

FIGURES 40 TO 47

Figures 40 to 47 focus on average sales volume for average, better, and best performers and the percentage premium paid to better and best performers. These tables are discussed in greater detail elsewhere in this report.

FIGURES 48 TO 57

To compare sales compensation and volume levels for the average of the median range of responses, you will want to consult Figures 48 to 57. These tables provide average total cash compensation for all plans combined and sales volume figures broken out for company size, product or service sold, type of buyer, and industry for average, better, and best performers.

FIGURES 58 TO 67

In order to provide a look at the higher range (third-quartile) responses, we have included Figures 58 to 67, which examine the relationship between total cash compensation for all plans combined and sales volume for the third-quartile level. If your company is higher-paying, you will want to consult these tables for a look at the upper range of survey responses.

Finally, in each section where data tables appear, a breakout of the data is provided wherever possible by company size, type of products or services sold, type of buyer of those products or services, as well as by specific industry group. Often a small amount of representation is better than none at all. However, in order to ensure the confidentiality of the responses of any individual participant, we do not report data for any particular category with fewer than seven companies submitting information.

PUTTING THE DATA TO WORK — AN EXAMPLE

So what does all this mean to us? The following example may help clarify any concepts that remain unclear.

Example: You're a sales manager for an electronics company that has annual gross sales of around $15 million. You want to see if your senior salespeople are being compensated at, above, or below the industry average. You use a combination plan (base salary plus incentive) for your senior salespeople.

How to proceed: There are several ways or combinations of ways to approach this problem. You may decide, for example, that you're interested in taking a look at how similar size companies in a variety of industries compensate their senior salespeople so that you can get a general idea of prevailing compensation levels. This step will enable you to see whether your particular industry is higher- or lower-paying than the general average for your size of company.

Looking at Figure 14, you see that other firms in your company's size category pay their senior salespeople who are on a combination plan $41,300 in salary and another $24,100 in incentive for a total of $65,400. You also see in Figure 14 that there is an industry breakout for the electronics industry. (General classifications of types of companies represented in the industry breakouts can be found in Section 15.) Here you note that senior reps on a combination plan earn $40,500 in salary and $25,600 in incentive for a total of $66,100 — a little higher than the median pay for companies in your size range. Remember that the figures on this table encompass our entire range of responses and include all levels of salespeople, regardless of ability, and all companies, regardless of whether they are average-paying or higher-paying companies.

We need to see if we can refine the data a bit. Moving to Figure 24, Average Total Cash Compensation for Senior Sales Reps, you see that senior salespeople in your company's size range ($5 million to $25 million) earn between $55,000 and $82,000 annually. This gives us the range of responses from average performer to best performer. In other words, this is the compensation a senior salesperson on a combination plan could expect to earn in an average company with annual sales of $5 million to $25 million, depending, of course, on the variables of industry, geographic location, salesperson ability, and so on.

When you look at your particular industry — in this case, the electronics industry — you see a total compensation range of $70,000 to $100,000 annually. Looking at Figure 24, you easily can see the progression of compensation from average performer to best performer. Because the compensation range by size of company and by industry is similar, you now have two "benchmarks" to work with. But based on our research thus far, it is clear that the electronics industry is higher-paying than many industries.

If your company is "higher-paying," you'll want to take a look at Figure 62, Sales Compensation and Volume Levels—Third Quartile—Senior Sales Reps. This table provides a look at the higher range of responses.

You also might want to refer to Section 11 to compare overall compensation differences based on geographic sections of the country. Generally speaking, overall compensation tends to be higher in the New England and Mid-Atlantic states than in the South Atlantic, East South Central, and Mountain States. (See Section 11 for more detail.)

All surveys are based on extremes — in other words, a full range of responses is analyzed to determine what compensation levels are most likely to be paid by similar companies not participating in the survey and provide guidelines to help you determine compensation levels. Use your own judgment when applying these figures to your own organization.

This survey provides thorough breakouts of the data to enable you to examine certain segments of responses. Your figures will differ based on the particular idiosyncrasies of your own company, its geographic location, and other factors. In looking at the range of data, however, you will be able to determine how your company compares with other companies of similar size in a similar industry.

As mentioned previously, all the data tables contained in this survey are self-explanatory. Many of the tables that do not deal directly with compensation data include a brief commentary noting changes over the last survey period. It is suggested that all this data be carefully considered when making judgments based on the material in this survey.

A word of caution: Survey results are generated from a collection of widely varying responses and are therefore based on extremes. The data presented here is intended to provide guidelines as to prevailing practices and emerging trends.

It is not uncommon for us to receive calls from individual salespeople wanting to know exactly how much they should be making in their particular companies — or how much of a raise they should ask for during their annual reviews. No survey can provide that kind of specific information.

All companies of a similar size in a similar industry do not pay their salespeople exactly the same. If that were the case, you'd already know how much everyone in your industry was paying for each survey position. Although this may seem obvious, it's worth mentioning if only to remind users of this survey that all data contained within the survey should be applied with good judgment.

Executive Summary

Senior salespeople have something to cheer about! The booming U.S. economy has helped boost senior sales rep earnings 6.8 percent over the past two years. Average annual earnings for senior salespeople now stand at $68,000, according to our new survey data.

Intermediate reps (those with one to three years of sales experience) and entry level sales reps fared less well. Intermediate reps earn $46,000 per year, the same figure we reported two years ago. Entry level reps now earn $35,000, a loss of 2.7 percent over the survey period. (Note: Compensation figures represent the median of average pay as reported by survey respondents.) Chart 1 summarizes these findings:

CHART 1

Position	Median 1996 Total Cash Compensation	Median 1998 Total Cash Compensation	% Difference
Senior Rep	$63,700	$68,000	6.8%
Intermediate Rep	46,000	46,000	0%
Entry Level Rep	36,000	35,000	(2.7%)

Although senior salespeople appear to be meeting the challenges of selling in an increasingly complex marketplace, intermediate and entry level reps need to "get up to speed."

What's Changed

1. Downsizing. Over the past few years, many buyer/seller relationships have changed. Corporate restructuring has changed how companies conduct business. Longtime relationships between salespeople and purchasing agents have been altered, and new faces on both sides of the desk have slowed down the selling process.

Success strategy: Make sure your reps network within companies to establish and maintain relationships with all those involved in the buying process.

2. Partnering. As companies reduce the number of suppliers they do business with, the more difficult it has become to unseat the competition. More and more companies have won long-term contracts as a firm's favored or single supplier. This has simplified the selling process for preferred companies. But any lapses in quality or service that result in the loss of such accounts will have a greater negative impact on the bottom line.

Success strategy: Make sure your reps perform "added-value" activities within such accounts to reinforce your company's leadership position. One caution: Buyers will continue to look for the best value at the best price. This means that today's added value will become tomorrow's expected value. Make sure you will still be able to compete without sacrificing profit margins.

3. Cost cutting. Even though the economy is booming, companies are still watching their pennies. Waste will not be tolerated by corporate management. All expenditures — routine and big-ticket — will have to be accounted for. Purchasing agents continue to be held accountable for what they buy. Quality, price, and delivery are all items to pay special attention to in the presentation of products and services.

Success strategy: Make sure your salespeople clearly quantify any savings, such as time, money, or labor, in terms the buyer can understand. Your reps also should make sure the buyer can communicate these ideas to other influential people in the company. Your salespeople need to work with buyers as partners in business to develop trusting working relationships that will endure.

4. Technology. In just a few short years, the Internet has changed how buyers gather information. Salespeople often find they are presenting the same information their competitors are presenting. This is often the same information the buyer has just downloaded from the Internet. The result: Buyers no longer rely on salespeople the way they did in the past.

Success strategy: Your reps will need to think one step beyond the competition and mine little-known information sources. They will need to refocus on the individual needs of the customer and present unique solutions to "common" problems.

ADDITIONAL SURVEY HIGHLIGHTS

Figure 1 on page 20 presents the Dartnell Profile of the American Sales Professional. Please note that the figures are national averages; more detailed breakouts can be found on the tables indicated and elsewhere in this survey.

Average age of salespeople: The average age of today's sales professional is 37.5 years old and has not varied significantly over the last several editions of the survey.

Women in the sales force: Women continue to have a significant impact on the sales profession and now represent 24.3 percent of the total number of salespeople in this year's survey.

Education: The educational level of today's sales professional is higher now than at any time in the history of the survey and confirms that companies are continuing to hire only the best-qualified individuals. Currently, 65.6 percent of today's salespeople have a college degree.

Length of service: Today's sales professional is likely to remain with his or her company an average of 6.8 years, down from 7.4 years in our previous survey. This figure has remained fairly constant over the past 12, years which indicates a fair degree of stability in sales forces. The overall turnover rate in this year's survey is 15.2 percent, up slightly from the 14.1 percent turnover rate reported two years ago.

Sales calls per day: On average, salespeople make 3.0 sales calls per day. This figure has not changed significantly since the last survey period. In 1982, survey respondents reported that salespeople made an average of six calls per day. As noted elsewhere in this survey, today's sales managers are putting more emphasis on the quality of the calls their salespeople make and are less likely to set daily call quotas for their salespeople. This is also the result of improved methods of qualifying prospects and pre-planning the sales call. In other words, today's sales professional is working smarter — not harder.

Number of calls needed to close the sale: It now takes an average of 3.8 sales calls to close a sale, about the same as two years ago. Back in 1982, it took an average of five calls to close a sale. One reason for the improvement: Today's prospects are better qualified than in years past, making it more likely that a sale will be made.

Field expenses: The average cost of keeping a salesperson in the field now stands at $16,000 per year — unchanged from two years ago.

Value of benefits: Today's sales professional receives an average of $7,614 in benefits — the same as two years ago. More often than not, employees tend to take the benefits provided by their employers for granted. This "additional income" should not be overlooked either in the total compensation package or as a lure in recruiting prospects for the sales force.

Annual sales volume: Average annual sales volume now stands at $1,394,260 — essentially unchanged from survey results two years ago. However, senior salespeople are selling significantly more. (See Figure 40 for more detail.)

How salespeople spend their time: Today's sales professional spends approximately 48.2 hours a week on the job compared with 46.9 hours reported in 1996. Of that time, 54 percent is spent on selling activities; 46 percent on nonselling activities — essentially the same percentage split as reported two years ago. Time spent in face-to-face contact with customers or prospects is 13.9 hours a week, or 28.8 percent of the total available working time — down 2.2 percent in two years.

Cost of training: Companies now spend an average of $7,079 per year on training per salesperson. This is a sharp decline from the $7,937 figure reported two years ago. However, this decline is due to larger companies cutting back; smaller companies, those with up to $100 million in annual sales, have increased spending in this area. (See Figure 88.)

Cost of a sales call: The "average cost of a sales call" varies so widely, based on size of company and industry, that reporting any one single figure would be meaningless — and misleading. Clearly, smaller companies that cover small geographic areas spend considerably less money on field expenses than large companies that sell both nationally and internationally. The size of individual territories and where the company is located can have a dramatic effect on these costs as well. Consider, for example, two sales reps, one of whom is located in New York City, the other in Texas. Our New York City salesperson may have one skyscraper as his or her entire territory; our Texas-based salesperson may have to travel 50 to 100 miles or more between sales calls. Further, some salespeople travel extensively, only returning home on the weekends. Our Texas rep would spend considerably more on on-the-road expenses than would a salesperson who returns home every evening. (See immediately below for a discussion of the average cost of a sales call.)

THE "AVERAGE" COST OF A SALES CALL — WHAT DOES IT MEAN TO YOU?

Users of this survey who would like to determine "benchmark" figures for the average cost of a sales call in their particular industries or company-size groups can easily do so by using data from this survey.

Quite simply, the average cost of a sales call is calculated by dividing the average annual total cost of keeping your typical senior salesperson in the field by the total number of sales calls he or she makes per year. Average annual total expenses are determined by adding together data for total compensation, field expenses, and benefits.

For example, let's say you want to determine the average cost of a sales call for a top-performing senior salesperson in the chemicals field. Consult Figure 71 to determine the average cost of field expenses ($21,300) and the average cost of benefits ($13,000). See Figure 62 for third-quartile total cash compensation figures ($124,000). Add these figures together to determine total annual expenses to keep this salesperson in the field

($21,300 + $13,000 + $124,000 = $158,300). See Figure 104 to determine the average number of sales calls made per day in the communications industry (3.1). To determine the total number of sales calls made per year, multiply the average number of calls made per day (3.1) by the average number of workdays in a year. Although the average number of workdays varies by company, most salespeople work approximately 225 days a year. Multiplying 3.1 by 225 gives us the total number of sales calls made per year (697.5). Divide the total annual costs ($158,300) by total annual sales calls (697.5) to determine the average cost of a sales call (in this case, $226.95).

THE SURVEY AS A WHOLE

When we perform the same calculation for the survey as a whole, combining all levels of salespeople, all sizes of companies, and the entire range of industries, our average cost of a sales call is approximately $109 — or about one-third the amount frequently quoted by other research groups. This is understandably confusing.

MAKING SENSE OF IT ALL

To make some sense out of this, let's begin by taking a look at the Dartnell questionnaire. Basically, the Dartnell questionnaire asks the respondent to combine total compensation and total field expenses plus benefits and divide that amount by the total number of sales calls made per year. All computations are compiled on a per-rep basis. To compute the number of sales calls made each year by each rep, respondents are asked to multiply the average number of sales calls per day by 225 days — the average number of days worked by most salespeople.

For example, let's say my "average senior salesperson" makes a total of $60,000 in salary and commissions per year. Let's also say that it costs me an additional $15,000 per year in expenses. This includes travel reimbursement, lodging, etc. I also spend another $8,000 in benefits for this individual on health insurance and the like. That gives me a total of $83,000, or what it costs per year to keep that rep in the field. This hypothetical rep makes about four calls per day, or 900 calls per year. Dividing $83,000 by 900 gives me $92.22 — the cost of an "average" sales call in my particular business.

Here's another approach that gets to the real crux of the matter. Let's say that I accept the frequently quoted figure of $295 as the cost of an "average" sales call. Let's further assume that my average rep makes an average of three calls per day. Multiplying three by 225 gives us 675 sales calls per year for each rep. Now if we multiply $295 by 675, we get a total of $199,125 — the total cost to keep an "average" senior sales rep in the field on a per-year basis.

Most people would agree that they do not spend an average of nearly $200,000 to keep one of their salespeople in the field. Working the "cost of an average sales call" formula backward can give you a better insight into the reasonableness of this figure.

When all is said and done, the figure given for the cost of an average sales call only makes sense when it is compared with how profitable those sales calls are. Any company concerned with rising selling costs should take a look at what it is getting for those costs.

Here's a procedure for companies to follow to determine what they are getting in exchange for the money they spend on sales calls:

1. Determine the average cost of a sales call for your particular business, using the Dartnell formula.
2. Determine the average number of calls required for your salespeople to make a sale.
3. Determine the average dollar amount of an "average" sale.
4. Multiply the answer to No. 1 above by the answer to No. 2.
5. Divide the answer to No. 3 above by the answer to No. 4 above.

Your answer to No. 5 is the number of dollars of total revenue generated for every dollar spent on sales call costs. If this figure falls within the defined objectives of your company — great! If not, determine where the problem lies.

WHAT THIS DATA MEANS TO YOU: A LOOK AT STATISTICAL ANALYSIS

In sales, the bottom line is results! Because this is the case, consider the significance of being able to accurately identify — and even predict — industry-wide trends. Wouldn't your company prosper if you could increase the bottom line while actually decreasing your spending? Wouldn't your own worth to your company increase if you could more accurately see into the future? This is possible when you play the numbers game known as statistical analysis.

In sales management, statistical analysis can be used to assist you in planning, hiring, training, monitoring, and compensating your sales force.

WHAT IS IT, AND HOW CAN IT WORK TO YOUR ADVANTAGE?

Simply stated, it is the study of statistics as they occur and relate to your industry. More specifically, it is the process of using historical statistics to search for patterns, and characteristics of those patterns, that have produced favorable results in the past. The thinking here is that, although no one can know what the future holds, you may be able to use historical data to accurately identify successful trends in your specific industry.

For example, every sales department in the world has to deal with the problem of hiring new salespeople. This is as true today as it was in the past. Because this is true, there is a wealth of historical information directly related to this specific process that can be studied and evaluated.

What is the average education level of the top-producing salespeople in your industry? Is there any correlation between the age of a salesperson and the success he or she is likely to have in your specific industry? What is the optimum experience level of a new recruit in your industry? Knowing the answers to these questions would likely help you to hire more efficiently.

Consider the cost of training your new hires. Do you train your new recruits yourself, or do you use an external training source? Is the method of training that you use as effective as other methods of training that may exist in your industry? How much does it cost you to train your salespeople? How does this compare to what your competitors are spending to train their salespeople?

Statistical analysis can be especially helpful in monitoring your salespeople and making them more productive. How much of your sales team's time is actually spent selling? How much time is spent traveling? How many calls does it take them, on average, to close a sale? Is there any direct relation to the hours spent on a particular account and the profitability of that account? You may be surprised at the answers you find to these questions, and so may your salespeople.

What compensation method do you use? Should you consider changing it? What mix of incentive and base pay is producing the best results? What is working in your specific industry?

To be sure, there is no foolproof management tool that can guarantee you will be successful. However, if you take the time to study pertinent historical data, you may discover that you can, indeed, learn from other people's mistakes. What's more, with sales being a numbers game, you can increase your odds of being successful by following trends that lead to success!

CONTENT SUMMARY

Dartnell's *30th Sales Force Compensation Survey* is divided into three parts containing a total of 15 sections to help you quickly find the data, information, and analysis you need to make informed sales compensation decisions. Before working extensively with the data, however, we strongly recommend that you read Section 3, "How to Use This Survey." This material will help you understand the data tables and enable you to get the most out of this survey.

This content summary consists of two parts:

1. Where to Find What: A Guide to the Survey's Contents
2. Terminology Used in This Survey.

1. WHERE TO FIND WHAT: A GUIDE TO THE SURVEY'S CONTENTS

PART I

Section 1: Welcome to our 30th Survey Edition! A brief description of what you can expect to find in this survey, along with commentary on the additions and enhancements over the 29th edition.

Section 2: Survey Methodology. Provides information on survey participants, how data was obtained, and effective date of survey.

Section 3: How to Use This Survey. An explanation of the data tables, examples of how to determine compensation levels for any sales position, and general guidelines for using and applying the data in this survey.

Section 4: Executive Summary. The Dartnell profile of the 1998 sales professional is presented along with a brief rundown on how this year's data compares with previous findings. Data in this section includes the average age, educational level, and length of service of sales representatives as well as the average number of face-to-face calls made per day and the average number of calls needed to close the sale. Section 4 also contains overall average figures for typical field expense costs, the value of benefits, training costs, annual sales volume per salesperson, how the typical salesperson spends the workweek, and the yearly compensation of senior, intermediate, and entry-level salespeople.

Section 5: Content Summary. Includes a descriptive account of the survey's contents and an explanation of the terminology used along with suggestions on how to use the survey.

PART II

Section 6: Current Levels of Pay. Current and projected levels of pay for sales representatives are presented. This section contains tables which address: projected earnings and merit increases for senior sales representatives, the type of compensation plan used, and the base salary/incentive split used to determine total compensation.

*   Figures 10–19 exhibit the average pay levels for each of the 10 sales positions surveyed by plan type and all plans combined.

FIGURE 1

DARTNELL PROFILE: THE AMERICAN
SALES PROFESSIONAL — NATIONAL AVERAGES

		FURTHER DETAIL PROVIDED IN
• 37.5 YEARS OLD		
• 75.7% ARE MALE		FIGURE 100, PAGE 171
• 24.3% ARE FEMALE		FIGURE 100, PAGE 171
• 65.6% HAVE A COLLEGE DEGREE		FIGURE 101, PAGE 173
• LENGTH OF SERVICE	6.8 YEARS PER REP	
• SALES CALLS PER DAY	3.0	FIGURE 104, PAGE 181
• NUMBER OF CALLS TO CLOSE	3.8	FIGURE 104, PAGE 181
• FIELD EXPENSES COST	$16,000	FIGURE 71, PAGE 119
• VALUE OF BENEFITS	$7,614	FIGURE 40, PAGE 79
• ANNUAL SALES VOLUME	$1,394,260	FIGURE 99, PAGE 165
• AUTOMOBILES*		
– COMPANY–OWNED	34.5%	FIGURE 72, PAGE 122
– COMPANY–LEASED	30.8%	FIGURE 73, PAGE 123
– PERSONAL (MILEAGE)	62.9%	FIGURE 74, PAGE 124

• SPENDS ON AVERAGE 48.2 HOURS PER WEEK AS FOLLOWS:

TASK	PERCENT OF WEEKLY TIME
– SELLING FACE-TO-FACE	28.8% (13.9 HOURS)
– SELLING OVER THE PHONE	25.1 (12.1 HOURS)
– ADMINISTRATIVE TASKS	16 (7.7 HOURS)
– WAITING/TRAVELING	17.4 (8.4 HOURS)
– SERVICE CALLS	12.7 (6.1 HOURS)

• COMPENSATION		
– ENTRY LEVEL REP MAKES	$35,000	FIGURE 26, PAGE 62
– INTERMEDIATE REP MAKES	$46,000	FIGURE 25, PAGE 61
– SENIOR REP MAKES	$68,000	FIGURE 24, PAGE 60
• COSTS TO TRAIN	$7,079	FIGURE 88, PAGE 143

*TOTAL EXCEEDS 100% DUE TO MULTIPLE RESPONSES.

- Figures 20–29 exhibit the average total cash compensation for average, better, and best performers in each of the 10 survey positions.
- Figures 30–39 exhibit the average base salary and average total compensation for all plans for average, better, and best performers in each survey position.

Section 7: Pay and Performance. The relationship between pay and performance is examined through the following exhibits:

- Figure 40 looks at the average annual sales volume for intermediate and senior sales representatives by average, better, and best performers.
- Figures 41–47 exhibit the compensation levels of better and best performers as a percentage increase over average performers.
- Figures 48–57 exhibit compensation levels and sales volume generated by average, better, and best performers.
- Figures 58–67 exhibit third-quartile compensation levels and sales volume generated by average, better, and best performers.
- Figure 68 exhibits top performers' productivity as compared to average performers' productivity.
- Figure 69 exhibits senior salesperson productivity by better and best performers.

Section 8: Expenses, Benefits, Training. This section reviews the cost of sales, field expenses, benefits, and training. Specific areas looked at include:

- Figure 70 — sales force cost as a percent of sales.
- Figure 71 — field expenses and benefits cost per senior salesperson.
- Figures 72–85 — pay practices by selected field expense items.
- Figure 86 — specific benefits offered to salespeople.
- Figure 87 — methods of training used by companies.
- Figure 88 — length and cost of training new hires.
- Figure 89 — length, cost, and type of training for experienced reps.

Section 9: Incentive Plan Design Practices. This section focuses on typical incentive plan design practices of survey participants.

- Figures 90–93 examine the relationship between activities sales managers regard as critically important and whether these performance measures are included in their companies' compensation plan design. Specific performance measures looked at include selling to major accounts, retaining existing customers, finding new accounts, and reducing selling costs.
- Figure 94 examines the importance of profit contribution versus sales rep and sales manager incentives.
- Figures 95–97 focus on the degree of sales force effectiveness and include an examination of how effectively sales forces perform the tasks that sales managers say are important.
- Figure 98 looks at how commissions are paid — on sales volume, profitability, a combination of sales volume and profitability, or some other measure.
- Figure 99 shows the experience level preferred in newly hired salespeople.

Section 10: A Portrait of Today's Sales Force. This section takes a look at the sales force as a unit and focuses on the percentage of women in the sales force, the educational level of today's salespeople, typical spans of supervisory control, how salespeople spend their time, face-to-face selling statistics, the changing size of today's sales forces, and the use of manufacturers' representatives.

- Figure 100 shows the percentage of women in the sales force and the percentage of women who are sales managers.
- Figure 101 reviews the educational level of the responding companies' sales forces.
- Figure 102 shows the typical spans of supervisory control.
- Figure 103 illustrates how salespeople divide their time between selling and non-selling activities.
- Figure 104 focuses on face-to-face selling and reports on the average number of calls needed to close a sale and the average number of sales calls made per day.
- Figures 105 and 106 take a look at the changing size and turnover patterns of today's sales forces.
- Figure 107 reports on the use of manufacturers' representatives.

Section 11: Geographic Breakouts. A look at selected data for the nine major geographic regions that comprise the United States Data breakouts include percentage of companies anticipating higher senior salesperson earnings in 1999; percentage of companies anticipating lower senior salesperson earnings in 1999; average percent merit increase; total cash compensation for senior, intermediate, and entry level salespeople; total cost of field expenses and benefits; percentage of companies paying the entire cost of the following expense items: home photocopier, home fax machine, car phone, laptop computer; length of training and cost of training for new hires; time spent on ongoing training and cost of training for experienced salespeople; degree of sales force effectiveness; women in the sales force; salesperson educational level; how salespeople spend their time — total work hours per week, total hours per week spent on selling activities, total hours per week spent selling face-to-face; number of calls needed to close a sale; number of sales calls per day; the changing size of sales forces; and salesperson turnover rates.

PART III

Section 12: A Look Ahead. This section suggests what changes in sales and sales management we can expect to see as we move toward the year 2000. Also in this section we look at the trends, practices, and opinions that help add to "the big picture" of selling. Included here are such things as:

- Whether technology is simplifying — or complicating — salespeople's work.
- Whether they are using the Internet — and, if so, how?
- If salespeople think their sales compensation plan is fair.
- If they feel they are paid fairly, underpaid, or overpaid.
- Whether more compensation would make them more productive.
- How they respond when they see dishonesty in the field.
- The kinds of dishonesty salespeople see in the business world.
- How they rank a variety of common nonfinancial incentives.

Section 13: Aligning Your Compensation Plan with Your Business Plan. In this section, we take a look at some of the basics of business planning and compensation plan design so you can get more out of your compensation plan.

Section 14: Trends in Sales Compensation: What Enlightened Companies Are Doing to Boost Performance. Twelve case histories look at the compensation plans of companies in a variety of industries to see how others have leveraged their plans to boost performance. These case histories may well give you additional ideas on how you can adjust your pay plan to make it even more effective.

Section 15: Participating Companies by Standard Industrial Classification (SIC) Code 4-Digit Listings. This section concludes the survey with a listing of SIC codes used by survey participants. A list of position descriptions surveyed is also included. Please refer to this listing when matching survey positions with positions within your own company.

2. TERMINOLOGY USED IN THIS SURVEY

The following explanations of terminology used in this survey will help you more fully understand the data configurations presented:

- **Average** — Average, when used in connection with dollar amounts, always refers to the average of the median range. In all other instances, average figures represent true averages of responses received.
- **Median** — The median is the figure that is in the middle of all values arranged from lowest to highest — that is, half of the set of numbers fall above the median and half fall below it. The advantage of using the median is that it is not affected by extremes at either the high or low end of the range and thus provides a truer picture of the data.
- **Median range** — The median range is the middle 50 percent of responses — that is, those responses that fall between the 25th and 75th percentile of the entire range of responses.

- **Third quartile** — The third quartile is also referred to as the 75th percentile. It is the figure that is higher than 75 percent of all figures reported, but lower than 25 percent of the figures reported. Third-quartile figures enable us to look at the higher range of the data reported.
- **Better performer** — Better performers are those individuals who rank in the top 25 percent of their respective sales forces.
- **Best performer** — Best performers are those individuals who rank at the top of the survey sample. Compensation figures for best performer represent the top end of the scale in any particular breakout of the data. Similarly, sales volume data given for the best performer is generated from highest reported figures.
- **N/R** — An N/R entry in the data tables indicates that although data was received, the figure is not released due to insufficient sample size.
- **0.0** — A 0.0 entry in the data tables indicates that no data was received for that data category.
- **Salary-only plan** — A salary-only plan compensates the individual on the basis of a fixed yearly amount.
- **Incentive-only plan** — An incentive-only plan compensates the individual an agreed-upon amount upon the successful completion of certain tasks and activities. Earnings are based entirely on the performance of the individual.
- **Combination plan** — A combination plan is a combination of the salary and incentive plans. An individual on this plan is paid an annual sum in the form of salary, but earns additional (incentive) compensation on the basis of performance.

We suggest you refer to these definitions whenever data or explanations in the text seem unclear.

Position descriptions: The following position definitions are used throughout this survey and are repeated in Section 15 as a convenience to readers:

1. **Top Marketing Exec** — Typical title: Vice President of Marketing. Directs marketing functions and may oversee international operations, as well as field marketing support and field service. Reports to CEO, President, or Division President.
2. **Top Sales Exec** — Typical title: Vice President of Sales. Directs U.S. sales, has minimal marketing responsibilities, and may oversee field service. Reports to CEO, President, Division President, or Top Marketing Executive.
3. **Regional Sales Manager** — Manages specific region, industry, product, or distributor sales. Reports to Top Sales Executive.
4. **District Sales Manager** — Manages a more limited region, industry, or product segment. Reports to Regional Sales Manager.
5. **Senior Sales Rep** — A salesperson with three or more years of sales experience.
6. **Intermediate Sales Rep** — A salesperson with one to three years of sales experience.
7. **Entry Level Sales Rep** — A salesperson with less than one year of sales experience.
8. **National or Major Account Sales Manager** — Segments accounts and develops account strategies. Manages only National or Major (Key) Account Reps. Reports to Top Sales Executive.
9. **National Account Rep** — Sells to national customers. Typically requires at least seven years of industry-specific experience. Reports to National Account Sales Manager.
10. **Major (Key) Account Rep** — Sells to major (key) accounts with a central purchasing point. Reports to National Account Sales Manager.

PART TWO — DATA

CURRENT LEVELS OF PAY

How much are those in the sales and marketing professions paid? How are they most likely to be paid — straight salary, straight commission, or a combination of the two? And if they're paid on a combination plan, what percent is likely to be salary and what percent is likely to be incentive? This section has the answers to all these questions and more.

You'll find complete data tables for current levels of pay for the 10 survey positions broken out by size of company, product or service sold, type of buyer, and industry. In addition, compensation data is broken out for most positions by average, better, and best performer. (For a discussion of the terminology used in this survey and a description of positions surveyed, see Section 5.)

Positions surveyed include:

- Top Marketing Executive
- Top Sales Executive

(Note that because most companies have only one top marketing and/or top sales executive, there is no better or best performer.)

- Regional Sales Manager
- District Sales Manager
- Senior Sales Representative
- Intermediate Representative
- Entry Level Sales Representative
- National/Major Account Manager
- National Account Representative
- Major (Key) Account Representative

Before using these tables, be sure to read the suggestions on how to use this survey presented in Section 3. The data tables in this section are comprehensive and, as such, may be confusing to first-time users of this survey. Additional suggestions for using each series of tables are also presented in this section.

Other tables in this section include data on projected earnings and merit increases for senior sales representatives, the type of compensation plan used, and the base salary/incentive split used to determine total compensation.

The compensation tables can be summarized as follows:

- Figures 10–19 exhibit the average pay levels for each of the 10 sales positions surveyed by plan type and all plans combined. For positions that you compensate on an all-salary or all-incentive plan, these tables provide all the data you need. For those paying on a combination plan, these tables provide salary, incentive, and total cash compensation figures for the entire range of survey respondents. If you use a combination plan, you'll want to consult the more comprehensive data tables in this section for additional breakouts that will more closely represent your particular company.
- Figures 20–29 exhibit average total cash compensation for average, better, and best performers for most positions surveyed. Because most companies have only one top marketing and/or one top sales executive, there are no better or best per-

formers in that position. Use these tables to determine average total cash compensation for those positions paid on a combination plan.

- Figures 30–39 exhibit average base salary and average total compensation for all plans for average, better, and best performers in the positions surveyed. Use these tables to determine the base salary for those individuals paid on a combination (salary + incentive) plan.

This year's survey, like previous editions, provides extensive breakouts of the data to enable you to look at it in a variety of ways — for example, median and third-quartile figures for average, better, and best performers. These breakouts give you the opportunity to examine the segment of the data that is most relevant to you and to make extensive comparisons.

GENERAL OVERVIEW

Chart 2 below summarizes compensation data for all 10 surveyed positions over the past two years. Note that this data includes only those individuals paid on a combination plan (salary plus incentive) and includes the entire range of responses. These figures, then, represent average total cash compensation for individuals in surveyed positions who are paid on a combination plan.

CHART 2

	1996			1998		
	SALARY ($000)	INCENTIVE ($000)	TOTAL ($000)	SALARY ($000)	INCENTIVE ($000)	TOTAL ($000)
TOP MARKETING EXECUTIVE	$100.6	$33.2	$133.8	$107.3	$29.2	$136.5
TOP SALES EXECUTIVE	91.2	31.5	122.7	91.0	29.0	119.9
REGIONAL SALES MANAGER	69.0	23.3	92.3	74.5	21.9	96.4
DISTRICT SALES MANAGER	61.8	22.0	83.7	64.5	20.3	84.8
SENIOR SALES REPRESENTATIVE	45.1	23.2	68.3	47.5	26.0	73.5
INTERMEDIATE REPRESENTATIVE	34.6	16.1	50.7	36.1	15.3	51.4
ENTRY LEVEL SALES REPRESENTATIVE	28.8	10.9	39.8	29.7	13.4	43.1
NATL./MAJOR ACCOUNT MGR.	66.9	18.7	85.6	72.2	26.0	98.2
NATIONAL ACCOUNT REPRESENTATIVE	58.8	17.4	76.1	60.9	25.5	86.4
MAJOR (KEY) ACCOUNT REPRESENTATIVE	54.6	16.6	71.2	57.4	22.9	80.3

Figure 2 dramatically illustrates that over the years, the earnings of senior salespeople have steadily increased — despite periods of economic slowdowns. Although this graphic does not include data for years prior to 1956, the average earnings for senior salespeople have never shown a decrease from one survey period to the next in the history of this survey. This is an enviable record that many other professions would be hard-pressed to match.

Additionally, earnings have shown a consistent trend to increase more rapidly in the sales profession than in most other professions. In fact, the sales profession, unlike other occupations, can show significant earnings increases in a poor economy. Salespeople, paid for what they are able to produce, are not tied to the restrictions — and the current uncertainties — of salaried corporate positions.

FIGURE 2 — CURRENT LEVEL OF PAY: SENIOR SALES REPS

Figure 2 shows the increases in average earnings of senior sales representatives since 1956. This graph dramatically illustrates that at no time in more than 40 years have the average annual earnings of senior salespeople decreased, even though the U.S. economy has gone through several recessions. This seems to suggest that a career in sales is "recession-proof," provided the individual has the necessary skills to succeed.

FIGURE 2

CURRENT LEVEL OF PAY: SENIOR SALESPERSON

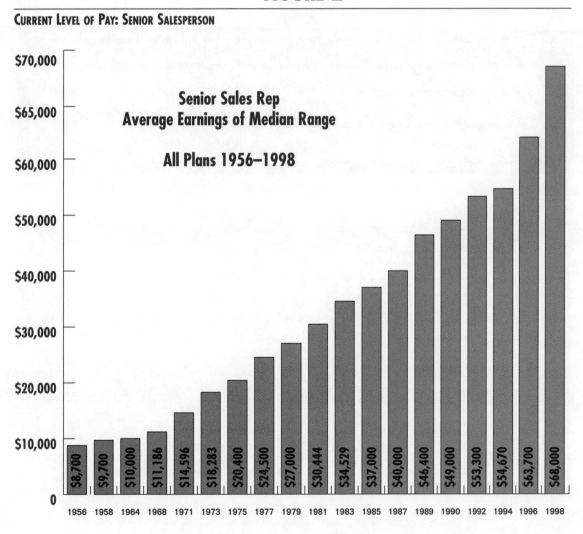

Senior Sales Rep
Average Earnings of Median Range

All Plans 1956–1998

Year	Earnings
1956	$8,700
1958	$9,700
1964	$10,000
1968	$11,186
1971	$14,596
1973	$18,283
1975	$20,400
1977	$24,500
1979	$27,000
1981	$30,444
1983	$34,529
1985	$37,000
1987	$40,000
1989	$46,400
1990	$49,000
1992	$53,300
1994	$54,670
1996	$63,700
1998	$68,000

FIGURE 3—PROJECTED SENIOR SALESPERSON EARNINGS IN 1999—INCREASES

Figure 3 shows that just over 88 percent of responding companies predict that their senior salespeople will earn more in 1999 than they will earn in 1998. Note that just slightly more than 17 percent of those companies said these increased earnings would come primarily from a change in their sales compensation plans. This means that the vast majority of those companies predicting higher senior sales representative earnings are basing those projections on increases in sales volume. This is a strong indication that companies continue to be optimistic about the future — a trend noted in other Dartnell surveys. In the previous survey period, 90.5 percent of companies predicted increased earnings for their senior sales reps. In 1994, 91.7 percent of responding companies predicted that senior sales representatives would earn more the following year. The stability of these figures over multiple survey periods indicates that the majority of companies are optimistic, even in periods of economic downturn.

(For geographic breakouts of this data, please see Section 11.)

FIGURE 3

**PROJECTED SENIOR SALESPERSON
EARNINGS IN 1999 — INCREASES**

	PERCENTAGE OF FIRMS PREDICTING HIGHER EARNINGS IN 1999	PERCENTAGE HIGHER	PERCENTAGE OF FIRMS INDICATING CHANGE IN COMPENSATION PLAN
COMPANY SIZE			
UNDER $5 MILLION	87.7%	11.5%	14.8%
$5MM–$25MM	91.8	12.3	16.7
$25MM–$100MM	87.1	9.5	17.3
$100MM–$250MM	87.5	10.6	27.3
OVER $250MM	79.4	9.4	20.0
PRODUCT OR SERVICE			
CONSUMER PRODUCTS	87.8	11.2	16.5
CONSUMER SERVICES	88.7	11.6	23.6
INDUSTRIAL PRODUCTS	88.7	11.3	13.4
INDUSTRIAL SERVICES	88.2	11.2	14.6
OFFICE PRODUCTS	82.8	13.5	10.0
OFFICE SERVICES	84.7	12.9	16.7
TYPE OF BUYER			
CONSUMERS	89.0	11.7	18.5
DISTRIBUTORS	88.7	11.2	16.2
INDUSTRY	87.1	11.2	14.8
RETAILERS	84.8	11.9	10.6
INDUSTRY			
BANKING	66.7	15.5	18.2
BUSINESS SERVICES	85.7	14.0	18.5
CHEMICALS	100.0	9.1	9.1
COMMUNICATIONS	77.8	11.4	31.2
CONSTRUCTION	100.0	11.7	0.0
EDUCATIONAL SERVICES	87.5	9.6	25.0
ELECTRONICS	89.5	12.6	11.8
ELECTRONIC COMPONENTS	80.0	10.6	33.3
FABRICATED METALS	95.5	10.2	17.4
FOOD PRODUCTS	100.0	8.0	0.0
HEALTH SERVICES	88.9	9.6	22.2
HOTELS AND OTHER LODGING PLACES	75.0	11.2	50.0
INSTRUMENTS	100.0	9.5	11.1
INSURANCE	90.5	10.2	22.7
MACHINERY	100.0	7.9	30.0
MANUFACTURING	82.4	12.9	0.0
OFFICE EQUIPMENT	81.2	10.5	21.4
PAPER AND ALLIED PRODUCTS	100.0	8.7	0.0
PHARMACEUTICALS	85.7	6.3	14.3
PRINTING AND PUBLISHING	94.4	9.8	11.1
REAL ESTATE	100.0	18.8	25.0
RETAIL	87.5	10.2	15.6
RUBBER/PLASTICS	100.0	6.4	20.0
TRANSPORTATION EQUIPMENT	100.0	7.8	14.3
WHOLESALE (CONSUMER GOODS)	90.7	12.0	17.1
OVERALL	**88.4%**	**11.2%**	**17.1%**

FIGURE 4 — PROJECTED SENIOR SALESPERSON EARNINGS IN 1999 — DECREASES

Fewer than 12 percent of responding companies predict that their senior sales representatives will earn less in 1999 than they will earn in 1998. Of these, 27.4 percent said these decreases would result from changes in their sales compensation plans. This figure is virtually unchaged from the data reported in our last survey period. In the 1996 survey period, 26.4 percent of respondents indicated that decreased earnings would result from changes in their compensation plans.

(For geographic breakouts of this data, please see Section 11.)

FIGURE 4

Projected Senior Salesperson Earnings in 1999 — Decreases

	Percentage of Firms Predicting Lower Earnings in 1999	Percentage Lower	Percentage of Firms Indicating Change in Compensation Plan
Company Size			
Under $5 Million	12.3%	11.5%	27.0%
$5MM–$25MM	8.2	9.2	20.4
$25MM–$100MM	12.9	4.5	28.1
$100MM–$250MM	12.5	7.5	42.9
Over $250MM	20.6	8.5	50.0
Product or Service			
Consumer Products	12.2	7.8	32.0
Consumer Services	11.3	9.5	29.7
Industrial Products	11.3	8.1	24.6
Industrial Services	11.8	10.4	32.6
Office Products	17.2	9.3	30.0
Office Services	15.3	9.9	32.6
Type of Buyer			
Consumers	11.0	9.1	32.6
Distributors	11.3	8.0	34.8
Industry	12.9	9.8	26.5
Retailers	15.2	8.7	40.9
Industry			
Banking	33.3	13.3	40.0
Business Services	14.3	11.1	35.0
Communications	22.2	15.0	0.0
Construction	0.0	10.0	0.0
Educational Services	12.5	3.0	66.7
Electronics	10.5	7.5	0.0
Electronic Components	20.0	0.0	66.7
Fabricated Metals	4.5	9.0	12.5
Food Products	0.0	0.0	0.0
Health Services	11.1	0.0	100.0
Hotels and Other Lodging Places	25.0	0.0	100.0
Insurance	9.5	8.4	25.0
Manufacturing	17.6	13.3	40.0
Office Equipment	18.8	7.0	0.0
Paper and Allied Products	0.0	0.0	0.0
Pharmaceuticals	14.3	5.0	25.0
Printing and Publishing	5.6	8.2	42.9
Retail	12.5	5.2	18.2
Rubber/Plastics	0.0	0.0	0.0
Wholesale (Consumer Goods)	9.3	6.9	29.4
Overall	**11.6%**	**8.9%**	**27.4%**

FIGURE 5 — AVERAGE PERCENT MERIT INCREASE

The average 1997 merit increase for salespeople averaged 5.4 percent, up from the 4.9 percent increase projected by respondents to our previous survey. It's interesting to note that companies of all sizes, with the exception of companies over $250 million in annual sales, are predicting similar merit increases for the next two years. In our last survey period, smaller companies predicted higher increases than their larger counterparts.

(For geographic breakouts of this data, please see Section 11.)

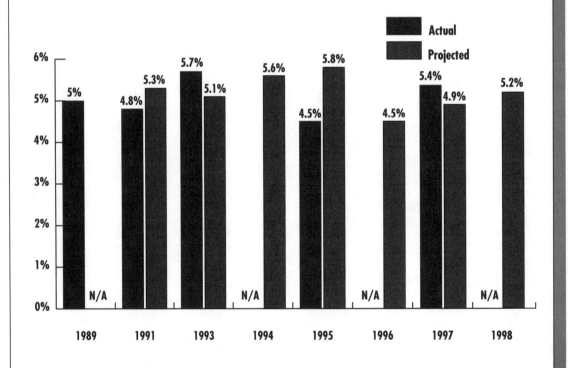

FIGURE 5

AVERAGE PERCENT MERIT INCREASE

	1997	PROJECTED 1998	PROJECTED 1999
COMPANY SIZE			
UNDER $5 MILLION	5.4%	5.3%	5.6%
$5MM–$25MM	6.4	5.7	6.2
$25MM–$100MM	4.5	4.7	5.2
$100MM–$250MM	5.0	5.6	6.5
OVER $250MM	3.7	3.6	3.8
PRODUCT OR SERVICE			
CONSUMER PRODUCTS	4.4	4.7	5.0
CONSUMER SERVICES	5.1	5.1	5.5
INDUSTRIAL PRODUCTS	5.5	5.3	5.9
INDUSTRIAL SERVICES	5.5	5.4	6.1
OFFICE PRODUCTS	4.6	5.0	5.3
OFFICE SERVICES	6.4	5.8	6.2
TYPE OF BUYER			
CONSUMERS	5.4	5.2	5.7
DISTRIBUTORS	5.2	5.0	5.5
INDUSTRY	5.5	5.2	5.8
RETAILERS	4.9	4.6	5.0
INDUSTRY			
BANKING	5.0	5.2	4.8
BUSINESS SERVICES	7.2	6.1	6.1
CHEMICALS	3.5	3.6	3.6
COMMUNICATIONS	5.1	5.1	5.3
CONSTRUCTION	4.0	5.0	5.7
EDUCATIONAL SERVICES	9.5	7.2	8.3
ELECTRONICS	4.9	5.1	5.2
ELECTRONIC COMPONENTS	4.2	4.6	4.6
FABRICATED METALS	4.0	4.2	4.8
FOOD PRODUCTS	4.0	6.0	4.0
HEALTH SERVICES	4.4	4.9	6.0
HOTELS AND OTHER LODGING PLACES	3.7	3.7	3.8
INSTRUMENTS	4.3	4.9	5.0
INSURANCE	4.8	4.3	4.6
MACHINERY	2.8	3.5	5.1
MANUFACTURING	7.5	5.8	8.5
OFFICE EQUIPMENT	4.2	5.1	4.3
PAPER AND ALLIED PRODUCTS	3.5	4.0	6.0
PHARMACEUTICALS	4.3	4.1	4.5
PRINTING AND PUBLISHING	3.7	3.9	4.3
RETAIL	5.3	5.0	5.1
TRANSPORTATION EQUIPMENT	3.8	4.0	5.2
WHOLESALE (CONSUMER GOODS)	6.1	4.8	4.9
OVERALL	**5.4%**	**5.2%**	**5.6%**

FIGURE 6 — COMPENSATION PLAN TYPE USED: SENIOR SALES REPRESENTATIVES

The combination plan (base salary plus an incentive) remains the compensation plan of choice. In our 1982 survey, for example, just over 50 percent of responding companies used this type of pay plan to compensate their senior salespeople. Today, this figure stands at nearly 70 percent (68.2%) of responding companies, slightly lower than our 1996 data. In our previous survey, combination plans were used by 76.9 percent of responding companies. A "salary-only" pay plan is used by 12.8 percent of responding companies and 19.0 percent prefer the "incentive-only" option. Over the years, the number of companies on the "salary-only" or "incentive-only" plan has fluctuated, sometimes significantly. Here's a summary over the past 14 years:

	SALARY ONLY	INCENTIVE ONLY
1984	22%	21.4%
1986	20	30
1988	27	24
1990	7	19.2
1992	8.1	24.2
1994	14.6	19.7
1996	7.6	15.5
1998	12.8	19.0

The greatest movement has been in the number of companies embracing the "salary-only" plan. (See Figure 14 for greater detail.)

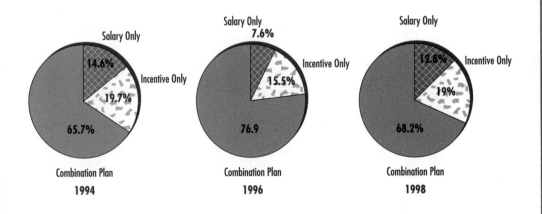

FIGURE 6

SENIOR SALES REP: COMPENSATION PLAN TYPE USED

	PERCENTAGE OF COMPANIES USING		
	SALARY ONLY	INCENTIVE ONLY	COMBINATION PLAN
COMPANY SIZE			
UNDER $5 MILLION	16.9%	26.2%	56.9%
$5MM–$25MM	10.2	19.4	70.4
$25MM–$100MM	11.3	14.5	74.2
$100MM–$250MM	17.4	21.7	60.9
OVER $250MM	12.9	9.7	77.4
PRODUCT OR SERVICE			
CONSUMER PRODUCTS	13.3	20.4	66.3
CONSUMER SERVICES	15.6	24.0	60.4
INDUSTRIAL PRODUCTS	9.8	14.3	75.9
INDUSTRIAL SERVICES	12.5	11.5	76.0
OFFICE PRODUCTS	3.0	21.2	75.8
OFFICE SERVICES	6.4	21.8	71.8
TYPE OF BUYER			
CONSUMERS	15.2	23.2	61.6
DISTRIBUTORS	12.7	17.8	69.5
INDUSTRY	10.5	15.3	74.2
RETAILERS	8.7	23.3	68.0
INDUSTRY			
BANKING	0.0	16.7	83.3
BUSINESS SERVICES	7.0	14.0	79.1
CHEMICALS	10.0	10.0	80.0
COMMUNICATIONS	16.7	8.3	75.0
CONSTRUCTION	20.0	0.0	80.0
EDUCATIONAL SERVICES	33.3	16.7	50.0
ELECTRONICS	8.3	0.0	91.7
ELECTRONIC COMPONENTS	20.0	0.0	80.0
FABRICATED METALS	7.7	15.4	76.9
FOOD PRODUCTS	100.0	0.0	0.0
HEALTH SERVICES	0.0	33.3	66.7
HOTELS AND OTHER LODGING PLACES	12.5	0.0	87.5
INSTRUMENTS	0.0	0.0	100.0
INSURANCE	18.8	31.2	50.0
MACHINERY	0.0	0.0	100.0
MANUFACTURING	33.3	11.1	55.6
OFFICE EQUIPMENT	0.0	7.7	92.3
PAPER AND ALLIED PRODUCTS	33.3	33.3	33.3
PHARMACEUTICALS	14.3	0.0	85.7
PRINTING AND PUBLISHING	7.1	42.9	50.0
REAL ESTATE	20.0	60.0	20.0
RETAIL	11.5	38.5	50.0
RUBBER/PLASTICS	16.7	33.3	50.0
TRANSPORTATION EQUIPMENT	20.0	0.0	80.0
WHOLESALE (CONSUMER GOODS)	12.1	30.3	57.6
OVERALL	**12.8%**	**19.0%**	**68.2%**

FIGURE 7 — METHODS OF COMPENSATION

The data on this table refers to the percentage of responding companies predominately using either straight-salary, incentive-only, or combination pay plans to compensate the 10 survey positions. Should you compare the data on this table with the data on Figure 6, keep in mind that the data tables report on different segments of the sales force. Figure 6 refers to senior salespeople only, and **Figure 7** includes all positions surveyed. The data can be more easily understood by remembering, for example, that many companies use a straight-salary plan to compensate their new hires and move them over to a combination plan after they have completed training.

By the same token, a company may pay most company sales positions on a combination-type basis, yet have a significant number of senior salespeople compensated on an "incentive-only" plan. These two tables, taken together, help us see the dynamics and variations in sales compensation plans.

METHODS OF COMPENSATION (FOR ALL POSITIONS COMBINED)

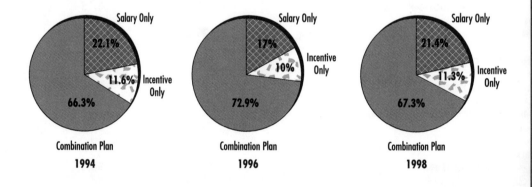

FIGURE 7

METHODS OF COMPENSATION

	PERCENTAGE OF COMPANIES USING		
	STRAIGHT SALARY	INCENTIVE ONLY	COMBINATION PLAN
COMPANY SIZE			
UNDER $5 MILLION	33.7%	13.7%	52.6%
$5MM–$25MM	17.6	10.7	71.7
$25MM–$100MM	14.1	10.0	75.9
$100MM–$250MM	16.5	10.0	73.6
OVER $250MM	13.7	8.3	77.9
PRODUCT OR SERVICE			
CONSUMER PRODUCTS	19.9	15.1	64.9
CONSUMER SERVICES	26.6	17.1	56.3
INDUSTRIAL PRODUCTS	17.1	7.3	75.6
INDUSTRIAL SERVICES	18.4	5.7	75.8
OFFICE PRODUCTS	12.1	11.1	76.8
OFFICE SERVICES	17.1	11.4	71.5
TYPE OF BUYER			
CONSUMERS	28.2	17.1	54.7
DISTRIBUTORS	23.9	9.6	66.5
INDUSTRY	18.3	8.6	73.1
RETAILERS	18.3	12.0	69.8
INDUSTRY			
BANKING	10.4	24.6	65.0
BUSINESS SERVICES	17.2	7.5	75.3
CHEMICALS	11.9	4.8	83.3
COMMUNICATIONS	11.6	9.7	78.7
CONSTRUCTION	11.4	10.0	78.6
EDUCATIONAL SERVICES	48.9	5.6	45.6
ELECTRONICS	7.2	2.3	90.5
ELECTRONIC COMPONENTS	43.3	0.0	56.7
FABRICATED METALS	18.0	9.1	72.9
FOOD PRODUCTS	75.0	0.0	25.0
HEALTH SERVICES	27.8	19.4	52.8
HOTELS AND OTHER LODGING PLACES	15.6	0.0	84.4
INSTRUMENTS	8.3	0.0	91.7
INSURANCE	35.9	25.3	38.7
MACHINERY	19.9	0.0	80.1
MANUFACTURING	38.8	3.5	57.6
OFFICE EQUIPMENT	8.2	2.1	89.8
PAPER AND ALLIED PRODUCTS	25.0	25.0	50.0
PHARMACEUTICALS	18.7	0.0	81.3
PRINTING AND PUBLISHING	23.4	22.5	54.1
REAL ESTATE	41.0	37.1	21.9
RETAIL	26.0	23.4	50.6
RUBBER/PLASTICS	30.5	19.5	50.0
TRANSPORTATION EQUIPMENT	16.7	7.1	76.1
WHOLESALE (CONSUMER GOODS)	18.2	14.7	67.0
OVERALL	**21.4%**	**11.3%**	**67.3%**

FIGURE 8 — BASE SALARY/INCENTIVE SPLIT

The base salary/incentive split in this year's survey is 59 percent salary and 41 percent incentive, an insignificant change from the 58/42 split reported two years ago. This figure has remained relatively constant over the last several editions of the survey. It is worth noting, however, that the base salary/incentive ratio has undergone significant change over the last 16 years. Our survey from 1982, for example, notes that base salaries representing 80 percent of total pay were common. Over the years, there has been a trend to reduce the percentage of base salary as part of the entire compensation package, enabling companies to put more money into incentive programs, while at the same time reducing fixed expenses. In the years ahead, it is likely that companies will continue to reduce the percentage of base salary as part of total pay in an effort to further reduce fixed costs and pay these monies out as incentives instead. As we move toward the year 2000, look for inventive and creative uses of incentives to become much more common than they are today.

Base Salary/Incentive Split (As a Percent of Total Compensation)

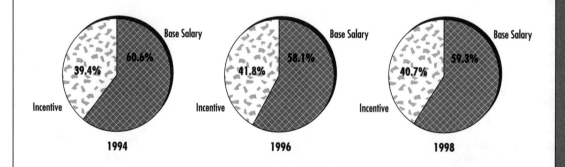

FIGURE 8

Base Salary/Incentive Split

	Average Percent Salary	Average Percent Incentive (Commission, Bonus)
Company Size		
Under $5 Million	62.6%	37.4%
$5MM–$25MM	57.7	42.3
$25MM–$100MM	57.9	42.1
$100MM–$250MM	59.5	40.5
Over $250MM	57.5	42.5
Product or Service		
Consumer Products	57.6	42.4
Consumer Services	55.9	44.1
Industrial Products	62.6	37.4
Industrial Services	62.4	37.6
Office Products	50.9	49.1
Office Services	52.3	47.7
Type of Buyer		
Consumers	55.8	44.2
Distributors	63.0	37.0
Industry	61.0	38.9
Retailers	56.4	43.6
Industry		
Banking	34.8	65.2
Business Services	56.5	43.5
Chemicals	70.8	29.2
Communications	57.8	42.2
Construction	59.1	40.9
Educational Services	73.3	26.7
Electronics	67.4	32.6
Electronic Components	85.3	14.7
Fabricated Metals	63.0	37.0
Food Products	95.0	5.0
Health Services	61.9	38.1
Hotels and Other Lodging Places	79.9	20.1
Instruments	65.8	34.2
Insurance	49.8	50.2
Machinery	76.6	23.4
Manufacturing	73.2	26.7
Office Equipment	62.2	37.8
Paper and Allied Products	55.0	45.0
Pharmaceuticals	75.0	25.0
Printing and Publishing	51.7	48.3
Real Estate	26.4	73.6
Retail	40.3	59.7
Rubber/Plastics	50.8	49.2
Transportation Equipment	68.6	31.4
Wholesale (Consumer Goods)	53.9	46.1
Overall	**59.3%**	**40.7%**

FIGURE 9 — HOW SALES EXECS AND REPS ARE PAID

How the 10 positions in our survey are compensated can provide insight into the actual selling responsibilities of the position. It makes sense that the more a particular position is compensated through the use of an incentive (commission), the more likely it is that the position carries responsibility for actually making sales. **Figure 9** on the opposite page shows how the 10 sales positions in the Dartnell survey are compensated. Note that the table carries the added information that the data is "incumbent-weighted" — that is, final figures are based on the total number of people in each position represented in the survey. In looking at the data, we can see, for example, that because nearly 63 percent of the national account reps included in this survey are paid on some type of salary plus commission basis, we can conclude that most individuals in that position represented in the survey have selling or direct sales responsibility. On the other hand, because nearly 53 percent of the top marketing executives in this survey are paid on either a straight salary or salary plus bonus plan, it is safe to assume that although these individuals may have overall responsibility for the sales performance of their respective companies, they often have no direct responsibility for making actual sales.

FIGURE 9

HOW SALES EXECS AND REPS ARE PAID
(ALL RESPONDENTS) INCUMBENT-WEIGHTED

	STRAIGHT SALARY	STRAIGHT COMM.	COMM. & BONUS	SALARY & COMM.	SALARY & BONUS	SALARY, BONUS, & COMM.
SURVEY POSITION						
1. TOP MARKETING EXECUTIVE	15.43%	3.35%	1.30%	8.18%	37.36%	34.39%
2. TOP SALES EXECUTIVE	9.17%	2.81%	1.63%	10.80%	12.28%	63.02%
3. REGIONAL SALES MANAGER	8.21%	0.65%	0.52%	23.47%	26.08%	41.07%
4. DISTRICT SALES MANAGER	36.72%	0.19%	0.00%	7.57%	29.05%	26.46%
5. SENIOR SALES REP	17.05%	14.23%	2.15%	29.53%	21.30%	15.72%
6. INTERMEDIATE SALES REP	16.78%	19.49%	0.99%	19.96%	24.28%	18.49%
7. ENTRY LEVEL SALES REP	23.56%	5.70%	2.46%	22.47%	13.83%	31.98%
8. NATL./MAJ. ACCOUNT MANAGER	18.08%	0.00%	1.41%	25.71%	10.73%	44.07%
9. NATIONAL ACCOUNT REP	36.99%	3.47%	0.87%	4.62%	11.27%	42.77%
10. MAJOR (KEY) ACCOUNT REP	19.69%	8.29%	8.29%	16.06%	16.06%	31.61%

Figures 10–19 — Compensation Tables: Average Sales Compensation Pay Levels By Plan Type and All Plans Combined

Before drawing conclusions based on the data contained in the following tables, we suggest you familiarize yourself with the material presented in Section 3 on how to use this survey. This material not only provides general guidelines on how to use the data, but also contains a specific example of how to solve a typical research problem using the data.

The following tables (Figures 10–19) exhibit the average pay levels for each of the 10 sales positions surveyed by plan type and all plans combined. The positions surveyed are:

- Top Marketing Executive
- Top Sales Executive
- Regional Sales Manager
- District Sales Manager
- Senior Sales Representative (three or more years of experience)
- Intermediate Sales Representative (one to three years of experience)
- Entry Level Sales Representative (less than one year of experience)
- National/Major Account Manager
- National Account Representative
- Major (Key) Account Representative

(A more detailed description of each of these positions can be found in Section 5.)

These tables provide compensation data for those individuals paid on a combination plan, broken out by salary (base) pay and incentive pay; data for those paid on an all-incentive plan; and data for those paid on an all-salary plan. Average total cash compensation data for all plans is also provided. Note that the data on these tables includes the full range of responses for each position surveyed.

For those individuals on a salary-only or incentive-only plan, these tables provide a complete picture of average annual total compensation. However, for those individuals paid on a combination plan, you'll want to refer to Figures 20–39 for more extensive breakouts of the data.

(For geographic breakouts of selected portions of this data, please see Section 11.)

FIGURE 10

AVERAGE SALES COMPENSATION PAY LEVELS BY PLAN TYPE
AND ALL PLANS COMBINED ($000)

TOP MARKETING EXECUTIVE

	SALARY AND INCENTIVE			ALL-INCENTIVE PLAN	ALL-SALARY PLAN	AVERAGE TOTAL CASH COMPENSATION FOR ALL PLANS
	SALARY	INCENTIVE	TOTAL			
COMPANY SIZE						
UNDER $5 MILLION	$88.8	$18.3	$107.1	$100.0	$108.8	$101.0
$5MM–$25MM	75.8	13.8	89.7	74.8	84.0	82.7
$25MM–$100MM	111.0	33.6	144.6	146.5	142.0	135.4
$100MM–$250MM	135.4	35.0	170.4	N/R	N/R	166.1
OVER $250MM	152.0	53.5	205.5	N/R	250.0	233.5
PRODUCT OR SERVICE						
CONSUMER PRODUCTS	113.4	37.7	151.1	123.8	99.6	135.5
CONSUMER SERVICES	90.3	31.4	121.6	105.4	92.2	106.7
INDUSTRIAL PRODUCTS	108.6	29.1	137.7	N/R	122.2	127.1
INDUSTRIAL SERVICES	101.3	31.1	132.4	61.0	106.2	117.7
OFFICE PRODUCTS	139.3	39.2	178.5	70.0	90.5	179.8
OFFICE SERVICES	106.0	36.0	142.1	74.2	90.0	109.7
TYPE OF BUYER						
CONSUMERS	95.4	31.6	127.1	89.5	89.5	97.3
DISTRIBUTORS	116.9	36.4	153.3	120.0	130.7	141.9
INDUSTRY	107.4	30.5	137.9	74.2	100.1	120.5
RETAILERS	121.4	32.5	153.9	152.7	113.2	145.7
INDUSTRY						
BANKING	90.4	54.6	145.1	52.0	N/R	139.8
BUSINESS SERVICES	77.5	27.2	104.7	105.0	136.0	119.9
CHEMICALS	125.0	37.5	162.5	N/R	N/R	147.5
COMMUNICATIONS	90.0	31.2	121.2	N/R	65.0	123.3
CONSTRUCTION	70.0	2.4	72.4	90.0	N/R	86.7
EDUCATIONAL SERVICES	85.0	15.0	100.0	N/R	150.0	116.7
ELECTRONICS	120.0	20.6	140.6	N/R	175.0	161.7
ELECTRONIC COMPONENTS	92.5	24.4	116.9	N/R	N/R	135.0
FABRICATED METALS	115.0	38.2	153.2	N/R	N/R	152.4
HEALTH SERVICES	115.0	39.0	153.9	70.0	43.0	76.5
HOTELS AND OTHER LODGING PLACES	110.6	23.0	133.6	N/R	55.0	109.5
INSTRUMENTS	112.3	26.7	139.0	N/R	N/R	139.0
INSURANCE	154.5	60.0	214.5	N/R	70.6	113.6
MACHINERY	117.5	17.5	135.0	N/R	N/R	147.5
MANUFACTURING	120.0	14.9	134.9	N/R	85.0	95.8
OFFICE EQUIPMENT	140.0	31.3	171.3	N/R	17.0	176.0
PHARMACEUTICALS	181.7	63.3	245.0	N/R	125.0	217.5
PRINTING AND PUBLISHING	97.8	32.3	130.1	61.0	175.0	122.5
RETAIL	120.1	30.7	150.9	203.0	40.0	116.8
TRANSPORTATION EQUIPMENT	85.0	15.0	100.0	N/R	N/R	100.0
WHOLESALE (CONSUMER GOODS)	92.5	7.6	100.2	N/R	125.0	100.0
OVERALL	**$107.3**	**$29.2**	**$136.5**	**$99.0**	**$105.1**	**$121.0**

FIGURE 11

**AVERAGE SALES COMPENSATION PAY LEVELS BY PLAN TYPE
AND ALL PLANS COMBINED ($000)**

TOP SALES EXECUTIVE

	SALARY AND INCENTIVE			ALL-INCENTIVE PLAN	ALL-SALARY PLAN	AVERAGE TOTAL CASH COMPENSATION FOR ALL PLANS
	SALARY	INCENTIVE	TOTAL			
COMPANY SIZE						
UNDER $5 MILLION	$74.8	$12.6	$87.4	$93.3	$103.6	$77.2
$5MM–$25MM	64.4	18.1	82.5	82.0	85.3	81.7
$25MM–$100MM	101.4	35.1	136.5	94.0	103.4	124.0
$100MM–$250MM	117.9	31.2	149.1	N/R	185.0	152.0
OVER $250MM	125.9	55.9	181.8	N/R	300.0	220.2
PRODUCT OR SERVICE						
CONSUMER PRODUCTS	96.5	35.4	131.9	106.8	112.5	121.3
CONSUMER SERVICES	73.7	31.2	105.0	95.8	93.5	88.5
INDUSTRIAL PRODUCTS	86.5	27.8	114.2	N/R	105.8	109.9
INDUSTRIAL SERVICES	80.9	29.1	110.0	58.5	103.2	106.6
OFFICE PRODUCTS	100.2	42.0	142.2	60.0	90.0	141.4
OFFICE SERVICES	87.7	40.9	128.6	75.2	108.3	113.1
TYPE OF BUYER						
CONSUMERS	78.3	33.1	111.4	70.7	89.2	90.2
DISTRIBUTORS	94.0	31.9	125.9	100.8	115.1	118.5
INDUSTRY	89.8	29.9	119.7	75.2	104.6	109.2
RETAILERS	112.8	35.8	148.6	107.8	111.9	135.4
INDUSTRY						
BANKING	78.0	106.9	184.9	N/R	N/R	233.5
BUSINESS SERVICES	71.4	32.9	104.3	109.5	128.0	112.4
CHEMICALS	112.5	27.4	139.9	N/R	N/R	143.0
ELECTRONICS	90.8	25.4	116.2	N/R	125.0	125.0
ELECTRONIC COMPONENTS	75.0	7.5	82.5	N/R	121.0	110.5
FABRICATED METALS	94.5	29.9	124.4	N/R	N/R	113.4
HEALTH SERVICES	93.7	32.3	126.0	60.0	N/R	88.0
HOTELS AND OTHER LODGING PLACES	78.3	35.0	113.3	N/R	N/R	113.3
MACHINERY	145.0	9.0	154.0	N/R	N/R	158.3
MANUFACTURING	108.0	15.4	123.4	N/R	67.5	90.0
OFFICE EQUIPMENT	119.0	32.3	151.3	N/R	N/R	166.3
PHARMACEUTICALS	183.8	44.4	228.1	N/R	185.0	240.0
PRINTING AND PUBLISHING	86.9	21.5	108.4	58.5	150.0	112.0
RETAIL	91.0	27.3	118.3	123.0	48.0	69.0
TRANSPORTATION EQUIPMENT	85.0	17.5	102.5	N/R	80.0	95.0
WHOLESALE (CONSUMER GOODS)	83.0	24.5	107.5	59.0	140.0	97.2
OVERALL	**$91.0**	**$29.0**	**$119.9**	**$87.8**	**$105.8**	**$108.9**

FIGURE 12

AVERAGE SALES COMPENSATION PAY LEVELS BY PLAN TYPE
AND ALL PLANS COMBINED ($000)

REGIONAL SALES MANAGER

| | SALARY AND INCENTIVE | | | ALL-INCENTIVE PLAN | ALL-SALARY PLAN | AVERAGE TOTAL CASH COMPENSATION FOR ALL PLANS |
	SALARY	INCENTIVE	TOTAL			
COMPANY SIZE						
UNDER $5 MILLION	$84.1	$5.8	$89.9	$60.0	$46.0	$54.2
$5MM–$25MM	61.9	19.5	81.3	103.7	72.2	72.9
$25MM–$100MM	74.2	26.2	100.4	107.2	100.0	94.0
$100MM–$250MM	76.2	25.9	102.1	N/R	N/R	96.5
OVER $250MM	93.4	18.9	112.3	N/R	92.5	97.6
PRODUCT OR SERVICE						
CONSUMER PRODUCTS	82.3	20.6	102.9	134.5	62.8	86.8
CONSUMER SERVICES	76.5	17.3	93.8	97.2	65.6	76.8
INDUSTRIAL PRODUCTS	71.0	19.6	90.7	80.0	71.4	81.6
INDUSTRIAL SERVICES	71.3	19.0	90.4	N/R	58.8	81.1
OFFICE PRODUCTS	73.9	30.3	104.3	62.3	53.5	99.0
OFFICE SERVICES	75.8	32.4	108.2	103.7	50.0	107.2
TYPE OF BUYER						
CONSUMERS	68.8	17.9	86.7	98.4	71.8	78.7
DISTRIBUTORS	73.1	22.7	95.9	92.3	65.4	84.3
INDUSTRY	74.0	20.4	94.3	95.8	65.3	84.5
RETAILERS	81.6	25.3	106.9	97.2	51.4	94.8
INDUSTRY						
BUSINESS SERVICES	73.6	35.7	109.3	60.0	67.5	99.6
CHEMICALS	83.7	18.7	102.4	N/R	N/R	85.0
EDUCATIONAL SERVICES	60.0	21.2	81.2	N/R	55.0	80.0
ELECTRONICS	56.0	9.0	65.0	N/R	N/R	74.8
ELECTRONIC COMPONENTS	75.8	9.2	85.0	N/R	70.0	66.7
FABRICATED METALS	77.3	29.3	106.5	80.0	N/R	82.1
MACHINERY	111.7	8.8	120.4	N/R	50.0	107.3
MANUFACTURING	66.9	18.0	85.0	N/R	62.0	76.6
OFFICE EQUIPMENT	87.1	41.8	128.9	N/R	45.0	113.0
PHARMACEUTICALS	122.4	31.6	154.1	N/R	N/R	169.9
PRINTING AND PUBLISHING	75.9	20.0	95.9	N/R	N/R	88.3
RETAIL	67.5	7.8	75.2	134.5	N/R	95.0
WHOLESALE (CONSUMER GOODS)	53.7	16.0	69.7	N/R	82.5	68.6
OVERALL	**$74.5**	**$21.9**	**$96.4**	**$96.4**	**$67.4**	**$84.7**

FIGURE 13

AVERAGE SALES COMPENSATION PAY LEVELS BY PLAN TYPE AND ALL PLANS COMBINED ($000)

DISTRICT SALES MANAGER

	SALARY AND INCENTIVE			ALL-INCENTIVE PLAN	ALL-SALARY PLAN	AVERAGE TOTAL CASH COMPENSATION FOR ALL PLANS
	SALARY	INCENTIVE	TOTAL			
COMPANY SIZE						
UNDER $5 MILLION	$52.9	$15.0	$68.0	$100.0	$32.5	$64.1
$5MM–$25MM	58.5	18.8	77.3	N/R	65.0	69.3
$25MM–$100MM	66.5	23.6	90.2	N/R	85.0	91.1
$100MM–$250MM	60.0	17.2	77.2	N/R	N/R	80.3
OVER $250MM	80.9	22.2	103.2	N/R	69.4	83.1
PRODUCT OR SERVICE						
CONSUMER PRODUCTS	68.8	19.6	88.3	100.0	55.0	84.6
CONSUMER SERVICES	63.7	20.3	84.0	100.0	56.7	77.4
INDUSTRIAL PRODUCTS	65.4	18.9	84.2	100.0	69.6	82.6
INDUSTRIAL SERVICES	62.1	21.1	83.2	100.0	67.5	80.5
OFFICE PRODUCTS	61.6	16.4	78.1	100.0	N/R	80.4
OFFICE SERVICES	61.8	23.9	85.7	100.0	40.0	78.5
TYPE OF BUYER						
CONSUMERS	59.4	17.9	77.3	100.0	72.5	75.3
DISTRIBUTORS	63.1	20.9	84.0	N/R	69.4	79.2
INDUSTRY	65.8	20.4	86.2	100.0	64.6	81.3
RETAILERS	62.8	21.3	84.1	N/R	45.0	79.1
INDUSTRY						
BUSINESS SERVICES	55.2	33.0	88.1	N/R	50.0	62.1
CHEMICALS	54.6	15.8	70.4	N/R	N/R	51.8
ELECTRONIC COMPONENTS	65.0	7.8	72.8	N/R	65.0	60.2
FABRICATED METALS	59.8	26.4	86.2	N/R	N/R	96.9
INSURANCE	65.3	38.3	103.7	N/R	70.0	75.5
OFFICE EQUIPMENT	89.0	23.1	112.1	N/R	N/R	118.6
PRINTING AND PUBLISHING	57.7	16.0	73.7	N/R	N/R	67.3
WHOLESALE (CONSUMER GOODS)	49.0	11.0	60.0	N/R	54.2	68.9
OVERALL	**$64.5**	**$20.3**	**$84.8**	**$100.0**	**$61.0**	**$78.0**

FIGURE 14

AVERAGE SALES COMPENSATION PAY LEVELS BY PLAN TYPE
AND ALL PLANS COMBINED ($000)

SENIOR SALES REP

| | SALARY AND INCENTIVE | | | ALL-INCENTIVE PLAN | ALL-SALARY PLAN | AVERAGE TOTAL CASH COMPENSATION FOR ALL PLANS |
	SALARY	INCENTIVE	TOTAL			
COMPANY SIZE						
UNDER $5 MILLION	$46.3	$17.4	$63.7	$61.8	$49.9	$51.8
$5MM–$25MM	41.3	24.1	65.4	75.4	63.5	62.8
$25MM–$100MM	48.8	28.5	77.4	144.1	71.9	71.4
$100MM–$250MM	47.0	18.3	65.3	257.5	85.0	85.6
OVER $250MM	60.1	37.9	98.0	229.8	80.3	100.9
PRODUCT OR SERVICE						
CONSUMER PRODUCTS	56.3	30.3	86.6	88.2	62.3	72.1
CONSUMER SERVICES	47.9	29.3	77.1	83.6	52.6	61.7
INDUSTRIAL PRODUCTS	46.6	25.9	72.5	104.1	78.1	66.5
INDUSTRIAL SERVICES	46.9	30.8	77.7	101.4	51.0	61.7
OFFICE PRODUCTS	46.0	39.2	85.3	171.3	N/R	84.6
OFFICE SERVICES	42.5	38.9	81.5	117.1	50.0	81.9
TYPE OF BUYER						
CONSUMERS	47.6	27.3	75.0	82.8	56.2	63.6
DISTRIBUTORS	48.4	27.6	76.0	71.7	83.1	68.9
INDUSTRY	47.8	26.6	74.4	96.3	70.0	68.9
RETAILERS	54.7	29.9	84.6	129.3	77.4	76.0
INDUSTRY						
BANKING	50.1	87.8	137.8	N/R	N/R	177.4
BUSINESS SERVICES	38.4	47.2	85.6	96.0	42.5	71.5
CHEMICALS	55.8	14.8	70.5	N/R	N/R	62.9
COMMUNICATIONS	25.2	23.0	48.2	N/R	59.0	50.6
CONSTRUCTION	31.7	36.7	68.3	N/R	61.7	58.9
EDUCATIONAL SERVICES	47.5	32.5	80.0	110.0	89.7	99.8
ELECTRONICS	40.5	25.6	66.1	N/R	90.0	62.7
ELECTRONIC COMPONENTS	56.4	18.5	74.8	N/R	50.0	72.4
FABRICATED METALS	56.7	12.6	69.3	97.5	N/R	66.1
HOTELS AND OTHER LODGING PLACES	41.3	9.1	50.4	N/R	N/R	49.1
INSURANCE	38.5	25.7	64.2	68.6	55.0	62.8
MANUFACTURING	41.4	21.6	63.0	70.0	93.4	67.4
OFFICE EQUIPMENT	53.8	27.6	81.5	64.3	N/R	69.1
PHARMACEUTICALS	68.9	34.2	103.2	N/R	85.0	108.3
PRINTING AND PUBLISHING	39.6	16.8	56.4	122.8	52.3	71.4
RETAIL	30.5	29.6	60.2	213.8	24.3	61.0
TRANSPORTATION EQUIPMENT	36.5	18.0	54.5	N/R	110.0	64.6
WHOLESALE (CONSUMER GOODS)	37.1	9.6	46.7	130.7	66.3	59.8
OVERALL	**$47.5**	**$26.0**	**$73.5**	**$122.9**	**$64.9**	**$68.0**

FIGURE 15

AVERAGE SALES COMPENSATION PAY LEVELS BY PLAN TYPE AND ALL PLANS COMBINED ($000)

INTERMEDIATE SALES REP

	SALARY AND INCENTIVE			ALL-INCENTIVE PLAN	ALL-SALARY PLAN	AVERAGE TOTAL CASH COMPENSATION FOR ALL PLANS
	SALARY	INCENTIVE	TOTAL			
COMPANY SIZE						
UNDER $5 MILLION	$24.4	$12.7	$37.1	$40.8	$30.0	$35.5
$5MM–$25MM	30.7	14.8	45.5	43.8	39.6	42.8
$25MM–$100MM	42.1	15.7	57.9	68.6	38.2	50.2
$100MM–$250MM	34.8	15.4	50.2	57.3	N/R	51.2
OVER $250MM	48.7	17.7	66.3	119.6	65.0	62.8
PRODUCT OR SERVICE						
CONSUMER PRODUCTS	39.4	16.0	55.4	49.1	42.0	50.0
CONSUMER SERVICES	33.1	15.9	49.0	57.0	27.2	44.0
INDUSTRIAL PRODUCTS	37.3	12.1	49.4	54.8	47.1	46.2
INDUSTRIAL SERVICES	38.4	15.3	53.8	57.9	35.4	47.4
OFFICE PRODUCTS	35.2	24.3	59.6	50.0	N/R	56.0
OFFICE SERVICES	32.8	24.4	57.2	49.6	30.0	55.5
TYPE OF BUYER						
CONSUMERS	32.1	15.7	47.8	58.6	27.6	44.5
DISTRIBUTORS	39.0	17.4	56.4	43.0	49.8	48.7
INDUSTRY	36.8	14.8	51.6	52.3	41.9	46.9
RETAILERS	37.6	17.2	54.9	56.1	40.9	48.6
INDUSTRY						
BANKING	33.7	2.2	35.9	190.0	N/R	86.9
BUSINESS SERVICES	33.0	32.3	65.3	49.3	35.0	43.4
CHEMICALS	39.8	10.9	50.7	N/R	N/R	41.8
COMMUNICATIONS	29.9	12.5	42.4	N/R	N/R	80.1
EDUCATIONAL SERVICES	37.5	25.0	62.5	70.0	33.0	57.5
ELECTRONICS	36.2	9.0	45.3	N/R	N/R	38.7
ELECTRONIC COMPONENTS	49.2	27.0	76.2	N/R	45.0	65.8
FABRICATED METALS	49.2	10.3	59.5	55.0	N/R	50.2
HOTELS AND OTHER LODGING PLACES	33.4	6.8	40.2	N/R	N/R	41.1
INSURANCE	33.2	18.0	51.3	40.0	32.5	39.7
MACHINERY	46.2	3.8	50.0	N/R	N/R	60.8
MANUFACTURING	25.0	30.0	55.0	37.5	47.7	42.6
OFFICE EQUIPMENT	38.2	22.2	60.4	53.0	N/R	57.0
PHARMACEUTICALS	58.3	13.9	72.2	N/R	N/R	83.9
PRINTING AND PUBLISHING	29.7	7.4	37.1	53.8	36.2	39.7
RETAIL	26.8	18.4	45.2	49.9	22.5	42.1
WHOLESALE (CONSUMER GOODS)	26.5	8.0	34.5	54.8	50.0	42.3
OVERALL	**$36.1**	**$15.3**	**$51.4**	**$57.0**	**$38.9**	**$46.4**

FIGURE 16

AVERAGE SALES COMPENSATION PAY LEVELS BY PLAN TYPE
AND ALL PLANS COMBINED ($000)

ENTRY LEVEL SALES REP

	SALARY AND INCENTIVE			ALL-INCENTIVE PLAN	ALL-SALARY PLAN	AVERAGE TOTAL CASH COMPENSATION FOR ALL PLANS
	SALARY	INCENTIVE	TOTAL			
COMPANY SIZE						
UNDER $5 MILLION	$22.1	$6.0	$28.0	$18.2	$22.6	$27.0
$5MM–$25MM	26.1	10.3	36.3	56.5	26.4	31.8
$25MM–$100MM	31.1	14.9	46.0	44.3	32.9	39.1
$100MM–$250MM	32.5	8.8	41.4	29.2	25.0	35.8
OVER $250MM	39.3	26.9	66.2	10.4	54.5	56.3
PRODUCT OR SERVICE						
CONSUMER PRODUCTS	32.1	19.4	51.5	34.6	25.3	38.6
CONSUMER SERVICES	26.8	17.1	43.9	24.4	23.9	30.6
INDUSTRIAL PRODUCTS	32.1	14.9	47.0	39.2	35.7	38.3
INDUSTRIAL SERVICES	31.7	18.4	50.1	47.9	26.7	39.4
OFFICE PRODUCTS	30.1	24.8	54.9	36.8	18.3	43.1
OFFICE SERVICES	27.5	20.3	47.8	55.4	24.3	38.5
TYPE OF BUYER						
CONSUMERS	27.6	17.2	44.8	30.8	24.1	32.7
DISTRIBUTORS	31.4	15.4	46.8	36.6	34.6	39.2
INDUSTRY	30.6	14.4	45.0	50.7	29.7	37.0
RETAILERS	30.2	16.4	46.6	28.0	29.3	35.9
INDUSTRY						
BANKING	34.6	46.3	80.9	N/R	N/R	87.7
BUSINESS SERVICES	26.9	15.7	42.6	64.9	27.5	34.8
CHEMICALS	32.1	10.7	42.8	N/R	N/R	36.0
COMMUNICATIONS	19.0	14.1	33.1	N/R	30.5	31.4
EDUCATIONAL SERVICES	27.8	11.2	39.0	N/R	32.0	44.8
ELECTRONICS	28.8	6.9	35.6	N/R	N/R	27.8
ELECTRONIC COMPONENTS	45.0	27.0	72.0	N/R	40.0	61.3
FABRICATED METALS	44.8	8.1	52.8	32.0	N/R	37.4
HOTELS AND OTHER LODGING PLACES	28.0	5.1	33.1	N/R	N/R	33.1
INSURANCE	27.5	11.2	38.7	26.7	25.0	30.4
MACHINERY	31.2	3.7	34.9	N/R	N/R	60.0
MANUFACTURING	34.0	12.7	46.7	N/R	36.0	43.1
OFFICE EQUIPMENT	32.5	12.1	44.6	N/R	N/R	36.3
PHARMACEUTICALS	45.9	13.3	59.2	N/R	N/R	65.2
PRINTING AND PUBLISHING	22.0	3.1	25.1	49.3	29.2	32.4
RETAIL	24.0	16.0	40.0	24.6	18.4	32.5
WHOLESALE (CONSUMER GOODS)	25.9	5.5	31.4	40.4	30.0	31.7
OVERALL	**$29.7**	**$13.4**	**$43.1**	**$40.2**	**$28.6**	**$35.5**

FIGURE 17

AVERAGE SALES COMPENSATION PAY LEVELS BY PLAN TYPE
AND ALL PLANS COMBINED ($000)

NATIONAL/MAJOR ACCOUNT MANAGER

	SALARY AND INCENTIVE			ALL-INCENTIVE PLAN	ALL-SALARY PLAN	AVERAGE TOTAL CASH COMPENSATION FOR ALL PLANS
	SALARY	INCENTIVE	TOTAL			
COMPANY SIZE						
UNDER $5 MILLION	$45.5	$6.9	$52.4	N/R	$52.5	$60.0
$5MM–$25MM	54.7	11.4	66.2	93.0	72.8	72.8
$25MM–$100MM	72.1	31.2	103.2	N/R	62.3	86.6
$100MM–$250MM	88.1	44.2	132.3	N/R	N/R	121.7
OVER $250MM	77.8	23.0	100.7	N/R	107.5	104.8
PRODUCT OR SERVICE						
CONSUMER PRODUCTS	69.3	23.0	92.3	93.0	N/R	88.9
CONSUMER SERVICES	57.6	23.4	81.0	N/R	N/R	78.4
INDUSTRIAL PRODUCTS	69.2	15.2	84.4	93.0	83.9	85.2
INDUSTRIAL SERVICES	71.4	26.0	97.4	93.0	81.3	98.8
OFFICE PRODUCTS	72.3	34.8	107.1	93.0	N/R	93.3
OFFICE SERVICES	74.7	43.7	118.4	93.0	N/R	105.2
TYPE OF BUYER						
CONSUMERS	63.2	23.6	86.8	93.0	N/R	86.6
DISTRIBUTORS	64.8	26.4	91.3	93.0	82.2	87.3
INDUSTRY	76.6	25.9	102.5	93.0	N/R	95.1
RETAILERS	65.1	28.7	93.8	93.0	N/R	90.6
INDUSTRY						
CHEMICALS	93.3	18.7	112.0	N/R	N/R	97.8
ELECTRONICS	71.7	8.1	79.8	N/R	N/R	86.4
ELECTRONIC COMPONENTS	61.9	15.6	77.6	N/R	95.0	90.8
MACHINERY	86.7	5.8	92.5	N/R	100.0	405.2
OFFICE EQUIPMENT	55.5	27.8	83.2	N/R	N/R	75.9
PRINTING AND PUBLISHING	63.3	15.0	78.3	N/R	62.3	69.7
WHOLESALE (CONSUMER GOODS)	N/R	N/R	N/R	93.0	77.7	80.5
OVERALL	**$72.2**	**$26.0**	**$98.2**	**$93.0**	**$79.8**	**$88.6**

FIGURE 18

AVERAGE SALES COMPENSATION PAY LEVELS BY PLAN TYPE AND ALL PLANS COMBINED ($000)

NATIONAL ACCOUNT REP

	SALARY AND INCENTIVE			ALL-INCENTIVE PLAN	ALL-SALARY PLAN	AVERAGE TOTAL CASH COMPENSATION FOR ALL PLANS
	SALARY	INCENTIVE	TOTAL			
COMPANY SIZE						
$5MM–$25MM	$39.3	$5.5	$44.8	$57.2	$67.5	$49.1
$25MM–$100MM	65.9	48.1	114.0	N/R	60.0	79.8
$100MM–$250MM	54.4	10.2	64.7	N/R	N/R	68.3
OVER $250MM	66.7	13.0	79.7	N/R	74.2	80.9
PRODUCT OR SERVICE						
CONSUMER PRODUCTS	69.8	18.7	88.5	71.0	N/R	79.4
CONSUMER SERVICES	56.1	12.0	68.0	N/R	N/R	64.5
INDUSTRIAL PRODUCTS	57.8	30.0	87.9	71.0	72.1	76.1
INDUSTRIAL SERVICES	62.6	21.0	83.6	71.0	72.5	77.3
OFFICE PRODUCTS	69.9	11.0	80.9	57.2	N/R	72.4
OFFICE SERVICES	71.3	17.4	88.7	57.2	N/R	72.7
TYPE OF BUYER						
CONSUMERS	56.0	13.2	69.2	57.2	N/R	59.2
DISTRIBUTORS	60.9	28.1	89.1	57.2	65.8	62.8
INDUSTRY	68.8	19.4	88.2	57.2	N/R	79.6
RETAILERS	54.4	15.1	69.5	71.0	N/R	63.9
INDUSTRY						
ELECTRONIC COMPONENTS	75.0	11.7	86.7	N/R	72.5	77.2
MANUFACTURING	65.0	15.6	80.6	N/R	60.0	59.3
OFFICE EQUIPMENT	61.8	14.7	76.5	N/R	N/R	66.8
PRINTING AND PUBLISHING	60.4	8.8	69.2	N/R	N/R	45.1
OVERALL	**$60.9**	**$25.5**	**$86.4**	**$57.2**	**$68.3**	**$71.2**

FIGURE 19

**AVERAGE SALES COMPENSATION PAY LEVELS BY PLAN TYPE
AND ALL PLANS COMBINED ($000)**

MAJOR (KEY) ACCOUNT REP

	SALARY AND INCENTIVE			ALL-INCENTIVE PLAN	ALL-SALARY PLAN	AVERAGE TOTAL CASH COMPENSATION FOR ALL PLANS
	SALARY	INCENTIVE	TOTAL			
COMPANY SIZE						
UNDER $5 MILLION	$44.7	$5.8	$50.5	N/R	N/R	$50.5
$5MM–$25MM	45.0	10.2	55.2	48.0	42.5	51.0
$25MM–$100MM	58.7	21.8	80.4	80.0	83.8	78.4
$100MM–$250MM	72.6	70.8	143.3	N/R	N/R	144.1
OVER $250MM	72.5	20.4	92.9	N/R	80.0	99.1
PRODUCT OR SERVICE						
CONSUMER PRODUCTS	64.4	20.2	84.5	48.0	90.0	83.6
CONSUMER SERVICES	51.1	15.7	66.8	N/R	55.0	63.8
INDUSTRIAL PRODUCTS	58.3	15.0	73.3	64.0	83.0	74.3
INDUSTRIAL SERVICES	55.9	16.4	72.3	48.0	62.5	66.7
OFFICE PRODUCTS	70.7	43.4	114.2	48.0	110.0	90.9
OFFICE SERVICES	58.6	42.6	101.3	48.0	80.0	74.2
TYPE OF BUYER						
CONSUMERS	54.9	17.0	71.9	48.0	76.2	70.0
DISTRIBUTORS	62.5	23.4	86.0	48.0	66.0	79.4
INDUSTRY	59.8	28.7	88.5	64.0	85.0	77.1
RETAILERS	61.2	18.4	79.6	48.0	80.0	73.5
INDUSTRY						
BUSINESS SERVICES	74.2	71.6	145.9	N/R	35.0	60.0
ELECTRONIC COMPONENTS	61.2	24.9	86.2	N/R	50.0	74.1
OFFICE EQUIPMENT	58.1	11.8	69.9	N/R	N/R	60.2
WHOLESALE (CONSUMER GOODS)	N/R	N/R	N/R	64.0	125.0	95.0
OVERALL	**$57.4**	**$22.9**	**$80.3**	**$64.0**	**$72.5**	**$72.1**

FIGURES 20–29 — COMPENSATION TABLES: AVERAGE TOTAL CASH COMPENSATION FOR AVERAGE, BETTER, AND BEST PERFORMERS (MEDIAN AND THIRD QUARTILE)

You'll want to use these tables to determine total cash compensation for those people paid on a combination plan. Remember, use tables 10–19 to determine total cash compensation for those individuals on either a "salary-only" or "incentive-only" plan. Here's how this group of tables works:

Figures 20–29 show how much average, better, and best performers in various positions earn at typical-paying ("median") companies and higher-paying (third-quartile) companies. The positions surveyed are:

- Top Marketing Executive
- Top Sales Executive
- Regional Sales Manager
- District Sales Manager
- Senior Sales Representative (three or more years of experience)
- Intermediate Sales Representative (one to three years of experience)
- Entry Level Sales Representative (less than one year of experience)
- National/Major Account Manager
- National Account Representative
- Major (Key) Account Representative

Note: Because most companies have only one top marketing executive and/or one top sales executive, there is no better or best performer for that position. Therefore, the data for these two positions encompasses the full range of responses received.

Here are some suggestions on how to use these tables:

1. Determine the relative level you should be paying at — median, above median, below median, highest, etc.
2. Determine the relative skill level of the person in the position for which you are analyzing compensation. Is this individual an average performer, a better performer, or a top (best) performer?
3. Select the comparison groups that are the most similar to your company. Potential comparison groups might be based on company size, type of buyer, type of product or service sold, or industry.
4. Use the pay levels on the tables you've selected as guides when analyzing pay levels in your organization.
5. Remember that these data tables provide figures for total cash compensation. You still will need to break the total compensation you select into its base salary and incentive components. Figures 30–39 will help you determine salary levels for combined plans.

FIGURE 20

AVERAGE TOTAL CASH COMPENSATION

TOP MARKETING EXECUTIVE

	MEDIAN ($000)	THIRD QUARTILE ($000)
COMPANY SIZE		
UNDER $5 MILLION	$90.0	$150.0
$5MM–$25MM	72.0	125.0
$25MM–$100MM	130.0	175.0
$100MM–$250MM	145.0	250.0
OVER $250MM	240.0	250.0
PRODUCT OR SERVICE		
CONSUMER PRODUCTS	130.0	203.0
CONSUMER SERVICES	100.0	150.0
INDUSTRIAL PRODUCTS	125.0	185.0
INDUSTRIAL SERVICES	110.0	165.0
OFFICE PRODUCTS	160.0	275.0
OFFICE SERVICES	94.5	175.0
TYPE OF BUYER		
CONSUMERS	90.0	160.0
DISTRIBUTORS	145.0	200.0
INDUSTRY	115.0	175.0
RETAILERS	144.0	230.0
INDUSTRY		
BANKING	62.0	270.0
BUSINESS SERVICES	110.0	150.0
CHEMICALS	150.0	162.5
COMMUNICATIONS	110.0	160.0
ELECTRONICS	175.0	200.0
ELECTRONIC COMPONENTS	120.0	150.0
FABRICATED METALS	135.0	195.0
HEALTH SERVICES	70.0	82.9
HOTELS AND OTHER LODGING PLACES	105.0	150.0
INSURANCE	85.0	189.0
MACHINERY	125.0	170.0
MANUFACTURING	98.0	115.0
OFFICE EQUIPMENT	144.0	250.0
PHARMACEUTICALS	185.0	250.0
PRINTING AND PUBLISHING	125.0	148.0
RETAIL	67.0	203.0
WHOLESALE (CONSUMER GOODS)	95.0	160.0
OVERALL	**$120.0**	**$175.0**

FIGURE 21

AVERAGE TOTAL CASH COMPENSATION

TOP SALES EXECUTIVE

	MEDIAN ($000)	THIRD QUARTILE ($000)
COMPANY SIZE		
UNDER $5 MILLION	$73.0	$120.0
$5MM–$25MM	80.0	118.0
$25MM–$100MM	125.0	160.0
$100MM–$250MM	145.0	185.0
OVER $250MM	240.0	280.0
PRODUCT OR SERVICE		
CONSUMER PRODUCTS	123.0	180.0
CONSUMER SERVICES	84.0	130.0
INDUSTRIAL PRODUCTS	107.0	156.0
INDUSTRIAL SERVICES	107.0	156.0
OFFICE PRODUCTS	125.0	250.0
OFFICE SERVICES	118.0	185.0
TYPE OF BUYER		
CONSUMERS	84.0	150.0
DISTRIBUTORS	123.0	160.0
INDUSTRY	107.0	160.0
RETAILERS	130.0	235.0
INDUSTRY		
BANKING	172.0	295.0
BUSINESS SERVICES	118.0	150.0
CHEMICALS	130.0	156.0
COMMUNICATIONS	78.0	130.0
CONSTRUCTION	68.5	89.2
ELECTRONICS	130.0	160.0
ELECTRONIC COMPONENTS	107.0	125.0
FABRICATED METALS	123.6	140.0
HEALTH SERVICES	60.0	116.0
INSTRUMENTS	90.0	100.0
MACHINERY	160.0	200.0
MANUFACTURING	75.0	140.0
OFFICE EQUIPMENT	144.0	275.0
PHARMACEUTICALS	235.0	270.0
PRINTING AND PUBLISHING	125.0	150.0
RETAIL	70.0	99.0
WHOLESALE (CONSUMER GOODS)	85.0	180.0
OVERALL	**$110.0**	**$160.0**

FIGURE 22

AVERAGE TOTAL CASH COMPENSATION

REGIONAL SALES MANAGER

	AVERAGE PERFORMER		BETTER PERFORMER		BEST PERFORMER	
	MEDIAN ($000)	THIRD QUARTILE ($000)	MEDIAN ($000)	THIRD QUARTILE ($000)	MEDIAN ($000)	THIRD QUARTILE ($000)
COMPANY SIZE						
UNDER $5 MILLION	$50.0	$65.0	N/R	N/R	$50.0	$50.0
$5MM–$25MM	65.0	84.0	70.0	85.0	82.0	90.0
$25MM–$100MM	90.0	102.0	90.0	N/R	106.0	115.0
$100MM–$250MM	90.0	120.0	108.0	120.0	120.0	130.0
OVER $250MM	97.5	115.0	100.0	135.0	115.0	135.0
PRODUCT OR SERVICE						
CONSUMER PRODUCTS	90.0	113.0	N/R	N/R	85.0	115.0
CONSUMER SERVICES	65.0	100.0	70.0	135.0	85.0	N/R
INDUSTRIAL PRODUCTS	74.0	100.0	81.0	100.0	100.0	120.0
INDUSTRIAL SERVICES	80.0	117.5	N/R	N/R	90.0	134.0
OFFICE PRODUCTS	91.5	150.0	98.0	150.0	120.0	200.0
OFFICE SERVICES	91.5	160.0	100.0	170.0	120.0	200.0
TYPE OF BUYER						
CONSUMERS	75.0	100.0	N/R	N/R	75.0	115.0
DISTRIBUTORS	80.0	113.0	83.0	N/R	90.0	115.0
INDUSTRY	80.0	105.0	83.0	108.0	104.0	125.0
RETAILERS	90.0	135.0	100.0	156.0	105.0	200.0
INDUSTRY						
BUSINESS SERVICES	90.0	120.0	108.0	170.0	134.0	N/R
CHEMICALS	95.0	95.0	N/R	105.0	105.0	115.0
COMMUNICATIONS	32.0	160.0	49.8	N/R	N/R	N/R
EDUCATIONAL SERVICES	65.0	120.0	120.0	120.0	120.0	120.0
ELECTRONICS	56.0	63.0	76.0	83.0	97.0	106.0
ELECTRONIC COMPONENTS	70.0	90.0	N/R	100.0	8.0	120.0
FABRICATED METALS	81.1	86.0	N/R	88.0	100.0	104.0
HEALTH SERVICES	50.0	105.0	62.0	N/R	75.0	75.0
HOTELS AND OTHER LODGING PLACES	53.0	54.0	57.0	61.0	64.0	68.0
INSTRUMENTS	60.0	65.0	85.0	95.0	110.0	125.0
INSURANCE	30.0	80.0	N/R	N/R	N/R	N/R
MACHINERY	97.5	140.0	N/R	N/R	110.0	135.0
MANUFACTURING	69.0	95.0	N/R	N/R	85.0	126.0
OFFICE EQUIPMENT	115.0	175.0	N/R	N/R	120.0	200.0
PHARMACEUTICALS	195.0	215.0	N/R	235.0	85.0	255.0
PRINTING AND PUBLISHING	91.5	102.0	98.0	122.0	110.0	142.0
RETAIL	75.0	113.0	95.0	156.0	N/R	N/R
WHOLESALE (CONSUMER GOODS)	70.0	74.0	71.0	75.0	N/R	90.0
OVERALL	**$80.0**	**$102.0**	**$84.0**	**$110.0**	**$104.0**	**$121.0**

FIGURE 23

AVERAGE TOTAL CASH COMPENSATION

DISTRICT SALES MANAGER

	AVERAGE PERFORMER		BETTER PERFORMER		BEST PERFORMER	
	MEDIAN ($000)	THIRD QUARTILE ($000)	MEDIAN ($000)	THIRD QUARTILE ($000)	MEDIAN ($000)	THIRD QUARTILE ($000)
COMPANY SIZE						
UNDER $5 MILLION	$75.0	$100.0	N/R	N/R	$51.2	$60.0
$5MM–$25MM	70.0	90.0	N/R	90.0	50.0	90.0
$25MM–$100MM	85.0	105.0	N/R	N/R	65.0	90.0
$100MM–$250MM	60.0	85.0	75.0	95.0	90.0	110.0
OVER $250MM	65.0	130.0	80.0	140.0	95.0	155.0
PRODUCT OR SERVICE						
CONSUMER PRODUCTS	85.0	110.0	N/R	131.0	90.0	N/R
CONSUMER SERVICES	76.0	100.0	N/R	140.0	80.0	N/R
INDUSTRIAL PRODUCTS	75.0	100.0	75.0	100.0	90.0	115.0
INDUSTRIAL SERVICES	76.0	102.5	N/R	N/R	90.0	105.0
OFFICE PRODUCTS	60.0	102.5	68.0	N/R	90.0	120.0
OFFICE SERVICES	75.0	100.0	90.0	100.0	N/R	140.0
TYPE OF BUYER						
CONSUMERS	75.0	100.0	N/R	N/R	64.0	80.0
DISTRIBUTORS	65.0	100.0	75.0	N/R	85.0	105.0
INDUSTRY	80.0	103.0	N/R	N/R	85.0	115.0
RETAILERS	71.0	102.5	N/R	N/R	80.0	90.0
INDUSTRY						
BUSINESS SERVICES	60.0	80.0	90.0	90.0	N/R	N/R
CHEMICALS	65.0	78.0	N/R	N/R	30.0	65.0
ELECTRONIC COMPONENTS	65.0	85.0	N/R	95.0	5.0	110.0
FABRICATED METALS	82.0	103.0	108.0	131.0	115.0	138.0
INSURANCE	75.0	76.0	N/R	N/R	80.0	80.0
MACHINERY	55.0	130.0	N/R	N/R	50.0	85.0
MANUFACTURING	60.0	143.0	N/R	N/R	N/R	N/R
OFFICE EQUIPMENT	115.0	130.0	N/R	140.0	120.0	155.0
PHARMACEUTICALS	110.0	184.0	196.0	196.0	220.0	220.0
PRINTING AND PUBLISHING	70.0	80.0	N/R	N/R	50.0	90.0
WHOLESALE (CONSUMER GOODS)	58.0	75.0	75.0	80.0	90.0	95.0
OVERALL	**$75.0**	**$100.0**	**$75.0**	**N/R**	**$80.0**	**$110.0**

FIGURE 24

AVERAGE TOTAL CASH COMPENSATION

SENIOR SALES REP

	AVERAGE PERFORMER		BETTER PERFORMER		BEST PERFORMER	
	MEDIAN ($000)	THIRD QUARTILE ($000)	MEDIAN ($000)	THIRD QUARTILE ($000)	MEDIAN ($000)	THIRD QUARTILE ($000)
COMPANY SIZE						
UNDER $5 MILLION	$47.5	$70.0	N/R	N/R	$45.0	$65.0
$5MM–$25MM	55.0	75.0	55.0	N/R	60.0	82.0
$25MM–$100MM	65.0	95.0	67.5	N/R	89.0	115.0
$100MM–$250MM	57.0	85.0	70.0	120.0	93.0	200.0
OVER $250MM	86.0	109.0	96.0	140.0	135.0	158.0
PRODUCT OR SERVICE						
CONSUMER PRODUCTS	63.0	90.0	67.5	100.0	77.0	125.0
CONSUMER SERVICES	50.0	75.0	60.0	85.0	65.0	108.0
INDUSTRIAL PRODUCTS	56.0	77.0	65.0	85.0	80.0	119.0
INDUSTRIAL SERVICES	53.0	80.0	60.0	85.0	70.0	119.0
OFFICE PRODUCTS	70.0	100.0	80.0	120.0	118.0	200.0
OFFICE SERVICES	70.0	109.0	78.0	110.0	100.0	169.0
TYPE OF BUYER						
CONSUMERS	51.0	75.0	56.5	85.0	65.0	108.0
DISTRIBUTORS	60.0	85.0	63.5	85.0	80.0	108.0
INDUSTRY	60.0	85.0	64.5	85.0	80.0	120.0
RETAILERS	60.0	91.0	67.5	98.0	90.0	165.0
INDUSTRY						
BANKING	70.0	120.0	230.0	245.0	249.0	259.0
BUSINESS SERVICES	75.0	95.0	N/R	N/R	70.0	100.0
CHEMICALS	59.0	70.0	68.0	70.0	85.0	104.0
COMMUNICATIONS	45.0	53.0	N/R	64.5	60.0	220.0
CONSTRUCTION	50.0	50.0	65.0	100.0	75.0	N/R
EDUCATIONAL SERVICES	50.0	80.0	80.0	110.0	140.0	150.0
ELECTRONICS	70.0	70.0	N/R	80.0	80.0	100.0
ELECTRONIC COMPONENTS	50.0	70.0	80.0	87.5	95.0	135.0
FABRICATED METALS	56.0	63.0	63.5	69.0	N/R	93.0
HEALTH SERVICES	70.0	90.0	82.0	N/R	100.0	100.0
HOTELS AND OTHER LODGING PLACES	40.0	60.0	40.8	N/R	61.0	65.0
INSTRUMENTS	75.0	95.0	80.0	105.0	89.0	125.0
INSURANCE	57.0	70.0	60.0	73.5	80.0	92.0
MACHINERY	119.0	340.0	119.0	N/R	119.0	141.0
MANUFACTURING	55.0	77.0	65.0	N/R	81.2	90.0
OFFICE EQUIPMENT	70.0	90.0	N/R	142.0	82.0	N/R
PHARMACEUTICALS	100.0	120.0	120.0	144.0	N/R	158.0
PRINTING AND PUBLISHING	50.0	95.0	60.0	N/R	60.0	150.0
REAL ESTATE	80.0	174.7	120.0	285.0	250.0	N/R
RETAIL	43.0	80.0	53.0	N/R	63.0	108.0
RUBBER/PLASTICS	85.0	100.0	N/R	N/R	40.0	40.0
TRANSPORTATION EQUIPMENT	50.0	110.0	N/R	N/R	15.0	70.0
WHOLESALE (CONSUMER GOODS)	51.0	60.0	65.0	75.0	80.0	90.0
OVERALL	**$58.0**	**$85.0**	**$65.0**	**$87.5**	**$80.0**	**$120.0**

FIGURE 25

AVERAGE TOTAL CASH COMPENSATION

INTERMEDIATE SALES REP

	AVERAGE PERFORMER		BETTER PERFORMER		BEST PERFORMER	
	MEDIAN ($000)	THIRD QUARTILE ($000)	MEDIAN ($000)	THIRD QUARTILE ($000)	MEDIAN ($000)	THIRD QUARTILE ($000)
COMPANY SIZE						
UNDER $5 MILLION	$30.5	$45.0	$32.2	N/R	$34.2	N/R
$5MM–$25MM	40.0	50.0	45.0	50.0	50.0	58.0
$25MM–$100MM	45.0	60.0	45.5	N/R	54.0	70.0
$100MM–$250MM	32.5	60.0	45.0	70.0	80.0	80.0
OVER $250MM	60.0	70.0	66.0	80.0	90.0	100.0
PRODUCT OR SERVICE						
CONSUMER PRODUCTS	45.0	60.0	49.5	65.0	57.0	83.0
CONSUMER SERVICES	39.0	50.0	43.0	66.0	55.0	90.0
INDUSTRIAL PRODUCTS	43.0	51.8	45.0	55.0	53.0	80.0
INDUSTRIAL SERVICES	44.0	60.0	45.0	72.0	58.0	90.0
OFFICE PRODUCTS	46.8	62.0	50.0	72.0	80.0	100.0
OFFICE SERVICES	46.0	63.0	50.0	72.0	65.0	90.0
TYPE OF BUYER						
CONSUMERS	39.0	50.0	45.0	65.0	53.0	83.0
DISTRIBUTORS	45.0	60.0	46.0	66.0	57.0	80.0
INDUSTRY	44.0	60.0	45.0	63.0	52.0	80.0
RETAILERS	40.0	60.0	45.0	66.0	58.0	85.0
INDUSTRY						
BANKING	40.0	70.0	100.0	135.0	153.5	N/R
BUSINESS SERVICES	43.0	60.0	N/R	70.0	41.5	N/R
CHEMICALS	45.0	50.0	N/R	50.0	54.0	72.0
COMMUNICATIONS	31.0	67.0	63.0	92.0	103.0	124.5
EDUCATIONAL SERVICES	45.0	60.0	80.0	80.0	100.0	100.0
ELECTRONICS	32.0	50.0	43.0	72.0	52.0	90.0
ELECTRONIC COMPONENTS	45.0	60.0	72.0	80.0	80.0	125.0
FABRICATED METALS	48.5	51.8	49.0	N/R	50.0	52.0
HOTELS AND OTHER LODGING PLACES	38.5	43.8	N/R	45.5	41.0	N/R
INSURANCE	40.0	40.0	40.0	41.2	47.5	50.0
MACHINERY	47.0	65.0	60.0	90.5	70.0	96.5
MANUFACTURING	43.0	53.0	N/R	N/R	40.0	60.0
OFFICE EQUIPMENT	46.8	65.0	50.0	80.0	65.0	100.0
PHARMACEUTICALS	90.0	95.0	N/R	109.0	57.0	121.0
PRINTING AND PUBLISHING	32.5	50.0	42.0	55.0	50.0	80.0
REAL ESTATE	33.0	41.1	50.0	57.3	95.0	95.0
RETAIL	32.8	39.0	42.5	65.0	53.0	N/R
WHOLESALE (CONSUMER GOODS)	40.0	45.0	45.0	52.0	58.0	62.5
OVERALL	**$43.0**	**$60.0**	**$45.0**	**$63.0**	**$54.0**	**$80.0**

FIGURE 26

AVERAGE TOTAL CASH COMPENSATION

ENTRY LEVEL SALES REP

	AVERAGE PERFORMER		BETTER PERFORMER		BEST PERFORMER	
	MEDIAN ($000)	THIRD QUARTILE ($000)	MEDIAN ($000)	THIRD QUARTILE ($000)	MEDIAN ($000)	THIRD QUARTILE ($000)
COMPANY SIZE						
UNDER $5 MILLION	$25.0	$35.0	$30.0	N/R	$31.8	N/R
$5MM–$25MM	31.2	39.0	N/R	39.7	30.5	45.0
$25MM–$100MM	35.0	45.0	36.5	N/R	46.0	55.8
$100MM–$250MM	30.5	50.0	N/R	N/R	36.0	40.0
OVER $250MM	43.0	60.0	62.0	70.0	72.0	80.0
PRODUCT OR SERVICE						
CONSUMER PRODUCTS	34.0	43.0	40.0	50.0	52.0	75.0
CONSUMER SERVICES	25.2	35.0	31.3	43.0	40.0	55.8
INDUSTRIAL PRODUCTS	35.0	45.0	39.7	60.0	47.0	67.2
INDUSTRIAL SERVICES	35.0	50.0	40.0	60.0	50.0	68.0
OFFICE PRODUCTS	35.0	50.0	43.0	75.0	53.0	80.0
OFFICE SERVICES	34.0	50.0	41.0	60.0	52.0	60.5
TYPE OF BUYER						
CONSUMERS	30.0	40.0	35.0	47.0	41.5	60.0
DISTRIBUTORS	35.0	45.0	41.0	62.4	52.0	70.0
INDUSTRY	34.0	45.0	39.7	60.0	46.0	60.5
RETAILERS	32.0	43.0	36.5	50.0	42.5	75.0
INDUSTRY						
BUSINESS SERVICES	40.0	45.0	N/R	50.2	33.0	60.0
CHEMICALS	36.4	40.0	N/R	47.0	48.0	55.0
COMMUNICATIONS	25.0	45.0	30.5	N/R	30.5	30.5
EDUCATIONAL SERVICES	39.0	50.0	60.0	60.0	70.0	70.0
ELECTRONICS	27.0	30.0	N/R	38.0	20.0	47.0
ELECTRONIC COMPONENTS	40.0	55.0	67.0	75.0	80.0	120.0
FABRICATED METALS	45.0	52.0	47.0	68.0	N/R	N/R
HOTELS AND OTHER LODGING PLACES	31.2	33.5	N/R	36.5	36.0	N/R
INSURANCE	25.5	35.0	30.0	N/R	37.5	40.0
MACHINERY	37.0	55.0	66.0	80.0	72.0	90.0
MANUFACTURING	36.0	57.6	62.4	62.4	67.2	67.2
OFFICE EQUIPMENT	34.0	36.0	34.0	37.0	39.0	44.0
PHARMACEUTICALS	53.0	95.0	N/R	N/R	45.0	72.0
PRINTING AND PUBLISHING	24.0	30.5	35.0	60.0	38.0	68.0
REAL ESTATE	10.4	25.0	10.5	32.0	40.0	40.0
RETAIL	26.5	33.0	30.5	39.7	41.5	53.0
RUBBER/PLASTICS	46.0	65.0	N/R	N/R	50.0	50.0
TRANSPORTATION EQUIPMENT	32.0	45.0	N/R	N/R	10.0	10.0
WHOLESALE (CONSUMER GOODS)	30.0	35.0	40.0	42.0	42.5	60.0
OVERALL	**$32.0**	**$45.0**	**$35.0**	**$50.0**	**$44.0**	**$60.0**

FIGURE 27

Average Total Cash Compensation

National/Major Account Manager

	Average Performer		Better Performer		Best Performer	
	Median ($000)	Third Quartile ($000)	Median ($000)	Third Quartile ($000)	Median ($000)	Third Quartile ($000)
Company Size						
Under $5 Million	$57.0	$70.0	N/R	N/R	N/R	N/R
$5MM–$25MM	68.0	80.0	N/R	110.0	52.0	N/R
$25MM–$100MM	77.0	112.0	N/R	N/R	N/R	N/R
$100MM–$250MM	N/R	N/R	N/R	N/R	100.0	140.0
Over $250MM	90.0	125.0	98.0	N/R	120.0	145.0
Product or Service						
Consumer Products	80.0	100.0	92.5	110.0	108.0	125.0
Consumer Services	70.0	87.0	82.5	98.0	108.0	120.0
Industrial Products	76.0	95.0	85.0	105.0	108.0	120.0
Industrial Services	90.0	110.0	105.0	140.0	120.0	145.0
Office Products	87.0	112.0	98.0	140.0	108.0	140.0
Office Services	87.0	140.0	110.0	140.0	N/R	140.0
Type of Buyer						
Consumers	70.0	90.0	92.5	98.0	108.0	120.0
Distributors	77.5	100.0	98.0	115.0	120.0	140.0
Industry	90.0	112.0	92.5	N/R	108.0	125.0
Retailers	77.5	100.0	98.0	140.0	120.0	145.0
Industry						
Business Services	140.0	280.0	175.0	N/R	250.0	250.0
Chemicals	98.0	150.0	N/R	N/R	N/R	N/R
Electronics	87.0	90.0	N/R	98.0	77.0	120.0
Electronic Components	75.0	90.0	85.0	105.0	108.0	145.0
Manufacturing	95.0	100.0	105.0	105.0	120.0	120.0
Office Equipment	66.0	90.0	92.5	160.0	125.0	160.0
Pharmaceuticals	127.0	175.0	138.0	N/R	142.0	142.0
Printing and Publishing	65.0	77.0	N/R	N/R	65.0	100.0
Transportation Equipment	45.0	100.0	N/R	N/R	N/R	N/R
Wholesale (Consumer Goods)	68.0	76.0	110.0	115.0	120.0	120.0
Overall	**$85.0**	**$110.0**	**$92.5**	**$115.0**	**$108.0**	**$140.0**

FIGURE 28

AVERAGE TOTAL CASH COMPENSATION

NATIONAL ACCOUNT REP

	AVERAGE PERFORMER		BETTER PERFORMER		BEST PERFORMER	
	MEDIAN ($000)	THIRD QUARTILE ($000)	MEDIAN ($000)	THIRD QUARTILE ($000)	MEDIAN ($000)	THIRD QUARTILE ($000)
COMPANY SIZE						
UNDER $5 MILLION	$75.0	N/R	N/R	N/R	N/R	N/R
$5MM–$25MM	55.0	60.0	N/R	82.0	55.0	N/R
$25MM–$100MM	85.0	125.0	N/R	N/R	56.0	130.0
$100MM–$250MM	70.0	75.0	80.0	85.0	95.0	100.0
OVER $250MM	75.0	89.0	80.0	98.0	95.0	120.0
PRODUCT OR SERVICE						
CONSUMER PRODUCTS	87.0	100.0	N/R	N/R	108.0	120.0
CONSUMER SERVICES	55.0	87.0	55.0	N/R	N/R	N/R
INDUSTRIAL PRODUCTS	70.0	75.0	82.0	92.5	95.0	100.0
INDUSTRIAL SERVICES	75.0	88.0	N/R	N/R	56.0	120.0
OFFICE PRODUCTS	66.0	100.0	N/R	N/R	55.0	125.0
OFFICE SERVICES	87.0	133.0	N/R	N/R	55.0	120.0
TYPE OF BUYER						
CONSUMERS	55.0	75.0	55.0	82.0	55.0	120.0
DISTRIBUTORS	65.0	75.0	N/R	82.0	55.0	95.0
INDUSTRY	75.0	90.0	80.0	92.5	95.0	120.0
RETAILERS	60.0	87.0	N/R	N/R	56.0	120.0
INDUSTRY						
ELECTRONIC COMPONENTS	75.0	80.0	85.0	85.0	100.0	100.0
HEALTH SERVICES	30.0	85.0	30.0	N/R	55.0	130.0
MACHINERY	20.0	90.0	200.0	N/R	N/R	N/R
MANUFACTURING	70.0	74.8	N/R	80.0	19.5	95.0
OFFICE EQUIPMENT	66.0	90.0	N/R	92.5	125.0	125.0
PHARMACEUTICALS	89.0	125.0	98.0	N/R	108.0	108.0
PRINTING AND PUBLISHING	46.0	133.0	N/R	N/R	N/R	N/R
WHOLESALE (CONSUMER GOODS)	60.0	75.0	80.0	82.0	95.0	95.0
OVERALL	**$74.8**	**$88.0**	**N/R**	**$92.5**	**$95.0**	**$108.0**

64

FIGURE 29

AVERAGE TOTAL CASH COMPENSATION

MAJOR (KEY) ACCOUNT REP

	AVERAGE PERFORMER		BETTER PERFORMER		BEST PERFORMER	
	MEDIAN ($000)	THIRD QUARTILE ($000)	MEDIAN ($000)	THIRD QUARTILE ($000)	MEDIAN ($000)	THIRD QUARTILE ($000)
COMPANY SIZE						
UNDER $5 MILLION	$40.0	$85.0	N/R	N/R	N/R	N/R
$5MM–$25MM	51.0	60.0	54.0	60.0	58.0	60.0
$25MM–$100MM	80.0	85.0	90.0	100.0	110.0	115.0
$100MM–$250MM	70.0	184.0	77.0	N/R	85.0	N/R
OVER $250MM	87.0	87.0	95.0	97.0	120.0	120.0
PRODUCT OR SERVICE						
CONSUMER PRODUCTS	80.0	87.0	92.5	97.0	110.0	120.0
CONSUMER SERVICES	60.0	80.0	90.0	95.0	110.0	115.0
INDUSTRIAL PRODUCTS	70.0	87.0	77.0	95.0	110.0	120.0
INDUSTRIAL SERVICES	66.0	75.0	N/R	98.0	60.0	120.0
OFFICE PRODUCTS	80.0	100.0	92.5	N/R	120.0	125.0
OFFICE SERVICES	66.0	87.0	N/R	98.0	58.0	120.0
TYPE OF BUYER						
CONSUMERS	60.0	85.0	90.0	95.0	110.0	120.0
DISTRIBUTORS	66.0	87.0	92.5	98.0	120.0	120.0
INDUSTRY	70.0	90.0	92.5	97.0	108.0	120.0
RETAILERS	60.0	85.0	90.0	95.0	115.0	120.0
INDUSTRY						
BUSINESS SERVICES	35.0	85.0	N/R	N/R	N/R	N/R
ELECTRONICS	87.0	175.0	98.0	185.0	120.0	190.0
ELECTRONIC COMPONENTS	70.0	70.0	77.0	95.0	85.0	120.0
OFFICE EQUIPMENT	55.0	66.0	N/R	92.5	58.0	125.0
RETAIL	60.0	85.0	60.0	100.0	60.0	115.0
WHOLESALE (CONSUMER GOODS)	80.0	140.0	N/R	N/R	58.0	110.0
OVERALL	**$66.0**	**$85.0**	**$90.0**	**$97.0**	**$110.0**	**$120.0**

Figures 30–39 — Compensation Tables: Average Base Salary and Total Compensation for Combined Plans (Marketing, Management, and All Sales Positions)

Once you have determined total cash compensation for the comparator groups you have selected, you need to break out the base salary and incentive components. The following group of tables allows you to do just that.

Figures 30–39 present average base salary levels for all bonus-eligible individuals — in other words, those people in a combined compensation plan as opposed to a salary-only or an incentive-only plan. These tables will help you determine how much of the overall pay will take the form of salary for those people paid on a combined plan. Compensation figures are provided for average, better, and best performers, and are broken out by size of company, product or service sold, type of buyer, and industry. Note: Because most companies have only one top marketing executive and/or one top sales executive, there is no better or best performer for that position. Therefore, the data for these two positions encompasses the full range of responses received.

Here are some guidelines on how to use these tables:

1. Use these tables after you have used tables 20–29, which presented figures for total compensation.

2. Determine the optimal compensation plan type for each position in your organization. Do not feel obligated to select the same plan type for each job.

3. For each position in a combined plan (salary plus incentive), use these tables to help determine base salary levels.

FIGURE 30

AVERAGE BASE SALARY AND TOTAL COMPENSATION

TOP MARKETING EXECUTIVE

	AVERAGE BASE SALARY FOR BONUS-ELIGIBLE INDIVIDUALS ($000)	AVERAGE TOTAL CASH COMPENSATION FOR ALL PLANS ($000)
COMPANY SIZE		
UNDER $5 MILLION	$97.9	$101.0
$5MM–$25MM	71.1	82.7
$25MM–$100MM	107.5	135.4
$100MM–$250MM	149.1	166.1
OVER $250MM	152.5	233.5
PRODUCT OR SERVICE		
CONSUMER PRODUCTS	116.1	135.5
CONSUMER SERVICES	87.7	106.7
INDUSTRIAL PRODUCTS	104.3	127.1
INDUSTRIAL SERVICES	98.5	117.7
OFFICE PRODUCTS	149.6	179.8
OFFICE SERVICES	103.0	109.7
TYPE OF BUYER		
CONSUMERS	99.1	97.3
DISTRIBUTORS	116.7	141.9
INDUSTRY	106.2	120.5
RETAILERS	125.2	145.7
INDUSTRY		
BANKING	50.7	139.8
BUSINESS SERVICES	82.1	119.9
CHEMICALS	123.8	147.5
COMMUNICATIONS	65.0	123.3
CONSTRUCTION	70.0	86.7
EDUCATIONAL SERVICES	85.0	116.7
ELECTRONICS	120.0	161.7
ELECTRONIC COMPONENTS	90.0	135.0
FABRICATED METALS	132.4	152.4
FOOD PRODUCTS	75.0	N/R
HEALTH SERVICES	115.0	76.5
HOTELS AND OTHER LODGING PLACES	110.6	109.5
INSTRUMENTS	108.5	139.0
INSURANCE	154.5	113.6
MACHINERY	117.5	147.5
OFFICE EQUIPMENT	143.3	176.0
PHARMACEUTICALS	181.7	217.5
PRINTING AND PUBLISHING	109.8	122.5
RETAIL	134.2	116.8
RUBBER/PLASTICS	182.5	N/R
TRANSPORTATION EQUIPMENT	85.0	100.0
WHOLESALE (CONSUMER GOODS)	92.5	100.0
OVERALL	**$107.7**	**$121.0**

FIGURE 31

AVERAGE BASE SALARY AND TOTAL COMPENSATION

TOP SALES EXECUTIVE

	AVERAGE BASE SALARY FOR BONUS-ELIGIBLE INDIVIDUALS ($000)	AVERAGE TOTAL CASH COMPENSATION FOR ALL PLANS ($000)
COMPANY SIZE		
UNDER $5 MILLION	$89.7	$77.2
$5MM–$25MM	68.5	81.7
$25MM–$100MM	100.5	124.0
$100MM–$250MM	125.4	152.0
OVER $250MM	131.8	220.2
PRODUCT OR SERVICE		
CONSUMER PRODUCTS	105.8	121.3
CONSUMER SERVICES	76.9	88.5
INDUSTRIAL PRODUCTS	86.1	109.9
INDUSTRIAL SERVICES	83.3	106.6
OFFICE PRODUCTS	116.3	141.4
OFFICE SERVICES	101.5	113.1
TYPE OF BUYER		
CONSUMERS	89.5	90.2
DISTRIBUTORS	97.5	118.5
INDUSTRY	93.7	109.2
RETAILERS	124.0	135.4
INDUSTRY		
BANKING	71.0	233.5
BUSINESS SERVICES	96.2	112.4
CHEMICALS	110.0	143.0
COMMUNICATIONS	42.2	95.8
CONSTRUCTION	56.0	78.9
EDUCATIONAL SERVICES	100.0	N/R
ELECTRONICS	102.0	125.0
ELECTRONIC COMPONENTS	75.0	110.5
FABRICATED METALS	113.7	113.4
HEALTH SERVICES	92.5	88.0
HOTELS AND OTHER LODGING PLACES	78.3	113.3
INSTRUMENTS	63.3	95.0
INSURANCE	150.0	N/R
MACHINERY	145.0	158.3
MANUFACTURING	63.2	90.0
OFFICE EQUIPMENT	150.0	166.3
PAPER AND ALLIED PRODUCTS	100.0	N/R
PHARMACEUTICALS	183.8	240.0
PRINTING AND PUBLISHING	103.3	112.0
RETAIL	113.3	69.0
RUBBER/PLASTICS	100.0	N/R
TRANSPORTATION EQUIPMENT	85.0	95.0
WHOLESALE (CONSUMER GOODS)	85.0	97.2
OVERALL	**$98.0**	**$108.9**

FIGURE 32

Average Base Salary and Total Compensation

Regional Sales Manager

	Average Performer		Better Performer		Best Performer	
	Average Base Salary For Bonus-Eligible Individuals ($000)	Average Total Cash Comp. for All Plans ($000)	Average Base Salary For Bonus-Eligible Individuals ($000)	Average Total Cash Comp. for All Plans ($000)	Average Base Salary For Bonus-Eligible Individuals ($000)	Average Total Cash Comp. for All Plans ($000)
Company Size						
Under $5 Million	N/R	$53.3	N/R	N/R	N/R	N/R
$5MM–$25MM	51.9	66.9	57.3	70.8	65.4	80.6
$25MM–$100MM	74.4	89.3	N/R	N/R	78.4	103.8
$100MM–$250MM	69.8	95.9	73.8	N/R	83.0	110.8
Over $250MM	80.4	96.4	89.5	99.8	98.4	108.8
Product or Service						
Consumer Products	85.5	84.9	89.2	N/R	96.9	88.4
Consumer Services	73.6	72.4	84.2	83.4	93.4	N/R
Industrial Products	62.0	76.7	66.7	81.8	74.6	100.8
Industrial Services	63.7	82.3	69.0	82.6	76.0	95.3
Office Products	64.5	96.8	69.5	98.1	76.3	122.6
Office Services	63.0	103.4	70.8	109.4	76.9	122.6
Type of Buyer						
Consumers	70.0	75.9	73.6	N/R	86.0	85.1
Distributors	63.8	82.3	70.3	83.0	76.2	95.6
Industry	70.2	81.3	73.2	82.2	81.0	100.4
Retailers	75.1	90.6	N/R	102.2	79.6	111.6
Industry						
Business Services	66.2	93.8	75.0	122.8	82.0	135.0
Chemicals	77.0	88.8	82.5	N/R	100.0	89.5
Educational Services	40.0	80.0	N/R	N/R	N/R	N/R
Electronics	47.3	59.5	67.0	75.0	78.5	95.0
Electronic Components	60.0	75.0	N/R	N/R	N/R	N/R
Fabricated Metals	81.7	82.4	N/R	N/R	72.0	97.3
Hotels and Other Lodging Places	42.5	50.3	48.0	N/R	52.0	N/R
Instruments	60.0	62.5	N/R	86.7	N/R	N/R
Machinery	108.8	105.8	N/R	N/R	80.0	98.3
Manufacturing	36.0	75.3	36.0	N/R	36.0	105.5
Office Equipment	55.0	107.1	N/R	113.3	60.0	143.3
Pharmaceuticals	142.5	161.7	180.0	N/R	190.0	N/R
Printing and Publishing	72.3	92.1	73.3	N/R	83.3	101.8
Retail	70.0	79.3	85.0	102.2	100.0	N/R
Wholesale (Consumer Goods)	47.7	68.5	55.0	69.5	N/R	77.0
Overall	**$70.8**	**$81.3**	**$75.3**	**$84.9**	**$83.4**	**$100.4**

FIGURE 33

Average Base Salary and Total Compensation

District Sales Manager

	Average Performer		Better Performer		Best Performer	
	Average Base Salary For Bonus-Eligible Individuals ($000)	Average Total Cash Comp. for All Plans ($000)	Average Base Salary For Bonus-Eligible Individuals ($000)	Average Total Cash Comp. for All Plans ($000)	Average Base Salary For Bonus-Eligible Individuals ($000)	Average Total Cash Comp. for All Plans ($000)
Company Size						
Under $5 Million	$56.5	$68.8	N/R	N/R	$42.0	$53.7
$5MM–$25MM	49.9	69.9	N/R	N/R	33.0	54.8
$25MM–$100MM	66.5	87.6	83.8	N/R	N/R	73.8
$100MM–$250MM	46.7	68.3	N/R	79.3	50.0	95.0
Over $250MM	70.8	85.0	79.2	87.0	89.2	103.8
Product or Service						
Consumer Products	64.5	87.6	76.9	N/R	N/R	87.7
Consumer Services	59.3	78.2	76.5	85.4	79.0	N/R
Industrial Products	53.1	75.4	57.0	N/R	63.6	91.2
Industrial Services	55.5	79.0	N/R	N/R	61.3	77.0
Office Products	48.4	72.2	52.0	N/R	57.2	85.3
Office Services	54.9	74.2	55.2	82.6	60.5	83.4
Type of Buyer						
Consumers	49.4	76.8	50.4	N/R	N/R	64.6
Distributors	54.1	71.6	60.6	72.8	61.8	82.7
Industry	61.9	80.8	66.6	N/R	73.8	80.5
Retailers	56.4	73.3	58.6	N/R	N/R	76.7
Industry						
Business Services	60.0	63.8	N/R	74.1	42.0	N/R
Chemicals	53.3	64.0	56.0	N/R	60.0	47.5
Electronic Components	45.0	66.0	N/R	N/R	N/R	N/R
Fabricated Metals	51.0	76.7	71.5	99.7	71.5	114.3
Office Equipment	63.3	115.8	95.0	N/R	100.0	96.7
Printing and Publishing	55.2	71.5	N/R	N/R	35.0	56.7
Wholesale (Consumer Goods)	42.0	62.2	45.5	71.0	48.0	83.0
Overall	**$59.5**	**$76.9**	**$66.4**	**N/R**	**$66.9**	**$78.5**

FIGURE 34

AVERAGE BASE SALARY AND TOTAL COMPENSATION

SENIOR SALES REP

	AVERAGE PERFORMER		BETTER PERFORMER		BEST PERFORMER	
	AVERAGE BASE SALARY FOR BONUS-ELIGIBLE INDIVIDUALS ($000)	AVERAGE TOTAL CASH COMP. FOR ALL PLANS ($000)	AVERAGE BASE SALARY FOR BONUS-ELIGIBLE INDIVIDUALS ($000)	AVERAGE TOTAL CASH COMP. FOR ALL PLANS ($000)	AVERAGE BASE SALARY FOR BONUS-ELIGIBLE INDIVIDUALS ($000)	AVERAGE TOTAL CASH COMP. FOR ALL PLANS ($000)
COMPANY SIZE						
UNDER $5 MILLION	$35.4	$48.5	N/R	N/R	$50.0	$51.7
$5MM–$25MM	35.4	56.0	N/R	56.8	36.5	65.2
$25MM–$100MM	52.4	66.3	53.9	69.2	59.6	85.8
$100MM–$250MM	42.0	64.9	50.2	78.9	57.5	116.0
OVER $250MM	54.8	79.9	61.9	102.5	71.2	124.9
PRODUCT OR SERVICE						
CONSUMER PRODUCTS	66.3	65.7	N/R	70.9	64.5	86.6
CONSUMER SERVICES	57.9	54.3	N/R	58.5	54.8	70.0
INDUSTRIAL PRODUCTS	45.6	58.9	50.9	64.9	57.5	79.2
INDUSTRIAL SERVICES	49.5	57.5	55.8	61.9	61.7	74.4
OFFICE PRODUCTS	39.7	71.9	45.2	80.1	48.9	122.9
OFFICE SERVICES	37.9	69.6	43.3	76.5	49.4	111.3
TYPE OF BUYER						
CONSUMERS	56.5	54.5	N/R	59.8	53.0	74.6
DISTRIBUTORS	43.3	62.5	48.5	65.6	53.8	79.1
INDUSTRY	51.4	62.1	N/R	65.6	58.4	81.6
RETAILERS	56.5	64.0	N/R	66.1	52.4	93.0
INDUSTRY						
BANKING	36.0	95.0	65.0	N/R	72.0	N/R
BUSINESS SERVICES	39.8	69.3	N/R	N/R	49.5	70.2
CHEMICALS	48.8	62.0	60.0	N/R	81.3	73.0
COMMUNICATIONS	10.0	41.1	10.0	N/R	10.0	N/R
CONSTRUCTION	45.0	48.3	50.0	74.2	65.0	N/R
ELECTRONICS	46.7	55.5	67.5	67.7	77.5	85.7
ELECTRONIC COMPONENTS	36.0	55.0	38.0	70.2	40.0	92.0
FABRICATED METALS	55.8	58.8	N/R	60.9	61.7	72.0
HOTELS AND OTHER LODGING PLACES	39.8	44.1	N/R	N/R	44.5	57.6
INSURANCE	35.0	58.8	43.8	65.1	50.0	80.5
MANUFACTURING	32.2	61.3	32.2	65.1	32.2	83.7
OFFICE EQUIPMENT	42.5	67.7	51.0	85.0	52.5	N/R
PHARMACEUTICALS	80.0	101.7	100.0	110.3	105.0	N/R
PRINTING AND PUBLISHING	38.7	62.8	N/R	N/R	30.0	87.5
RETAIL	35.0	48.2	40.0	52.3	45.0	64.5
TRANSPORTATION EQUIPMENT	36.5	68.0	N/R	N/R	35.0	N/R
WHOLESALE (CONSUMER GOODS)	38.0	52.3	42.3	63.6	45.0	72.4
OVERALL	**$49.9**	**$61.1**	**$50.7**	**$65.2**	**$57.6**	**$80.2**

FIGURE 35

AVERAGE BASE SALARY AND TOTAL COMPENSATION

INTERMEDIATE SALES REP

	AVERAGE PERFORMER		BETTER PERFORMER		BEST PERFORMER	
	AVERAGE BASE SALARY FOR BONUS-ELIGIBLE INDIVIDUALS ($000)	AVERAGE TOTAL CASH COMP. FOR ALL PLANS ($000)	AVERAGE BASE SALARY FOR BONUS-ELIGIBLE INDIVIDUALS ($000)	AVERAGE TOTAL CASH COMP. FOR ALL PLANS ($000)	AVERAGE BASE SALARY FOR BONUS-ELIGIBLE INDIVIDUALS ($000)	AVERAGE TOTAL CASH COMP. FOR ALL PLANS ($000)
COMPANY SIZE						
UNDER $5 MILLION	$26.9	$34.7	$31.2	N/R	$33.8	$33.6
$5MM–$25MM	30.2	41.5	N/R	43.2	30.8	48.5
$25MM–$100MM	46.0	47.5	47.3	N/R	53.2	57.6
$100MM–$250MM	12.5	35.6	17.5	47.8	25.0	68.8
OVER $250MM	44.7	53.5	49.7	65.0	55.0	85.1
PRODUCT OR SERVICE						
CONSUMER PRODUCTS	44.6	45.5	51.0	48.7	55.9	60.8
CONSUMER SERVICES	36.5	38.6	45.8	48.1	52.1	62.0
INDUSTRIAL PRODUCTS	37.4	43.2	N/R	44.7	41.7	57.2
INDUSTRIAL SERVICES	40.8	44.9	42.0	49.4	48.5	62.5
OFFICE PRODUCTS	27.5	49.5	29.0	56.4	33.8	76.7
OFFICE SERVICES	28.1	48.4	33.2	52.8	38.0	69.5
TYPE OF BUYER						
CONSUMERS	34.4	39.1	41.1	46.8	46.2	59.0
DISTRIBUTORS	37.3	45.3	39.9	47.7	44.0	59.0
INDUSTRY	36.7	44.4	38.0	46.4	42.4	57.4
RETAILERS	36.2	42.8	39.0	47.0	43.8	61.4
INDUSTRY						
BANKING	32.3	55.0	60.0	N/R	68.0	N/R
BUSINESS SERVICES	35.0	46.0	N/R	N/R	N/R	41.8
COMMUNICATIONS	24.0	49.0	30.0	58.6	32.5	N/R
ELECTRONICS	33.3	41.0	47.5	46.7	55.0	57.3
FABRICATED METALS	50.7	49.1	N/R	49.2	46.0	51.0
HOTELS AND OTHER LODGING PLACES	33.2	38.1	35.0	39.3	35.0	N/R
INSURANCE	35.0	38.2	40.0	N/R	45.0	45.8
MACHINERY	45.0	56.0	75.0	N/R	80.0	N/R
OFFICE EQUIPMENT	35.0	52.4	N/R	61.5	35.0	76.0
PHARMACEUTICALS	62.5	76.0	65.0	N/R	70.0	N/R
PRINTING AND PUBLISHING	30.0	35.5	N/R	44.5	20.0	58.8
RETAIL	30.0	33.5	35.0	47.6	40.0	49.1
WHOLESALE (CONSUMER GOODS)	23.0	38.4	26.0	44.9	31.7	52.9
OVERALL	**$37.2**	**$43.1**	**$39.6**	**$46.4**	**$44.0**	**$57.4**

FIGURE 36

Average Base Salary and Total Compensation

Entry Level Sales Rep

	Average Performer		Better Performer		Best Performer	
	Average Base Salary For Bonus-Eligible Individuals ($000)	Average Total Cash Comp. for All Plans ($000)	Average Base Salary For Bonus-Eligible Individuals ($000)	Average Total Cash Comp. for All Plans ($000)	Average Base Salary For Bonus-Eligible Individuals ($000)	Average Total Cash Comp. for All Plans ($000)
Company Size						
Under $5 Million	$21.8	$25.8	$26.8	$30.3	$28.5	$39.9
$5MM–$25MM	23.7	32.2	24.2	N/R	26.0	33.0
$25MM–$100MM	33.6	35.5	N/R	36.9	38.0	47.8
$100MM–$250MM	28.0	33.2	29.3	N/R	N/R	35.2
Over $250MM	32.7	47.6	36.9	57.3	41.3	66.4
Product or Service						
Consumer Products	31.2	33.8	33.9	40.6	39.2	54.5
Consumer Services	26.5	27.8	31.5	33.4	36.1	42.0
Industrial Products	28.2	35.5	31.2	40.1	32.7	47.4
Industrial Services	28.2	36.2	30.5	41.2	34.7	50.7
Office Products	22.0	38.3	25.5	48.1	29.8	57.5
Office Services	21.8	34.8	25.9	40.7	29.5	49.5
Type of Buyer						
Consumers	26.0	30.3	30.4	35.7	34.4	46.5
Distributors	26.7	35.6	31.9	44.8	34.5	53.7
Industry	28.4	34.9	31.4	39.7	33.4	46.9
Retailers	27.2	32.6	28.6	37.3	32.3	48.7
Industry						
Business Services	28.4	34.6	29.7	N/R	32.3	39.2
Chemicals	33.3	36.1	40.0	N/R	45.0	44.3
Educational Services	15.6	44.5	N/R	N/R	N/R	N/R
Electronics	30.0	28.5	35.0	N/R	40.0	33.5
Fabricated Metals	44.0	43.7	60.0	44.3	N/R	N/R
Hotels and Other Lodging Places	28.7	32.4	33.0	N/R	N/R	N/R
Insurance	25.0	28.9	30.0	N/R	35.0	35.8
Machinery	28.8	46.0	42.5	66.7	47.5	77.7
Office Equipment	21.5	33.7	N/R	35.5	24.0	41.5
Pharmaceuticals	50.0	60.0	N/R	N/R	N/R	N/R
Printing and Publishing	18.0	27.1	24.0	41.5	30.0	48.5
Retail	26.7	26.7	30.7	33.7	34.7	39.9
Wholesale (Consumer Goods)	18.3	29.8	22.5	36.9	27.5	47.0
Overall	**$28.0**	**$33.3**	**$31.0**	**$36.5**	**$33.5**	**$45.0**

FIGURE 37

Average Base Salary and Total Compensation

National/Major Account Manager

	Average Performer		Better Performer		Best Performer	
	Average Base Salary For Bonus-Eligible Individuals ($000)	Average Total Cash Comp. for All Plans ($000)	Average Base Salary For Bonus-Eligible Individuals ($000)	Average Total Cash Comp. for All Plans ($000)	Average Base Salary For Bonus-Eligible Individuals ($000)	Average Total Cash Comp. for All Plans ($000)
Company Size						
Under $5 Million	$45.5	$63.5	N/R	N/R	N/R	N/R
$5MM–$25MM	53.3	70.8	N/R	N/R	31.0	N/R
$25MM–$100MM	74.0	88.7	N/R	N/R	70.0	56.0
$100MM–$250MM	110.0	107.5	N/R	110.0	70.0	115.0
Over $250MM	78.4	96.8	N/R	N/R	83.3	126.7
Product or Service						
Consumer Products	72.0	84.2	82.5	95.8	87.5	98.2
Consumer Services	60.0	72.8	80.0	N/R	90.0	89.3
Industrial Products	60.5	79.8	66.7	87.6	73.7	103.8
Industrial Services	64.3	88.4	70.0	107.1	75.2	122.6
Office Products	76.0	87.6	N/R	104.6	66.2	113.0
Office Services	87.5	101.4	N/R	107.6	65.2	117.0
Type of Buyer						
Consumers	60.0	76.3	80.0	91.0	80.0	109.3
Distributors	63.0	82.0	64.0	100.5	70.8	114.0
Industry	74.3	89.2	N/R	N/R	74.1	105.0
Retailers	64.0	80.5	65.0	104.7	72.0	123.0
Industry						
Chemicals	85.0	111.7	N/R	N/R	N/R	N/R
Electronics	66.7	78.3	70.0	N/R	77.5	N/R
Electronic Components	55.0	82.5	60.0	90.8	60.0	117.7
Machinery	75.0	N/R	85.0	N/R	100.0	N/R
Office Equipment	41.7	72.8	N/R	100.2	31.0	112.3
Printing and Publishing	55.0	67.3	N/R	N/R	70.0	57.7
Overall	**$71.1**	**$84.4**	**N/R**	**$89.8**	**$74.1**	**$108.2**

FIGURE 38

AVERAGE BASE SALARY AND TOTAL COMPENSATION

NATIONAL ACCOUNT REP

	AVERAGE PERFORMER		BETTER PERFORMER		BEST PERFORMER	
	AVERAGE BASE SALARY FOR BONUS-ELIGIBLE INDIVIDUALS ($000)	AVERAGE TOTAL CASH COMP. FOR ALL PLANS ($000)	AVERAGE BASE SALARY FOR BONUS-ELIGIBLE INDIVIDUALS ($000)	AVERAGE TOTAL CASH COMP. FOR ALL PLANS ($000)	AVERAGE BASE SALARY FOR BONUS-ELIGIBLE INDIVIDUALS ($000)	AVERAGE TOTAL CASH COMP. FOR ALL PLANS ($000)
COMPANY SIZE						
$5MM–$25MM	$31.5	$47.2	N/R	$49.0	N/R	N/R
$25MM–$100MM	76.3	85.5	N/R	N/R	60.0	67.0
$100MM–$250MM	18.0	56.3	22.0	67.3	30.0	81.3
OVER $250MM	61.2	78.2	66.5	81.4	70.8	96.0
PRODUCT OR SERVICE						
CONSUMER PRODUCTS	71.9	79.4	74.0	N/R	80.0	89.3
CONSUMER SERVICES	63.5	68.0	N/R	N/R	59.7	58.5
INDUSTRIAL PRODUCTS	49.6	70.1	51.0	83.9	60.0	84.8
INDUSTRIAL SERVICES	60.6	76.8	N/R	77.0	53.3	N/R
OFFICE PRODUCTS	65.3	74.5	N/R	N/R	64.7	87.2
OFFICE SERVICES	71.8	86.8	N/R	N/R	58.5	70.0
TYPE OF BUYER						
CONSUMERS	48.0	58.7	49.3	N/R	56.3	71.2
DISTRIBUTORS	67.4	64.1	N/R	N/R	52.2	59.3
INDUSTRY	64.4	78.2	N/R	N/R	61.9	90.7
RETAILERS	52.2	64.2	N/R	N/R	52.2	71.5
INDUSTRY						
OFFICE EQUIPMENT	38.0	66.7	N/R	N/R	N/R	N/R
PRINTING AND PUBLISHING	58.7	67.7	N/R	N/R	30.0	N/R
OVERALL	**$60.3**	**$70.4**	**N/R**	**N/R**	**$61.9**	**$77.4**

FIGURE 39

AVERAGE BASE SALARY AND TOTAL COMPENSATION

MAJOR (KEY) ACCOUNT REP

	AVERAGE PERFORMER		BETTER PERFORMER		BEST PERFORMER	
	AVERAGE BASE SALARY FOR BONUS-ELIGIBLE INDIVIDUALS ($000)	AVERAGE TOTAL CASH COMP. FOR ALL PLANS ($000)	AVERAGE BASE SALARY FOR BONUS-ELIGIBLE INDIVIDUALS ($000)	AVERAGE TOTAL CASH COMP. FOR ALL PLANS ($000)	AVERAGE BASE SALARY FOR BONUS-ELIGIBLE INDIVIDUALS ($000)	AVERAGE TOTAL CASH COMP. FOR ALL PLANS ($000)
COMPANY SIZE						
UNDER $5 MILLION	$44.7	$50.5	N/R	N/R	N/R	N/R
$5MM–$25MM	40.0	51.2	47.5	53.3	47.5	59.0
$25MM–$100MM	53.8	71.5	54.0	71.5	63.3	85.0
$100MM–$250MM	24.0	94.3	26.0	113.3	28.0	224.7
OVER $250MM	65.0	81.3	72.5	96.0	80.0	116.7
PRODUCT OR SERVICE						
CONSUMER PRODUCTS	60.0	72.4	71.2	93.6	80.0	113.2
CONSUMER SERVICES	41.9	56.4	53.6	69.5	61.6	81.0
INDUSTRIAL PRODUCTS	52.1	69.4	58.3	81.1	61.7	99.0
INDUSTRIAL SERVICES	55.0	62.0	58.3	76.8	61.7	89.5
OFFICE PRODUCTS	57.5	82.2	57.5	N/R	62.5	105.8
OFFICE SERVICES	38.2	65.7	47.0	73.2	51.0	89.0
TYPE OF BUYER						
CONSUMERS	41.9	60.6	53.6	76.7	61.6	92.6
DISTRIBUTORS	59.2	68.5	63.3	93.9	70.0	115.0
INDUSTRY	47.3	71.2	53.2	79.2	56.6	100.5
RETAILERS	55.0	65.8	73.3	84.4	83.3	101.2
INDUSTRY						
BUSINESS SERVICES	49.5	60.0	N/R	N/R	28.0	N/R
OFFICE EQUIPMENT	42.5	60.5	N/R	N/R	35.0	N/R
OVERALL	**$47.4**	**$64.1**	**$53.5**	**$76.4**	**$59.1**	**$95.8**

PAY AND PERFORMANCE

The link between pay and performance is one of the things that makes the study of sales compensation so interesting. Salespeople are one of the few remaining groups of nonself-employed people who can, through their own efforts, dramatically increase their annual earnings. And it's in the sales profession that the link between pay and performance has become the object of widespread study.

All this makes it easy to understand why sales and marketing executives never give up the search for that "perfect" pay plan — the one that drives salespeople to excel but does not financially strain the resources of the company. Does such a plan exist? No — at least not for long. Changes in product lines, company priorities, and changes in the makeup of the sales force itself put constant pressure on the sales compensation plan. But that doesn't mean that we don't constantly try to find the one plan — or combination of plans — that will make our companies successful beyond our wildest dreams. The right plan — at the right time — can make all the difference in the world. With exactly the right plan, we can point our salespeople in the direction we want them to take.

How much do salespeople earn compared with what they produce? How much more do top performers produce than their "average" counterparts? These are just two of the many questions this section examines in detail:

- Figure 40 looks at the average annual sales volume for intermediate and senior sales representatives by average, better, and best performers.
- Figures 41–47 exhibit the compensation levels of better and best performers as a percentage increase over average performers.
- Figures 48–57 exhibit compensation levels and sales volume levels generated by average, better, and best performers.
- Figures 58–67 exhibit third-quartile compensation levels and sales volume levels generated by average, better, and best performers.
- Figure 68 exhibits top performers' productivity as compared to average performers' productivity.
- Figure 69 exhibits senior salesperson productivity by better and best performers.

Although sales volume levels vary considerably by size of company, product or service sold, type of buyer, and industry, the data in this section provides "benchmark" figures you can use in comparing the productivity of your salespeople with salespeople in similar-size companies in similar industries.

In looking at the sales volume data in this section, remember that smaller companies generally report smaller sales volume levels per salesperson. This is due to the fact that many smaller companies have not yet developed a large, established base of customers. Much of the sales volume generated by these small companies comes from new business, which is harder to secure.

FIGURE 40 — SALESPERSON'S ANNUAL SALES VOLUME: AVERAGE MEDIAN RANGE FOR INTERMEDIATE AND SENIOR SALES REPS

Average annual sales volume for intermediate and senior sales reps combined is esssentially unchanged over the last survey period — $1,394,260 in this year's survey compared with $1,390,000 in 1996. Although this suggests that reps have not been able to increase their productivity over the past two years, a closer look at the data presents a different picture. When we look at reps in the "best performer" category, productivity gains are immediately apparent when compared with data from two years ago. Top performers in this year's survey averaged $1,959.9 in annual sales volume, a 17 percent increase over the $1,675.4 figure reported in 1996. As noted elsewhere in this survey, entry-level and intermediate reps did not show gains in earnings, an indication of static productivity. When we look at our "best performer data," we are looking at data for senior reps, who, you might recall, posted earnings gains of 6.8 percent. This supports results from a separate Dartnell survey: Top performers responding to that survey say they sold significantly more in 1997 than in 1996. (See Section 12 for details.)

Figure 40 presents average annual sales volume data for average, better, and best performers and looks specifically at the performance levels of intermediate and senior level salespeople. Sales volume levels for entry level salespeople, who may or may not have yet been assigned a territory, vary considerably and do not reflect the true potential of the individual. Intermediate and senior salespeople, on the other hand, provide "benchmark" data on average sales volume levels. Responses are broken out by company size, product or service sold, type of buyer, and industry. **Figure 40** provides a "quick-view" look at some of the data covered in detail in this section. Additional tables provide greater detail and should be consulted when comparing the sales volume levels of your salespeople with those reported by participants in this survey.

Remember, average sales volume levels can vary considerably by different sizes of companies in the same industry. For example, a large company in the electronic components industry will very likely report higher sales volume levels for its experienced salespeople than a smaller company in the same industry will report. Again, many larger companies have a significant number of long-standing accounts that place high dollar-volume orders on a regular basis. Smaller companies, trying to establish themselves, must often settle for "trial" orders that amount to significantly less dollar-volume gain.

FIGURE 40

SALESPERSON'S ANNUAL SALES VOLUME:
AVERAGE OF MEDIAN RANGE FOR INTERMEDIATE AND SENIOR SALES REPS

	AVERAGE PERFORMER ($000)	BETTER PERFORMER ($000)	BEST PERFORMER ($000)
COMPANY SIZE			
UNDER $5 MILLION	$363.2	$409.6	N/R
$5MM–$25MM	966.1	1,239.8	1,521.8
$25MM–$100MM	1,759.0	2,030.5	3,033.4
$100MM–$250MM	1,308.3	1,963.9	2,712.5
OVER $250MM	3,387.9	5,639.6	6,987.5
PRODUCT OR SERVICE			
CONSUMER PRODUCTS	981.1	1,408.1	1,798.2
CONSUMER SERVICES	876.1	1,154.8	1,492.4
INDUSTRIAL PRODUCTS	908.8	1,416.9	2,007.9
INDUSTRIAL SERVICES	868.2	1,386.4	2,086.6
OFFICE PRODUCTS	851.7	1,278.2	1,848.4
OFFICE SERVICES	753.8	956.8	1,295.9
TYPE OF BUYER			
CONSUMERS	829.1	1,135.9	1,583.1
DISTRIBUTORS	867.6	1,299.2	1,932.2
INDUSTRY	897.8	1,355.8	1,890.3
RETAILERS	838.7	1,309.1	1,880.1
INDUSTRY			
AGRICULTURE, FORESTRY AND FISHING	1,500.0	2,400.0	4,800.0
BANKING	11,200.0	15,375.0	28,875.0
BUSINESS SERVICES	776.8	848.2	1,219.6
CHEMICALS	1,381.2	2,330.0	4,373.8
COMMUNICATIONS	408.3	555.8	845.8
CONSTRUCTION	818.8	1,387.5	2,200.0
EDUCATIONAL SERVICES	479.7	825.0	1,200.0
ELECTRONICS	670.8	1,381.2	2,912.5
ELECTRONIC COMPONENTS	2,500.0	4,066.7	5,000.0
FABRICATED METALS	2,275.0	2,552.5	3,490.0
FOOD PRODUCTS	20,000.0	N/R	N/R
FURNITURE AND FIXTURES	4,058.3	7,987.5	12,000.0
HEALTH SERVICES	1,000.0	1,483.3	1,900.0
HOTELS AND OTHER LODGING PLACES	961.4	1,750.0	2,325.0
INSTRUMENTS	700.0	850.0	1,175.0
INSURANCE	644.0	939.2	1,077.5
MACHINERY	750.0	7,251.7	7,395.0
MANUFACTURING	875.4	1,428.1	2,078.3
OFFICE EQUIPMENT	809.3	896.7	N/R
PAPER AND ALLIED PRODUCTS	2,983.3	N/R	3,000.0
PHARMACEUTICALS	703.3	1,161.7	1,516.7
PRINTING AND PUBLISHING	796.2	1,369.0	1,945.0
REAL ESTATE	1,462.5	2,751.7	N/R
RETAIL	809.7	N/R	1,195.5
RUBBER/PLASTICS	775.0	N/R	N/R
TRANSPORTATION BY AIR	1,100.0	N/R	N/R
TRANSPORTATION EQUIPMENT	791.7	N/R	875.0
TRUCKING AND WAREHOUSING	800.0	1,100.0	1,500.0
WHOLESALE (CONSUMER GOODS)	1,175.0	1,568.8	2,097.5
OVERALL	**$957.9**	**$1,393.9**	**$1,959.9**

FIGURES 41–47 — PAY LEVELS FOR "BETTER" AND "BEST" PERFORMERS (MANAGEMENT AND ALL SALES POSITIONS)

As previously mentioned, one of the major attractions of the sales profession is the demonstrable link between pay and performance. Salespeople, more than any other group of employees, can directly influence the amount of annual compensation they receive, based on their own performance.

But although it is one thing to agree to pay better performers more, it's often quite another to agree on how that should be done. The following data tables shed some light on this issue. Section 9, "Incentive Plan Design Practices," contains more detail. (For a definition of "better" and "best" performers, see Section 5.)

Figures 41–47 show how much extra "better" and "best" performers are paid over and above what average performers earn. (The "percentage premium" is the additional compensation paid to better and best performers expressed as a percentage increase over compensation paid to average performers.) The premiums paid to better– and best–performing salespeople were calculated as follows:

1. The premiums reflect only those companies reporting average, third-quartile, and highest pay levels for positions with multiple individuals in those positions. (Because a company can have only one top marketing executive and one top sales executive, it can only report an average pay figure for that position.)

2. Paired pay comparisons were used within each company to compute the premium for better and best salespeople.

3. For "better" salespeople: The premium reflects the average of the percent differences between the reported third-quartile level and the average pay level for each relevant position in each company.

4. For "best" salespeople: The premium reflects the average of the percent differences between the reported highest pay level and the average pay level for each relevant position in each company.

5. The premiums are expressed as percentage premiums above the pay levels for average performers.

FIGURE 41

PERCENTAGE PREMIUM PAID TO BETTER AND
BEST PERFORMERS (COMPARED TO AVERAGE PERFORMERS)

REGIONAL SALES MANAGER

	BETTER PERFORMERS	BEST PERFORMERS
COMPANY SIZE		
$5MM–$25MM	28%	55%
$25MM–$100MM	22	47
$100MM–$250MM	17	33
OVER $250MM	15	29
PRODUCT OR SERVICE		
CONSUMER PRODUCTS	21	32
CONSUMER SERVICES	26	42
INDUSTRIAL PRODUCTS	24	45
INDUSTRIAL SERVICES	21	40
OFFICE PRODUCTS	18	30
OFFICE SERVICES	20	30
TYPE OF BUYER		
CONSUMERS	22	36
DISTRIBUTORS	21	38
INDUSTRY	21	41
RETAILERS	23	34
INDUSTRY		
BUSINESS SERVICES	24	40
CHEMICALS	17	43
ELECTRONICS	20	52
ELECTRONIC COMPONENTS	11	33
FABRICATED METALS	10	33
FOOD PRODUCTS	12	25
HEALTH SERVICES	24	50
HOTELS AND OTHER LODGING PLACES	10	23
INSTRUMENTS	43	88
MACHINERY	17	38
MANUFACTURING	28	72
OFFICE EQUIPMENT	20	27
PAPER AND ALLIED PRODUCTS	40	70
PHARMACEUTICALS	7	16
PRINTING AND PUBLISHING	15	32
RETAIL	25	38
WHOLESALE (CONSUMER GOODS)	11	24
OVERALL	**22%**	**42%**

FIGURE 42

PERCENTAGE PREMIUM PAID TO BETTER AND
BEST PERFORMERS (COMPARED TO AVERAGE PERFORMERS)

DISTRICT SALES MANAGER

	BETTER PERFORMERS	BEST PERFORMERS
COMPANY SIZE		
UNDER $5 MILLION	19%	42%
$5MM–$25MM	14	42
$25MM–$100MM	31	50
$100MM–$250MM	32	67
OVER $250MM	25	44
PRODUCT OR SERVICE		
CONSUMER PRODUCTS	25	42
CONSUMER SERVICES	28	45
INDUSTRIAL PRODUCTS	28	53
INDUSTRIAL SERVICES	25	49
OFFICE PRODUCTS	26	51
OFFICE SERVICES	23	50
TYPE OF BUYER		
CONSUMERS	20	30
DISTRIBUTORS	26	51
INDUSTRY	26	47
RETAILERS	22	44
INDUSTRY		
BUSINESS SERVICES	17	42
CHEMICALS	28	73
EDUCATIONAL SERVICES	67	133
ELECTRONIC COMPONENTS	12	29
FABRICATED METALS	33	60
MACHINERY	24	55
OFFICE EQUIPMENT	8	12
PHARMACEUTICALS	7	20
PRINTING AND PUBLISHING	25	50
TRANSPORTATION EQUIPMENT	50	75
WHOLESALE (CONSUMER GOODS)	12	30
OVERALL	**25%**	**49%**

FIGURE 43

PERCENTAGE PREMIUM PAID TO BETTER AND
BEST PERFORMERS (COMPARED TO AVERAGE PERFORMERS)

SENIOR SALES REP

	BETTER PERFORMERS	BEST PERFORMERS
COMPANY SIZE		
UNDER $5 MILLION	27%	63%
$5MM–$25MM	32	78
$25MM–$100MM	27	73
$100MM–$250MM	37	218
OVER $250MM	43	76
PRODUCT OR SERVICE		
CONSUMER PRODUCTS	41	73
CONSUMER SERVICES	43	85
INDUSTRIAL PRODUCTS	29	72
INDUSTRIAL SERVICES	31	70
OFFICE PRODUCTS	47	176
OFFICE SERVICES	41	130
TYPE OF BUYER		
CONSUMERS	43	86
DISTRIBUTORS	33	69
INDUSTRY	28	72
RETAILERS	43	139
INDUSTRY		
BANKING	103	136
BUSINESS SERVICES	23	63
CHEMICALS	28	84
COMMUNICATIONS	57	327
CONSTRUCTION	53	61
EDUCATIONAL SERVICES	71	180
ELECTRONICS	20	40
ELECTRONIC COMPONENTS	39	84
FABRICATED METALS	19	47
HEALTH SERVICES	17	43
HOTELS AND OTHER LODGING PLACES	19	63
INSTRUMENTS	9	25
INSURANCE	24	41
MACHINERY	15	29
MANUFACTURING	32	77
OFFICE EQUIPMENT	29	45
PHARMACEUTICALS	15	23
PRINTING AND PUBLISHING	32	120
REAL ESTATE	57	212
RETAIL	42	249
TRANSPORTATION EQUIPMENT	20	40
WHOLESALE (CONSUMER GOODS)	29	83
OVERALL	**32%**	**95%**

FIGURE 44

**PERCENTAGE PREMIUM PAID TO BETTER AND
BEST PERFORMERS (COMPARED TO AVERAGE PERFORMERS)**

INTERMEDIATE SALES REP

	BETTER PERFORMERS	BEST PERFORMERS
COMPANY SIZE		
UNDER $5 MILLION	18%	37%
$5MM–$25MM	20	49
$25MM–$100MM	30	53
$100MM–$250MM	32	84
OVER $250MM	29	96
PRODUCT OR SERVICE		
CONSUMER PRODUCTS	27	56
CONSUMER SERVICES	33	89
INDUSTRIAL PRODUCTS	21	50
INDUSTRIAL SERVICES	27	63
OFFICE PRODUCTS	31	79
OFFICE SERVICES	30	78
TYPE OF BUYER		
CONSUMERS	35	90
DISTRIBUTORS	28	58
INDUSTRY	24	55
RETAILERS	29	78
INDUSTRY		
BANKING	31	254
BUSINESS SERVICES	22	49
CHEMICALS	14	60
COMMUNICATIONS	48	178
CONSTRUCTION	12	38
EDUCATIONAL SERVICES	33	67
ELECTRONICS	25	54
ELECTRONIC COMPONENTS	60	123
FABRICATED METALS	10	19
HOTELS AND OTHER LODGING PLACES	21	42
INSTRUMENTS	8	14
INSURANCE	17	35
MACHINERY	29	45
MANUFACTURING	7	27
OFFICE EQUIPMENT	13	34
PHARMACEUTICALS	19	34
PRINTING AND PUBLISHING	38	85
REAL ESTATE	45	188
RETAIL	44	78
WHOLESALE (CONSUMER GOODS)	16	40
OVERALL	**26%**	**64%**

FIGURE 45

PERCENTAGE PREMIUM PAID TO BETTER AND
BEST PERFORMERS (COMPARED TO AVERAGE PERFORMERS)

ENTRY LEVEL SALES REP

	BETTER PERFORMERS	BEST PERFORMERS
COMPANY SIZE		
UNDER $5 MILLION	28%	48%
$5MM–$25MM	20	38
$25MM–$100MM	29	60
$100MM–$250MM	29	65
OVER $250MM	27	56
PRODUCT OR SERVICE		
CONSUMER PRODUCTS	33	59
CONSUMER SERVICES	32	64
INDUSTRIAL PRODUCTS	25	49
INDUSTRIAL SERVICES	26	52
OFFICE PRODUCTS	32	55
OFFICE SERVICES	28	57
TYPE OF BUYER		
CONSUMERS	30	59
DISTRIBUTORS	30	58
INDUSTRY	25	50
RETAILERS	31	60
INDUSTRY		
BANKING	0	4
BUSINESS SERVICES	22	56
CHEMICALS	28	80
EDUCATIONAL SERVICES	20	40
ELECTRONICS	26	57
ELECTRONIC COMPONENTS	68	144
HOTELS AND OTHER LODGING PLACES	20	64
INSTRUMENTS	5	11
INSURANCE	36	49
MACHINERY	34	59
MANUFACTURING	8	17
OFFICE EQUIPMENT	19	24
PHARMACEUTICALS	18	38
PRINTING AND PUBLISHING	30	56
REAL ESTATE	14	60
RETAIL	34	76
WHOLESALE (CONSUMER GOODS)	21	46
OVERALL	**26%**	**54%**

FIGURE 46

**Percentage Premium Paid to Better and
Best Performers (Compared to Average Performers)**

National Account Rep

	Better Performers	Best Performers
Company Size		
$5MM–$25MM	43%	83%
$100MM–$250MM	27	58
Over $250MM	8	27
Product or Service		
Consumer Products	16	33
Consumer Services	9	28
Industrial Services	34	71
Office Products	28	56
Office Services	33	61
Type of Buyer		
Consumers	27	56
Industry	20	43
Retailers	22	50
Industry		
Electronics	13	38
Electronic Components	13	33
Health Services	50	68
Hotels and Other Lodging Places	6	17
Manufacturing	14	36
Office Equipment	3	39
Pharmaceuticals	10	21
Printing and Publishing	54	104
Wholesale (Consumer Goods)	22	27
Overall	**26%**	**56%**

FIGURE 47

PERCENTAGE PREMIUM PAID TO BETTER AND
BEST PERFORMERS (COMPARED TO AVERAGE PERFORMERS)

MAJOR (KEY) ACCOUNT REP

	BETTER PERFORMERS	BEST PERFORMERS
COMPANY SIZE		
$5MM–$25MM	9%	22%
$25MM–$100MM	23	47
$100MM–$250MM	16	85
OVER $250MM	16	43
PRODUCT OR SERVICE		
CONSUMER PRODUCTS	21	48
CONSUMER SERVICES	22	47
INDUSTRIAL PRODUCTS	13	34
INDUSTRIAL SERVICES	15	35
OFFICE PRODUCTS	16	68
OFFICE SERVICES	18	67
TYPE OF BUYER		
CONSUMERS	18	46
DISTRIBUTORS	20	48
INDUSTRY	14	49
RETAILERS	22	52
INDUSTRY		
BUSINESS SERVICES	19	117
ELECTRONICS	9	23
ELECTRONIC COMPONENTS	23	46
HEALTH SERVICES	0	22
OFFICE EQUIPMENT	4	26
PHARMACEUTICALS	11	24
RETAIL	18	35
WHOLESALE (CONSUMER GOODS)	15	45
OVERALL	**16%**	**49%**

FIGURES 48–57 — SALES COMPENSATION AND VOLUME LEVELS: AVERAGE OF THE MEDIAN RANGE (MARKETING, MANAGEMENT, AND ALL SALES POSITIONS)

Now that we've determined what percentage premium "better" and "best" performers earn over and above their average counterparts, how much more do they produce? (See Section 5 for a definition of "better" and "best" performer.)

Figures 48–57 show the relationship between pay and performance by comparing data for average total cash compensation for all plans combined with data for average annual sales volume. The data is broken out to include average performers, better performers, and best performers.

Again, because there is just one top marketing executive and/or top sales executive at any one particular company, there is no better and best performer for those positions.

In comparing sales volume levels, it is helpful to remember that, generally speaking, average sales volume levels are lower in smaller companies. This makes sense when you consider that many of the smaller companies participating in the survey are relatively young or even start-up companies that have not yet had the opportunity to establish a strong foothold in the marketplace. These companies generally rely on attracting new business for corporate growth and, as such, the selling task is frequently more difficult than in more established companies. These larger companies rely heavily on repeat business to sustain growth, and over the years have developed large accounts that account for significant sales volume levels.

Keep in mind that although sales volume levels for individual performers in smaller companies are lower than what their counterparts in larger companies produce, the percentage of their sales compared with the volume of total company sales is significant.

Note: Sales volume figures for management positions frequently reflect a measure of overall job responsibility, especially in larger companies. However, in smaller companies, the top marketing executive, for example, may make actual sales. In this survey, for example, an examination of the returned questionnaires indicated that, indeed, top sales and marketing executives did have direct sales responsibilities in many, if not most, of the companies under $5 million in annual sales.

FIGURE 48

SALES COMPENSATION AND VOLUME LEVELS

TOP MARKETING EXECUTIVE

	TOTAL CASH COMP. FOR ALL PLANS COMBINED AVERAGE ($000)	SALES VOLUME AVERAGE* ($000)
COMPANY SIZE		
UNDER $5 MILLION	$82.5	$778.0
$5MM–$25MM	92.8	1,568.7
$25MM–$100MM	127.1	4,760.0
$100MM–$250MM	160.4	1,550.0
OVER $250MM	214.6	33,483.3
PRODUCT OR SERVICE		
CONSUMER PRODUCTS	120.8	1,140.0
CONSUMER SERVICES	103.7	1,325.8
INDUSTRIAL PRODUCTS	110.1	1,483.8
INDUSTRIAL SERVICES	105.7	1,404.7
OFFICE PRODUCTS	139.0	1,483.3
OFFICE SERVICES	109.6	1,308.1
TYPE OF BUYER		
CONSUMERS	87.0	1,449.7
DISTRIBUTORS	118.7	1,729.4
INDUSTRY	110.4	1,471.1
RETAILERS	125.2	1,085.0
INDUSTRY		
BANKING	97.2	2,480.0
BUSINESS SERVICES	112.3	1,147.5
CHEMICALS	140.6	N/R
COMMUNICATIONS	127.5	2,833.3
CONSTRUCTION	96.2	1,187.5
EDUCATIONAL SERVICES	86.2	N/R
ELECTRONICS	142.5	1,283.3
ELECTRONIC COMPONENTS	103.8	2,150.0
FABRICATED METALS	100.7	4,400.0
HEALTH SERVICES	64.5	4,333.3
HOTELS AND OTHER LODGING PLACES	92.5	1,153.3
INSTRUMENTS	135.0	N/R
INSURANCE	104.9	1,460.0
MACHINERY	108.2	N/R
MANUFACTURING	85.7	3,675.0
OFFICE EQUIPMENT	123.8	33,800.0
PHARMACEUTICALS	245.0	723.3
PRINTING AND PUBLISHING	103.8	1,150.0
REAL ESTATE	101.7	2,266.7
RETAIL	91.0	950.0
RUBBER/PLASTICS	190.0	N/R
TRANSPORTATION EQUIPMENT	126.7	3,100.0
WHOLESALE (CONSUMER GOODS)	89.3	1,016.2
OVERALL	**$107.5**	**$1,386.4**

*SALES VOLUME FIGURES FOR THIS POSITION ARE A MEASURE OF OVERALL JOB RESPONSIBILITY AND DO NOT NECESSARILY REFLECT ACTUAL SALES MADE.

FIGURE 49

SALES COMPENSATION AND VOLUME LEVELS

TOP SALES EXECUTIVE

	TOTAL CASH COMP. FOR ALL PLANS COMBINED AVERAGE ($000)	SALES VOLUME AVERAGE* ($000)
COMPANY SIZE		
UNDER $5 MILLION	$76.5	$615.0
$5MM–$25MM	87.8	1,710.9
$25MM–$100MM	115.0	5,150.0
$100MM–$250MM	146.5	19,950.0
OVER $250MM	207.5	32,462.5
PRODUCT OR SERVICE		
CONSUMER PRODUCTS	110.5	2,345.9
CONSUMER SERVICES	101.4	1,561.2
INDUSTRIAL PRODUCTS	98.8	1,466.5
INDUSTRIAL SERVICES	97.2	2,029.3
OFFICE PRODUCTS	113.9	1,559.5
OFFICE SERVICES	105.1	1,491.4
TYPE OF BUYER		
CONSUMERS	86.2	1,220.9
DISTRIBUTORS	109.6	2,710.6
INDUSTRY	99.3	1,574.1
RETAILERS	113.8	2,392.4
INDUSTRY		
BANKING	155.5	7,025.0
BUSINESS SERVICES	109.8	1,570.6
CHEMICALS	123.2	6,362.5
COMMUNICATIONS	93.5	450.0
CONSTRUCTION	78.7	1,000.0
EDUCATIONAL SERVICES	87.0	N/R
ELECTRONICS	101.7	2,200.0
ELECTRONIC COMPONENTS	104.2	2,666.7
FABRICATED METALS	86.8	2,627.5
FOOD PRODUCTS	N/R	4,250.0
HEALTH SERVICES	71.0	N/R
HOTELS AND OTHER LODGING PLACES	113.3	2,366.7
INSTRUMENTS	95.5	5,200.0
INSURANCE	90.8	N/R
MACHINERY	120.5	550.0
MANUFACTURING	84.0	2,750.0
OFFICE EQUIPMENT	93.2	1,000.0
PAPER AND ALLIED PRODUCTS	105.0	N/R
PHARMACEUTICALS	226.2	9,225.0
PRINTING AND PUBLISHING	113.6	3,210.0
REAL ESTATE	166.0	N/R
RETAIL	66.6	605.7
RUBBER/PLASTICS	85.0	N/R
TRANSPORTATION EQUIPMENT	105.0	N/R
WHOLESALE (CONSUMER GOODS)	88.5	1,575.0
OVERALL	**$99.0**	**$1,643.8**

*SALES VOLUME FIGURES FOR THIS POSITION ARE A MEASURE OF OVERALL JOB RESPONSIBILITY AND DO NOT NECESSARILY REFLECT ACTUAL SALES MADE.

FIGURE 50

REGIONAL SALES MANAGER

	AVERAGE PERFORMER		BETTER PERFORMER		BEST PERFORMER	
	TOTAL CASH COMP. FOR ALL PLANS COMBINED ($000)	SALES VOLUME* ($000)	TOTAL CASH COMP. FOR ALL PLANS COMBINED ($000)	SALES VOLUME* ($000)	TOTAL CASH COMP. FOR ALL PLANS COMBINED ($000)	SALES VOLUME* ($000)
COMPANY SIZE						
UNDER $5 MILLION	$57.2	$391.1	$59.5	$538.5	$87.7	$549.4
$5MM–$25MM	67.0	1,187.3	69.5	1,762.5	83.3	1,931.8
$25MM–$100MM	82.8	1,589.2	86.0	2,168.4	92.7	2,581.7
$100MM–$250MM	94.7	1,764.8	97.7	2,428.5	109.8	2,814.7
OVER $250MM	89.6	1,658.1	91.8	2,122.9	103.0	2,427.7
PRODUCT OR SERVICE						
CONSUMER PRODUCTS	79.6	1,139.9	82.3	1,444.3	88.9	1,578.7
CONSUMER SERVICES	70.8	1,199.2	76.5	1,462.0	89.5	1,968.9
INDUSTRIAL PRODUCTS	75.9	1,476.7	79.5	1,724.4	95.8	2,215.5
INDUSTRIAL SERVICES	77.1	1,430.2	82.7	1,457.0	92.5	1,683.2
OFFICE PRODUCTS	91.5	1,472.7	92.1	1,731.4	122.2	2,448.0
OFFICE SERVICES	85.8	1,176.5	88.2	1,206.6	117.5	1,578.6
TYPE OF BUYER						
CONSUMERS	72.3	1,066.6	76.6	1,367.5	90.3	1,831.0
DISTRIBUTORS	77.2	1,608.3	78.4	1,846.5	92.2	2,317.6
INDUSTRY	76.1	1,419.0	78.7	1,463.2	94.1	1,975.1
RETAILERS	79.9	1,099.7	87.6	1,329.3	106.5	1,504.6
INDUSTRY						
BANKING	N/R	N/R	N/R	N/R	104.0	1,705.7
BUSINESS SERVICES	80.3	825.0	85.2	1,133.2	101.2	1,736.6
CHEMICALS	79.0	1,563.3	77.0	1,508.8	88.8	2,392.8
ELECTRONICS	73.0	1,547.6	77.2	1,776.7	95.0	2,474.1
FABRICATED METALS	41.6	2,297.6	66.2	2,464.3	91.1	2,928.5
INSTRUMENTS	63.7	550.0	N/R	1,000.0	86.7	1,400.0
MACHINERY	72.5	562.4	98.3	2,077.3	101.9	3,562.4
MANUFACTURING	67.0	1,849.0	68.5	1,964.3	105.5	3,500.0
OFFICE EQUIPMENT	96.8	2,439.2	102.0	2,678.4	127.5	4,062.4
PHARMACEUTICALS	151.5	440.0	154.7	600.0	181.3	716.0
PRINTING AND PUBLISHING	78.2	1,531.2	92.0	3,047.6	92.2	3,344.0
RETAIL	75.0	N/R	N/R	N/R	102.2	2,761.9
RUBBER/PLASTICS	N/R	N/R	N/R	N/R	65.0	3,525.5
WHOLESALE (CONSUMER GOODS)	68.6	1,462.0	71.0	1,323.2	73.0	2,278.4
OVERALL	**$77.7**	**$1,503.3**	**$78.7**	**$1,547.6**	**$93.6**	**$2,015.6**

*SALES VOLUME FIGURES FOR THIS POSITION ARE A MEASURE OF OVERALL JOB RESPONSIBILITY AND DO NOT NECESSARILY REFLECT ACTUAL SALES MADE.

FIGURE 51

SALES COMPENSATION AND VOLUME LEVELS

DISTRICT SALES MANAGER

	AVERAGE PERFORMER		BETTER PERFORMER		BEST PERFORMER	
	TOTAL CASH COMP. FOR ALL PLANS COMBINED ($000)	SALES VOLUME* ($000)	TOTAL CASH COMP. FOR ALL PLANS COMBINED ($000)	SALES VOLUME* ($000)	TOTAL CASH COMP. FOR ALL PLANS COMBINED ($000)	SALES VOLUME* ($000)
COMPANY SIZE						
UNDER $5 MILLION	$46.4	$169.5	$53.7	$197.0	$60.5	$291.4
$5MM–$25MM	71.8	985.0	75.6	1,556.2	75.7	1,691.6
$25MM–$100MM	69.0	2,092.3	77.0	2,563.7	82.7	2,565.5
$100MM–$250MM	71.2	964.2	81.0	1,946.4	95.0	2,113.1
OVER $250MM	79.2	929.9	82.0	1,736.3	101.9	2,175.4
PRODUCT OR SERVICE						
CONSUMER PRODUCTS	79.6	1,288.2	80.7	1,692.8	92.7	1,824.4
CONSUMER SERVICES	67.3	620.0	76.4	776.6	90.0	1,144.0
INDUSTRIAL PRODUCTS	71.9	821.8	71.9	1,440.5	87.2	1,941.5
INDUSTRIAL SERVICES	75.2	766.7	78.5	1,362.3	80.9	1,667.5
OFFICE PRODUCTS	78.5	969.3	82.2	1,836.5	105.5	2,465.6
OFFICE SERVICES	79.8	580.5	91.2	1,285.8	102.9	1,879.8
TYPE OF BUYER						
CONSUMERS	74.0	1,245.5	74.5	1,438.8	91.5	1,651.5
DISTRIBUTORS	71.4	1,017.2	73.8	1,805.4	86.1	2,323.8
INDUSTRY	72.4	678.6	77.5	1,194.9	81.3	1,578.2
RETAILERS	71.8	1,371.4	73.8	1,911.5	80.4	1,973.6
INDUSTRY						
BUSINESS SERVICES	63.8	188.3	53.7	137.5	74.1	200.0
ELECTRONICS	N/R	N/R	N/R	N/R	103.8	958.3
ELECTRONIC COMPONENTS	N/R	N/R	N/R	963.1	62.5	1,882.1
FABRICATED METALS	76.7	2,316.7	99.7	2,445.5	114.3	3,032.1
INSURANCE	N/R	N/R	N/R	N/R	77.0	2,146.9
OFFICE EQUIPMENT	85.0	2,446.4	96.7	3,659.5	115.8	3,672.5
PHARMACEUTICALS	N/R	715.5	N/R	1,414.3	124.7	2,165.5
WHOLESALE (CONSUMER GOODS)	62.7	921.4	71.0	1,625.0	85.0	2,285.0
OVERALL	**$72.5**	**$990.3**	**$73.9**	**$1,544.7**	**$80.1**	**$1,687.6**

*SALES VOLUME FIGURES FOR THIS POSITION ARE A MEASURE OF OVERALL JOB RESPONSIBILITY AND DO NOT NECESSARILY REFLECT ACTUAL SALES MADE.

FIGURE 52

SALES COMPENSATION AND VOLUME LEVELS

SENIOR SALES REP

	AVERAGE PERFORMER		BETTER PERFORMER		BEST PERFORMER	
	TOTAL CASH COMP. FOR ALL PLANS COMBINED ($000)	SALES VOLUME ($000)	TOTAL CASH COMP. FOR ALL PLANS COMBINED ($000)	SALES VOLUME ($000)	TOTAL CASH COMP. FOR ALL PLANS COMBINED ($000)	SALES VOLUME ($000)
COMPANY SIZE						
UNDER $5 MILLION	$44.3	$381.2	$46.1	$423.5	$54.8	$429.7
$5MM–$25MM	57.1	1,141.1	59.1	1,350.1	73.3	1,680.3
$25MM–$100MM	64.8	1,636.6	67.3	2,292.8	88.3	3,232.5
$100MM–$250MM	63.7	1,312.5	75.2	1,709.8	106.9	2,105.2
OVER $250MM	71.1	1,525.3	93.0	2,001.7	126.2	2,521.7
PRODUCT OR SERVICE						
CONSUMER PRODUCTS	58.1	1,018.7	61.1	1,442.9	81.2	1,729.3
CONSUMER SERVICES	51.5	859.5	54.4	1,103.9	73.4	1,492.1
INDUSTRIAL PRODUCTS	59.5	995.4	65.7	1,595.9	83.9	1,994.1
INDUSTRIAL SERVICES	59.8	940.9	64.4	1,478.5	77.0	1,956.2
OFFICE PRODUCTS	71.7	960.3	81.6	1,325.2	115.4	1,489.9
OFFICE SERVICES	66.5	890.1	72.5	1,090.0	106.7	1,301.2
TYPE OF BUYER						
CONSUMERS	52.8	857.1	57.6	1,146.4	77.8	1,516.1
DISTRIBUTORS	59.9	976.5	64.2	1,391.0	81.7	1,934.2
INDUSTRY	61.3	1,021.2	67.7	1,446.7	87.2	2,021.0
RETAILERS	57.9	938.0	60.9	1,339.4	87.0	1,647.7
INDUSTRY						
BANKING	100.0	2,428.5	195.0	2,571.2	242.2	2,783.2
BUSINESS SERVICES	62.4	947.7	65.7	959.4	85.2	1,361.2
CHEMICALS	59.5	787.5	60.5	1,930.9	85.8	2,015.5
COMMUNICATIONS	43.2	416.7	55.9	575.0	123.5	866.7
CONSTRUCTION	48.3	900.0	58.0	2,082.1	61.2	2,300.0
EDUCATIONAL SERVICES	52.2	N/R	N/R	N/R	78.3	500.0
ELECTRONICS	60.3	677.8	69.5	1,462.5	93.8	2,558.0
ELECTRONIC COMPONENTS	55.0	3,166.7	70.2	4,233.3	92.0	5,333.3
FABRICATED METALS	63.2	2,241.1	69.7	2,875.0	72.0	3,012.5
HEALTH SERVICES	N/R	1,100.0	N/R	1,650.0	77.7	1,900.0
HOTELS AND OTHER LODGING PLACES	42.1	1,025.0	47.2	1,900.0	57.6	2,749.0
INSURANCE	54.4	642.4	60.5	960.0	81.8	1,115.0
MACHINERY	91.3	715.5	100.0	853.1	114.0	1,046.4
MANUFACTURING	59.0	971.8	60.0	1,361.6	77.8	2,731.3
OFFICE EQUIPMENT	63.2	1,028.3	66.6	1,075.0	73.4	1,235.7
PAPER AND ALLIED PRODUCTS	N/R	N/R	N/R	N/R	118.3	848.8
PHARMACEUTICALS	83.8	790.0	103.7	1,283.3	120.0	1,633.3
PRINTING AND PUBLISHING	55.9	1,020.0	65.7	1,204.0	86.2	2,259.3
REAL ESTATE	86.7	940.5	N/R	1,335.7	149.1	2,364.3
RETAIL	45.1	888.3	47.7	920.9	70.2	1,028.5
RUBBER/PLASTICS	45.5	N/R	68.0	N/R	126.0	825.0
TRANSPORTATION EQUIPMENT	44.3	N/R	49.7	N/R	54.3	1,033.3
WHOLESALE (CONSUMER GOODS)	52.8	1,278.6	64.7	1,754.2	76.4	2,320.0
OVERALL	**$58.5**	**$1,026.5**	**$64.5**	**$1,429.3**	**$84.0**	**$1,881.9**

FIGURE 53

SALES COMPENSATION AND VOLUME LEVELS

INTERMEDIATE SALES REP

	AVERAGE PERFORMER		BETTER PERFORMER		BEST PERFORMER	
	TOTAL CASH COMP. FOR ALL PLANS COMBINED ($000)	SALES VOLUME ($000)	TOTAL CASH COMP. FOR ALL PLANS COMBINED ($000)	SALES VOLUME ($000)	TOTAL CASH COMP. FOR ALL PLANS COMBINED ($000)	SALES VOLUME ($000)
COMPANY SIZE						
UNDER $5 MILLION	$35.7	$177.8	$43.2	$211.2	$43.5	$225.2
$5MM–$25MM	40.6	582.4	42.5	717.8	50.1	773.4
$25MM–$100MM	46.1	1,108.3	48.1	1,323.1	58.7	1,773.3
$100MM–$250MM	39.5	671.4	47.8	820.8	68.8	970.0
OVER $250MM	50.8	1,518.5	62.5	1,768.2	81.3	1,991.0
PRODUCT OR SERVICE						
CONSUMER PRODUCTS	42.7	634.2	49.7	910.3	60.7	1,064.4
CONSUMER SERVICES	39.2	674.1	48.9	1,016.0	63.7	1,031.1
INDUSTRIAL PRODUCTS	41.6	579.2	45.5	735.5	56.4	825.8
INDUSTRIAL SERVICES	45.8	500.5	49.7	826.9	60.0	1,107.6
OFFICE PRODUCTS	45.0	492.9	53.9	588.4	68.8	668.6
OFFICE SERVICES	45.0	431.6	52.2	546.1	64.6	648.1
TYPE OF BUYER						
CONSUMERS	37.7	572.5	45.0	905.1	56.2	951.4
DISTRIBUTORS	42.9	555.1	46.9	693.1	59.1	906.9
INDUSTRY	42.8	550.3	46.2	751.7	57.3	901.2
RETAILERS	41.1	612.8	47.7	830.0	61.2	1,064.1
INDUSTRY						
BANKING	57.0	2,154.4	83.3	2,749.9	120.5	3,136.5
BUSINESS SERVICES	41.7	434.1	42.0	505.0	49.5	596.9
CHEMICALS	38.4	467.5	41.0	721.7	63.0	1,413.3
COMMUNICATIONS	52.2	320.7	N/R	357.7	76.5	381.0
CONSTRUCTION	N/R	683.3	N/R	1,075.0	47.0	1,850.0
EDUCATIONAL SERVICES	N/R	N/R	N/R	N/R	46.7	500.0
ELECTRONICS	41.1	700.0	49.0	2,350.0	58.5	3,848.8
FABRICATED METALS	49.2	N/R	49.3	N/R	51.0	1,586.6
HOTELS AND OTHER LODGING PLACES	36.2	897.8	30.0	N/R	36.8	1,484.0
INSURANCE	35.0	450.0	38.8	550.0	45.8	737.5
MACHINERY	N/R	N/R	N/R	N/R	52.2	423.3
MANUFACTURING	36.2	337.5	36.2	992.0	46.7	1,658.7
OFFICE EQUIPMENT	46.5	335.0	55.2	423.7	67.5	577.5
PHARMACEUTICALS	64.0	675.0	65.3	935.0	80.0	1,100.0
PRINTING AND PUBLISHING	35.9	575.0	46.2	761.6	59.6	906.2
REAL ESTATE	N/R	866.7	N/R	1,262.5	34.7	1,436.7
RETAIL	33.1	356.8	46.5	475.6	54.3	687.8
WHOLESALE (CONSUMER GOODS)	37.8	1,016.7	45.9	1,435.7	53.9	1,508.3
OVERALL	**$41.3**	**$615.5**	**$47.2**	**$889.6**	**$58.9**	**$1,024.7**

FIGURE 54

SALES COMPENSATION AND VOLUME LEVELS

ENTRY LEVEL SALES REP

	AVERAGE PERFORMER		BETTER PERFORMER		BEST PERFORMER	
	TOTAL CASH COMP. FOR ALL PLANS COMBINED ($000)	SALES VOLUME ($000)	TOTAL CASH COMP. FOR ALL PLANS COMBINED ($000)	SALES VOLUME ($000)	TOTAL CASH COMP. FOR ALL PLANS COMBINED ($000)	SALES VOLUME ($000)
COMPANY SIZE						
UNDER $5 MILLION	$26.6	$93.3	$32.8	$96.3	$40.2	$100.0
$5MM–$25MM	32.3	301.4	33.7	304.1	38.9	353.6
$25MM–$100MM	34.4	778.3	38.0	780.0	46.6	960.6
$100MM–$250MM	30.5	591.2	31.4	641.7	35.2	950.0
OVER $250MM	40.9	897.0	53.3	978.1	63.6	1,217.9
PRODUCT OR SERVICE						
CONSUMER PRODUCTS	32.2	384.0	40.1	416.1	49.2	456.6
CONSUMER SERVICES	27.7	345.5	34.6	493.2	45.2	513.5
INDUSTRIAL PRODUCTS	34.1	441.6	38.2	478.5	46.2	486.9
INDUSTRIAL SERVICES	34.9	349.8	40.6	518.8	50.4	739.9
OFFICE PRODUCTS	33.4	306.4	41.3	298.6	50.3	349.5
OFFICE SERVICES	32.5	255.5	41.7	327.6	49.2	355.8
TYPE OF BUYER						
CONSUMERS	29.8	354.7	35.2	393.1	45.4	469.2
DISTRIBUTORS	33.4	372.0	41.6	453.5	50.9	556.9
INDUSTRY	33.5	356.8	39.1	439.6	47.1	514.7
RETAILERS	31.4	377.5	37.3	462.7	48.0	472.1
INDUSTRY						
BANKING	48.8	N/R	101.3	N/R	111.3	1,848.2
BUSINESS SERVICES	33.2	292.5	33.4	365.6	47.8	371.2
CHEMICALS	30.6	710.0	34.0	783.3	44.3	1,388.3
COMMUNICATIONS	29.8	150.0	N/R	206.0	49.8	240.5
CONSTRUCTION	N/R	N/R	N/R	N/R	32.8	533.3
EDUCATIONAL SERVICES	N/R	N/R	N/R	N/R	38.0	265.0
ELECTRONICS	28.5	750.0	31.0	1,433.3	39.0	1,833.3
FABRICATED METALS	38.2	N/R	27.3	N/R	44.3	1,600.0
HOTELS AND OTHER LODGING PLACES	N/R	N/R	N/R	N/R	31.2	616.7
INSURANCE	27.1	275.0	27.2	666.7	35.8	866.7
MACHINERY	42.3	404.7	66.7	N/R	77.7	590.0
OFFICE EQUIPMENT	32.5	511.7	40.2	441.8	46.0	608.3
PHARMACEUTICALS	42.5	800.0	42.7	990.0	49.5	1,203.3
PRINTING AND PUBLISHING	28.9	257.5	37.5	625.0	45.2	1,025.0
REAL ESTATE	N/R	408.0	N/R	619.0	20.1	780.0
RETAIL	26.6	211.5	33.3	241.8	39.3	336.8
TRANSPORTATION EQUIPMENT	28.3	N/R	34.0	N/R	34.7	1,291.7
WHOLESALE (CONSUMER GOODS)	30.3	633.3	34.6	708.3	39.0	987.5
OVERALL	**$32.1**	**$407.1**	**$37.3**	**$509.5**	**$45.4**	**$573.2**

FIGURE 55

SALES COMPENSATION AND VOLUME LEVELS

NATIONAL/MAJOR ACCOUNT MANAGER

	AVERAGE PERFORMER		BETTER PERFORMER		BEST PERFORMER	
	TOTAL CASH COMP. FOR ALL PLANS COMBINED ($000)	SALES VOLUME* ($000)	TOTAL CASH COMP. FOR ALL PLANS COMBINED ($000)	SALES VOLUME* ($000)	TOTAL CASH COMP. FOR ALL PLANS COMBINED ($000)	SALES VOLUME* ($000)
COMPANY SIZE						
UNDER $5 MILLION	N/R	N/R	N/R	N/R	$58.6	$462.5
$5MM–$25MM	69.5	1,172.1	72.5	916.7	94.0	1,268.6
$25MM–$100MM	70.7	2,100.0	80.0	2,598.2	90.0	2,986.6
$100MM–$250MM	95.8	698.8	110.0	1,716.7	115.0	2,646.4
OVER $250MM	91.1	2,380.8	97.2	2,404.7	119.2	3,407.0
PRODUCT OR SERVICE						
CONSUMER PRODUCTS	82.4	1,676.3	105.7	2,067.4	108.3	2,137.3
CONSUMER SERVICES	80.2	949.5	90.2	1,236.6	114.0	1,500.0
INDUSTRIAL PRODUCTS	77.6	1,621.4	90.1	1,813.7	106.1	2,176.6
INDUSTRIAL SERVICES	92.2	1,523.2	113.7	1,974.1	130.2	2,742.4
OFFICE PRODUCTS	80.2	1,195.0	113.7	1,227.5	116.0	1,257.6
OFFICE SERVICES	91.4	1,544.8	118.1	1,027.8	119.7	1,572.1
TYPE OF BUYER						
CONSUMERS	75.0	1,033.9	95.8	1,136.7	113.2	1,167.3
DISTRIBUTORS	82.2	1,666.0	104.1	1,870.5	112.2	2,283.3
INDUSTRY	86.3	1,778.8	96.5	2,094.6	111.0	2,192.1
RETAILERS	81.4	1,227.0	117.4	1,433.0	128.3	1,843.3
INDUSTRY						
BUSINESS SERVICES	N/R	N/R	N/R	N/R	132.5	2,518.1
ELECTRONICS	N/R	N/R	N/R	N/R	71.7	2,500.0
ELECTRONIC COMPONENTS	82.5	2,815.5	90.8	2,630.9	117.7	3,166.7
MACHINERY	N/R	N/R	N/R	N/R	394.0	546.4
MANUFACTURING	N/R	N/R	N/R	N/R	80.0	3,733.3
OFFICE EQUIPMENT	61.2	803.5	90.0	1,110.7	100.2	1,482.1
PHARMACEUTICALS	114.8	N/R	129.0	N/R	138.8	2,680.7
PRINTING AND PUBLISHING	N/R	N/R	57.7	N/R	67.3	1,395.2
WHOLESALE (CONSUMER GOODS)	N/R	N/R	N/R	N/R	81.3	3,841.6
OVERALL	**$80.5**	**$1,521.6**	**$97.6**	**$1,597.5**	**$108.7**	**$1,963.5**

*SALES VOLUME FIGURES FOR THIS POSITION ARE A MEASURE OF OVERALL JOB RESPONSIBILITY AND DO NOT NECESSARILY REFLECT ACTUAL SALES MADE.

FIGURE 56

SALES COMPENSATION AND VOLUME LEVELS

NATIONAL ACCOUNT REP

	AVERAGE PERFORMER		BETTER PERFORMER		BEST PERFORMER	
	TOTAL CASH COMP. FOR ALL PLANS COMBINED ($000)	SALES VOLUME ($000)	TOTAL CASH COMP. FOR ALL PLANS COMBINED ($000)	SALES VOLUME ($000)	TOTAL CASH COMP. FOR ALL PLANS COMBINED ($000)	SALES VOLUME ($000)
COMPANY SIZE						
$5MM–$25MM	$60.0	$583.3	N/R	N/R	$63.5	$1,723.2
$25MM–$100MM	51.0	1,061.6	67.0	2,533.3	75.3	3,482.1
$100MM–$250MM	60.3	N/R	67.3	N/R	81.3	2,682.3
OVER $250MM	77.8	1,490.5	85.4	2,022.0	102.8	2,147.8
PRODUCT OR SERVICE						
CONSUMER PRODUCTS	81.7	931.2	91.9	1,420.0	115.2	2,183.3
CONSUMER SERVICES	75.0	841.7	78.0	1,600.0	79.0	2,525.0
INDUSTRIAL PRODUCTS	77.5	1,105.8	86.2	759.8	107.0	1,309.3
INDUSTRIAL SERVICES	84.0	958.3	88.0	1,469.3	92.3	1,758.6
OFFICE PRODUCTS	84.1	1,632.1	95.7	1,231.2	114.2	1,922.6
OFFICE SERVICES	74.2	1,758.6	70.0	1,826.4	96.6	1,958.3
TYPE OF BUYER						
CONSUMERS	66.5	963.3	74.5	1,329.3	90.2	1,473.2
DISTRIBUTORS	69.1	1,398.9	72.6	1,684.7	77.7	1,827.5
INDUSTRY	80.6	1,374.4	85.4	1,440.6	95.0	1,636.6
RETAILERS	66.2	1,305.3	67.7	1,798.8	71.5	1,983.3
INDUSTRY						
BUSINESS SERVICES	N/R	975.0	N/R	2,208.3	73.0	2,633.3
PRINTING AND PUBLISHING	N/R	N/R	N/R	N/R	43.5	3,166.7
OVERALL	**$73.5**	**$1,202.6**	**$74.1**	**$1,753.9**	**$92.3**	**$1,782.5**

FIGURE 57

Sales Compensation and Volume Levels

Major (Key) Account Rep

	Average Performer		Better Performer		Best Performer	
	Total Cash Comp. for All Plans Combined ($000)	Sales Volume ($000)	Total Cash Comp. for All Plans Combined ($000)	Sales Volume ($000)	Total Cash Comp. for All Plans Combined ($000)	Sales Volume ($000)
Company Size						
Under $5 Million	N/R	N/R	N/R	N/R	N/R	N/R
$5MM–$25MM	48.0	970.3	54.5	1,252.6	75.8	1,384.5
$25MM–$100MM	65.7	1,723.2	66.9	1,861.6	80.0	3,000.0
$100MM–$250MM	68.7	1,723.2	113.3	2,446.4	224.7	2,761.9
Over $250MM	83.0	1,250.0	96.7	2,615.5	118.8	3,410.7
Product or Service						
Consumer Products	68.2	779.3	79.9	1,265.5	101.9	2,327.5
Consumer Services	62.3	507.7	77.2	850.0	101.2	1,225.0
Industrial Products	63.3	1,376.9	70.8	1,624.1	94.8	2,090.2
Industrial Services	65.8	1,137.5	66.3	1,348.8	88.2	1,523.2
Office Products	71.4	1,142.6	74.9	1,158.5	108.6	1,812.9
Office Services	63.2	884.0	73.8	1,318.2	97.0	2,071.8
Type of Buyer						
Consumers	64.9	739.4	74.9	984.9	99.8	1,905.1
Distributors	68.7	1,366.7	77.8	2,015.5	109.8	2,822.3
Industry	63.4	1,281.9	70.8	1,413.9	93.0	2,352.0
Retailers	61.9	1,333.3	66.9	1,991.1	94.3	2,632.1
Industry						
Business Services	40.3	525.0	43.9	1,250.0	70.5	1,883.3
Electronics	68.5	1,933.3	79.0	2,966.7	100.0	5,166.7
Retail	68.3	N/R	88.3	N/R	98.3	500.0
Wholesale (Consumer Goods)	N/R	N/R	N/R	1,648.8	86.7	2,423.3
Overall	**$61.1**	**$1,039.7**	**$71.8**	**$1,391.8**	**$92.2**	**$2,025.5**

FIGURES 58–67 — SALES COMPENSATION AND VOLUME LEVELS: THIRD QUARTILE
(MARKETING, MANAGEMENT, AND ALL SALES POSITIONS)

One of the many nice things about this survey is the ability to examine the data in a variety of ways. The following data tables enable us to look at different segments, or ranges of the data, to suit our differing purposes and objectives.

Figures 58–67 also examine the relationship between total compensation and sales volume produced and repeat the data configurations of Figures 48–57, but report third-quartile findings. Again, because the positions of top marketing executive and top sales executive are generally limited to one individual per organization, there is no data for better performers and best performers.

As you look at these tables, bear in mind that you are looking at the top 25 percent[1] range of responses received. If your company is higher-paying, these are the tables you should use. But even if your company pays in the "average" range, these tables provide insights into how well the top salespeople in a variety of industries perform.

You may find, through an examination of these tables, for example, that your best salespeople are near the top of the scale in terms of the volume they produce, but nearer the middle in terms of the overall compensation they earn. If that's the case, you might want to reexamine your compensation plan, its objectives, and possible implications for the future. Again, use the data in this survey with discretion and judgment.

FIGURE 58

TOP MARKETING EXECUTIVE

	TOTAL CASH COMP. FOR ALL PLANS COMBINED ($000)	SALES VOLUME* ($000)
COMPANY SIZE		
UNDER $5 MILLION	$110.0	$1,500.0
$5MM–$25MM	145.0	3,000.0
$25MM–$100MM	165.0	9,000.0
$100MM–$250MM	250.0	3,000.0
OVER $250MM	250.0	10,000.0
PRODUCT OR SERVICE		
CONSUMER PRODUCTS	185.0	2,000.0
CONSUMER SERVICES	150.0	3,000.0
INDUSTRIAL PRODUCTS	160.0	3,000.0
INDUSTRIAL SERVICES	160.0	3,000.0
OFFICE PRODUCTS	270.0	6,000.0
OFFICE SERVICES	170.0	2,250.0
TYPE OF BUYER		
CONSUMERS	150.0	4,000.0
DISTRIBUTORS	175.0	5,000.0
INDUSTRY	160.0	3,000.0
RETAILERS	200.0	2,000.0
INDUSTRY		
BANKING	175.0	6,500.0
BUSINESS SERVICES	150.0	2,000.0
CHEMICALS	162.5	80.0
COMMUNICATIONS	160.0	5,000.0
CONSTRUCTION	125.0	2,000.0
EDUCATIONAL SERVICES	120.0	100.0
ELECTRONICS	195.0	2,000.0
ELECTRONIC COMPONENTS	150.0	2,500.0
FABRICATED METALS	154.5	9,000.0
HEALTH SERVICES	75.0	7,000.0
HOTELS AND OTHER LODGING PLACES	105.0	1,760.0
INSTRUMENTS	145.0	16,000.0
INSURANCE	187.5	3,000.0
MACHINERY	127.0	40.0
MANUFACTURING	115.0	6,000.0
OFFICE EQUIPMENT	220.0	10,000.0
PHARMACEUTICALS	300.0	1,000.0
PRINTING AND PUBLISHING	148.0	2,000.0
REAL ESTATE	125.0	5,000.0
RETAIL	170.0	1,400.0
RUBBER/PLASTICS	350.0	26,000.0
TRANSPORTATION EQUIPMENT	150.0	7,000.0
WHOLESALE (CONSUMER GOODS)	145.0	2,000.0
OVERALL	**$154.5**	**$3,000.0**

*SALES VOLUME FIGURES FOR THIS POSITION ARE A MEASURE OF OVERALL JOB RESPONSIBILITY AND DO NOT NECESSARILY REFLECT ACTUAL SALES MADE.

FIGURE 59

SALES COMPENSATION AND VOLUME LEVELS — THIRD QUARTILE

TOP SALES EXECUTIVE

	TOTAL CASH COMP. FOR ALL PLANS COMBINED ($000)	SALES VOLUME* ($000)
COMPANY SIZE		
UNDER $5 MILLION	$110.0	$1,000.0
$5MM–$25MM	120.0	4,000.0
$25MM–$100MM	150.0	10,000.0
$100MM–$250MM	185.0	78,000.0
OVER $250MM	275.0	10,000.0
PRODUCT OR SERVICE		
CONSUMER PRODUCTS	157.0	11,000.0
CONSUMER SERVICES	150.0	5,000.0
INDUSTRIAL PRODUCTS	140.0	4,000.0
INDUSTRIAL SERVICES	125.0	5,000.0
OFFICE PRODUCTS	190.0	6,000.0
OFFICE SERVICES	150.0	4,000.0
TYPE OF BUYER		
CONSUMERS	130.5	3,000.0
DISTRIBUTORS	150.0	10,000.0
INDUSTRY	140.0	4,000.0
RETAILERS	170.0	11,000.0
INDUSTRY		
BANKING	210.0	11,000.0
BUSINESS SERVICES	140.0	4,000.0
CHEMICALS	156.0	20,000.0
COMMUNICATIONS	130.0	600.0
CONSTRUCTION	89.2	1,500.0
EDUCATIONAL SERVICES	110.0	100.0
ELECTRONICS	160.0	3,000.0
ELECTRONIC COMPONENTS	120.0	5,000.0
FABRICATED METALS	123.6	5,000.0
FOOD PRODUCTS	84.0	6,000.0
HEALTH SERVICES	116.0	650.0
HOTELS AND OTHER LODGING PLACES	155.0	5,400.0
INSTRUMENTS	100.0	10,000.0
INSURANCE	115.0	1,000.0
MACHINERY	160.0	1,000.0
MANUFACTURING	140.0	5,000.0
OFFICE EQUIPMENT	144.0	2,000.0
PAPER AND ALLIED PRODUCTS	120.0	850.0
PHARMACEUTICALS	270.0	35,000.0
PRINTING AND PUBLISHING	157.0	8,000.0
REAL ESTATE	278.0	370.0
RETAIL	90.0	840.0
RUBBER/PLASTICS	95.0	120.0
TRANSPORTATION EQUIPMENT	125.0	1,300.0
WHOLESALE (CONSUMER GOODS)	105.0	4,000.0
OVERALL	**$140.0**	**$5,000.0**

*SALES VOLUME FIGURES FOR THIS POSITION ARE A MEASURE OF OVERALL JOB RESPONSIBILITY AND DO NOT NECESSARILY REFLECT ACTUAL SALES MADE.

FIGURE 60

SALES COMPENSATION AND VOLUME LEVELS — THIRD QUARTILE

REGIONAL SALES MANAGER

	AVERAGE PERFORMER		BETTER PERFORMER		BEST PERFORMER	
	TOTAL CASH COMP. FOR ALL PLANS COMBINED ($000)	SALES VOLUME* ($000)	TOTAL CASH COMP. FOR ALL PLANS COMBINED ($000)	SALES VOLUME* ($000)	TOTAL CASH COMP. FOR ALL PLANS COMBINED ($000)	SALES VOLUME* ($000)
COMPANY SIZE						
UNDER $5 MILLION	$69.0	$600.0	$81.7	$750.0	$91.0	$1,000.0
$5MM–$25MM	85.0	2,000.0	90.0	3,000.0	110.0	3,000.0
$25MM–$100MM	98.0	2,339.2	102.0	3,500.0	110.0	3,800.0
$100MM–$250MM	120.0	3,000.0	120.0	3,446.4	145.0	4,339.2
OVER $250MM	110.0	2,696.0	135.0	3,446.4	135.0	3,852.8
PRODUCT OR SERVICE						
CONSUMER PRODUCTS	108.0	2,232.0	120.0	2,339.2	125.0	3,000.0
CONSUMER SERVICES	100.0	2,000.0	113.0	2,696.0	134.0	3,000.0
INDUSTRIAL PRODUCTS	100.0	2,713.6	100.0	3,000.0	120.0	3,852.8
INDUSTRIAL SERVICES	110.0	2,500.0	113.5	2,892.8	134.0	3,446.4
OFFICE PRODUCTS	145.0	2,892.8	150.0	3,000.0	204.0	4,124.8
OFFICE SERVICES	145.0	2,500.0	150.0	2,696.0	200.0	3,852.8
TYPE OF BUYER						
CONSUMERS	100.0	2,000.0	102.0	2,100.0	120.0	3,000.0
DISTRIBUTORS	100.0	2,892.8	105.0	3,000.0	110.0	4,000.0
INDUSTRY	100.0	2,713.6	100.0	3,000.0	121.0	3,852.8
RETAILERS	115.0	2,232.0	150.0	2,500.0	200.0	3,000.0
INDUSTRY						
BANKING	N/R	1,500.0	N/R	2,177.6	110.0	3,392.0
BUSINESS SERVICES	95.0	1,200.0	113.0	1,840.0	134.0	3,446.4
CHEMICALS	95.0	2,339.2	105.0	2,339.2	108.0	6,339.2
COMMUNICATIONS	132.0	12.0	80.0	13.0	157.0	18.0
CONSTRUCTION	N/R	1,100.0	N/R	2,000.0	90.0	3,000.0
EDUCATIONAL SERVICES	35.0	280.0	65.0	400.0	120.0	750.0
ELECTRONICS	83.0	2,000.0	105.0	3,000.0	106.0	3,446.4
FABRICATED METALS	50.0	3,000.0	81.1	5,000.0	100.0	5,000.0
FOOD PRODUCTS	50.0	3,446.4	55.0	2,232.0	60.0	4,892.8
HOTELS AND OTHER LODGING PLACES	54.0	1,800.0	57.0	1,800.0	64.0	3,000.0
INSTRUMENTS	66.0	600.0	95.0	1,000.0	110.0	1,500.0
INSURANCE	N/R	N/R	N/R	N/R	78.0	416.0
MACHINERY	90.0	678.4	135.0	3,500.0	140.0	5,678.4
MANUFACTURING	85.0	3,000.0	87.0	4,000.0	126.0	4,500.0
OFFICE EQUIPMENT	150.0	3,000.0	175.0	3,000.0	200.0	4,124.8
PAPER AND ALLIED PRODUCTS	50.0	N/R	70.0	N/R	85.0	3,000.0
PHARMACEUTICALS	195.0	480.0	235.0	600.0	255.0	732.0
PRINTING AND PUBLISHING	100.0	3,000.0	105.0	4,339.2	115.0	5,000.0
REAL ESTATE	N/R	270.0	N/R	350.0	102.0	450.0
RETAIL	75.0	2,000.0	61.0	3,000.0	156.0	6,285.6
RUBBER/PLASTICS	70.0	446.4	N/R	3,446.4	82.0	5,446.4
TRANSPORTATION EQUIPMENT	N/R	100.0	49.0	240.0	100.0	700.0
WHOLESALE (CONSUMER GOODS)	74.0	2,500.0	75.0	2,100.0	80.0	3,000.0
OVERALL	**$100.0**	**$2,892.8**	**$108.0**	**$3,000.0**	**$120.0**	**$3,800.0**

*SALES VOLUME FIGURES FOR THIS POSITION ARE A MEASURE OF OVERALL JOB RESPONSIBILITY AND DO NOT NECESSARILY REFLECT ACTUAL SALES MADE.

FIGURE 61

SALES COMPENSATION AND VOLUME LEVELS — THIRD QUARTILE

DISTRICT SALES MANAGER

	AVERAGE PERFORMER		BETTER PERFORMER		BEST PERFORMER	
	TOTAL CASH COMP. FOR ALL PLANS COMBINED ($000)	SALES VOLUME* ($000)	TOTAL CASH COMP. FOR ALL PLANS COMBINED ($000)	SALES VOLUME* ($000)	TOTAL CASH COMP. FOR ALL PLANS COMBINED ($000)	SALES VOLUME* ($000)
COMPANY SIZE						
UNDER $5 MILLION	$50.0	$288.0	$60.0	$400.0	$100.0	$500.0
$5MM–$25MM	90.0	2,000.0	108.0	2,000.0	115.0	2,140.0
$25MM–$100MM	94.0	3,200.0	90.0	3,446.4	100.0	3,900.0
$100MM–$250MM	85.0	1,356.8	95.0	2,446.4	110.0	4,000.0
OVER $250MM	100.0	1,446.4	115.0	3,446.4	125.0	3,785.6
PRODUCT OR SERVICE						
CONSUMER PRODUCTS	100.0	2,500.0	106.5	3,000.0	120.0	3,392.0
CONSUMER SERVICES	97.0	1,200.0	100.0	1,746.4	125.0	2,000.0
INDUSTRIAL PRODUCTS	97.0	1,300.0	100.0	2,300.0	115.0	3,392.0
INDUSTRIAL SERVICES	100.0	1,300.0	102.5	1,800.0	115.0	2,500.0
OFFICE PRODUCTS	100.0	2,400.0	115.0	3,785.6	140.0	4,124.8
OFFICE SERVICES	102.5	1,300.0	120.0	2,446.4	151.0	4,124.8
TYPE OF BUYER						
CONSUMERS	100.0	3,000.0	100.0	3,200.0	125.0	3,900.0
DISTRIBUTORS	95.0	2,000.0	98.0	3,000.0	120.0	4,000.0
INDUSTRY	100.0	1,285.6	103.0	2,300.0	120.0	3,392.0
RETAILERS	100.0	2,500.0	97.0	3,000.0	100.0	3,446.4
INDUSTRY						
BANKING	N/R	100.0	N/R	300.0	110.0	700.0
BUSINESS SERVICES	80.0	300.0	60.0	150.0	90.0	375.0
COMMUNICATIONS	92.0	1,000.0	97.0	2,000.0	125.0	2,000.0
CONSTRUCTION	N/R	2,500.0	N/R	3,200.0	77.0	3,900.0
ELECTRONICS	70.0	850.0	90.0	1,000.0	150.0	2,000.0
ELECTRONIC COMPONENTS	40.0	500.0	50.0	1,800.0	65.0	3,446.4
FABRICATED METALS	103.0	4,446.4	131.0	4,446.4	138.0	5,200.0
FOOD PRODUCTS	80.0	N/R	N/R	N/R	86.0	1,356.8
HOTELS AND OTHER LODGING PLACES	N/R	1,200.0	N/R	1,800.0	42.0	1,800.0
INSTRUMENTS	52.0	1,000.0	58.5	2,300.0	65.0	2,500.0
INSURANCE	60.0	N/R	80.0	N/R	87.0	5,820.8
MANUFACTURING	N/R	183.0	N/R	729.0	143.0	982.0
OFFICE EQUIPMENT	130.0	3,446.4	140.0	5,446.4	155.0	5,678.4
PHARMACEUTICALS	95.0	1,446.4	120.0	2,000.0	184.0	4,946.4
PRINTING AND PUBLISHING	75.0	2,446.4	80.0	4,000.0	90.0	5,446.4
RETAIL	100.0	425.0	130.0	200.0	130.0	4,390.0
RUBBER/PLASTICS	N/R	N/R	N/R	N/R	40.0	110.0
TRANSPORTATION EQUIPMENT	60.0	N/R	90.0	750.0	105.0	1,500.0
WHOLESALE (CONSUMER GOODS)	79.0	1,285.6	80.0	2,500.0	95.0	3,000.0
OVERALL	**$97.0**	**$2,000.0**	**$98.0**	**$2,500.0**	**$115.0**	**$3,250.0**

*SALES VOLUME FIGURES FOR THIS POSITION ARE A MEASURE OF OVERALL JOB RESPONSIBILITY AND DO NOT NECESSARILY REFLECT ACTUAL SALES MADE.

FIGURE 62

SALES COMPENSATION AND VOLUME LEVELS — THIRD QUARTILE

SENIOR SALES REP

	AVERAGE PERFORMER		BETTER PERFORMER		BEST PERFORMER	
	TOTAL CASH COMP. FOR ALL PLANS COMBINED ($000)	SALES VOLUME ($000)	TOTAL CASH COMP. FOR ALL PLANS COMBINED ($000)	SALES VOLUME ($000)	TOTAL CASH COMP. FOR ALL PLANS COMBINED ($000)	SALES VOLUME ($000)
COMPANY SIZE						
UNDER $5 MILLION	$60.0	$670.0	$65.0	$750.0	$82.0	$800.0
$5MM–$25MM	77.5	1,700.0	80.0	2,100.0	100.0	3,000.0
$25MM–$100MM	83.0	2,800.0	90.0	3,446.4	119.0	4,446.4
$100MM–$250MM	80.0	2,000.0	110.0	2,446.4	200.0	3,446.4
OVER $250MM	95.0	3,200.0	125.0	3,446.4	165.0	3,600.0
PRODUCT OR SERVICE						
CONSUMER PRODUCTS	85.0	2,000.0	95.0	2,339.2	125.0	2,800.0
CONSUMER SERVICES	70.0	1,600.0	80.0	2,000.0	111.0	2,500.0
INDUSTRIAL PRODUCTS	80.0	1,700.0	87.0	2,500.0	124.0	3,446.4
INDUSTRIAL SERVICES	80.0	1,700.0	98.0	2,500.0	120.0	3,446.4
OFFICE PRODUCTS	95.0	2,000.0	118.0	2,400.0	169.0	2,446.4
OFFICE SERVICES	95.0	1,800.0	110.0	1,892.8	165.0	2,225.0
TYPE OF BUYER						
CONSUMERS	70.0	1,597.0	85.0	2,000.0	120.0	2,500.0
DISTRIBUTORS	83.0	1,700.0	85.0	2,300.0	122.0	3,446.4
INDUSTRY	83.0	1,780.0	95.0	2,500.0	130.0	3,446.4
RETAILERS	87.0	1,700.0	90.0	2,100.0	140.0	2,600.0
INDUSTRY						
BANKING	125.0	2,500.0	230.0	3,446.4	249.0	4,803.2
BUSINESS SERVICES	80.0	1,500.0	90.0	1,600.0	122.5	2,500.0
CHEMICALS	65.0	1,000.0	75.0	3,000.0	124.0	3,446.4
COMMUNICATIONS	53.0	600.0	72.0	750.0	152.0	1,200.0
CONSTRUCTION	50.0	1,200.0	65.0	3,000.0	75.0	3,446.4
EDUCATIONAL SERVICES	80.0	500.0	110.0	750.0	140.0	900.0
ELECTRONICS	80.0	1,000.0	80.0	2,200.0	115.0	3,800.0
ELECTRONIC COMPONENTS	70.0	4,000.0	87.5	4,700.0	135.0	5,500.0
FABRICATED METALS	85.0	3,000.0	93.0	3,000.0	97.5	4,000.0
FOOD PRODUCTS	N/R	N/R	N/R	N/R	40.0	339.2
HEALTH SERVICES	82.0	1,200.0	25.0	2,500.0	90.0	3,000.0
HOTELS AND OTHER LODGING PLACES	46.5	1,200.0	57.0	2,000.0	65.0	3,498.0
INSTRUMENTS	75.0	1,250.0	80.0	1,500.0	89.0	2,100.0
INSURANCE	60.0	850.0	73.5	1,800.0	92.0	2,500.0
MACHINERY	119.0	1,500.0	125.0	2,000.0	141.0	2,500.0
MANUFACTURING	70.0	1,500.0	77.0	1,900.0	90.0	4,394.0
OFFICE EQUIPMENT	80.0	1,700.0	90.0	2,000.0	100.0	2,100.0
PAPER AND ALLIED PRODUCTS	80.0	1,000.0	100.0	1,500.0	250.0	3,000.0
PHARMACEUTICALS	100.0	1,500.0	120.0	2,000.0	142.0	2,200.0
PRINTING AND PUBLISHING	77.5	1,780.0	92.0	2,000.0	150.0	3,800.0
REAL ESTATE	135.0	2,000.0	100.5	2,446.4	285.0	6,000.0
RETAIL	70.0	1,597.0	80.0	1,700.0	115.0	1,900.0
RUBBER/PLASTICS	56.0	N/R	100.0	N/R	300.0	1,000.0
TRANSPORTATION EQUIPMENT	50.0	450.0	61.0	900.0	78.0	1,700.0
WHOLESALE (CONSUMER GOODS)	65.0	2,000.0	96.0	3,000.0	100.0	4,000.0
OVERALL	**$80.0**	**$2,000.0**	**$90.0**	**$2,500.0**	**$125.0**	**$3,446.4**

FIGURE 63

SALES COMPENSATION AND VOLUME LEVELS — THIRD QUARTILE

INTERMEDIATE SALES REP

	AVERAGE PERFORMER		BETTER PERFORMER		BEST PERFORMER	
	TOTAL CASH COMP. FOR ALL PLANS COMBINED ($000)	SALES VOLUME ($000)	TOTAL CASH COMP. FOR ALL PLANS COMBINED ($000)	SALES VOLUME ($000)	TOTAL CASH COMP. FOR ALL PLANS COMBINED ($000)	SALES VOLUME ($000)
COMPANY SIZE						
UNDER $5 MILLION	$47.0	$260.0	$60.0	$300.0	$60.0	$500.0
$5MM–$25MM	50.0	1,000.0	50.0	1,500.0	60.0	1,650.0
$25MM–$100MM	55.0	1,500.0	60.0	2,000.0	70.0	3,000.0
$100MM–$250MM	60.0	1,000.0	70.0	1,500.0	80.0	1,700.0
OVER $250MM	60.0	2,800.0	80.0	3,300.0	100.0	3,500.0
PRODUCT OR SERVICE						
CONSUMER PRODUCTS	60.0	1,200.0	66.0	1,750.0	85.0	2,000.0
CONSUMER SERVICES	50.0	1,446.4	67.1	2,000.0	90.0	2,000.0
INDUSTRIAL PRODUCTS	51.0	1,000.0	55.0	1,500.0	80.0	1,650.0
INDUSTRIAL SERVICES	60.0	1,000.0	72.0	1,500.0	85.0	2,000.0
OFFICE PRODUCTS	60.0	940.0	72.0	1,000.0	90.0	1,000.0
OFFICE SERVICES	62.0	700.0	70.0	800.0	85.0	1,000.0
TYPE OF BUYER						
CONSUMERS	50.0	1,100.0	60.0	1,800.0	83.0	2,000.0
DISTRIBUTORS	55.0	1,000.0	57.0	1,400.0	80.0	2,000.0
INDUSTRY	58.0	1,000.0	60.0	1,500.0	80.0	2,000.0
RETAILERS	57.0	1,100.0	66.0	1,700.0	85.0	2,000.0
INDUSTRY						
BANKING	60.0	4,446.4	100.0	4,124.8	153.5	5,339.2
BUSINESS SERVICES	58.0	800.0	65.0	800.0	78.0	1,000.0
CHEMICALS	42.0	850.0	45.0	2,000.0	72.0	4,000.0
COMMUNICATIONS	80.0	700.0	90.0	800.0	103.0	850.0
CONSTRUCTION	45.0	1,000.0	55.0	2,000.0	56.0	4,000.0
EDUCATIONAL SERVICES	60.0	600.0	80.0	800.0	100.0	1,000.0
ELECTRONICS	50.0	1,400.0	55.0	3,000.0	65.0	5,446.4
ELECTRONIC COMPONENTS	45.0	700.0	72.0	800.0	80.0	3,000.0
FABRICATED METALS	49.5	420.0	51.8	420.0	52.0	3,000.0
HOTELS AND OTHER LODGING PLACES	38.4	1,191.0	42.0	1,700.0	42.0	2,052.0
INSTRUMENTS	30.0	150.0	32.2	200.0	34.2	250.0
INSURANCE	40.0	800.0	50.0	700.0	50.0	1,800.0
MACHINERY	60.0	40.0	65.0	70.0	70.0	1,000.0
MANUFACTURING	37.5	500.0	43.0	2,000.0	60.0	4,000.0
OFFICE EQUIPMENT	60.0	500.0	66.0	721.0	85.0	1,300.0
PAPER AND ALLIED PRODUCTS	35.0	N/R	60.0	N/R	80.0	300.0
PHARMACEUTICALS	73.0	1,000.0	90.0	1,500.0	96.0	1,700.0
PRINTING AND PUBLISHING	49.0	1,000.0	55.0	1,250.0	73.5	1,500.0
REAL ESTATE	41.1	1,500.0	50.0	2,200.0	95.0	2,400.0
RETAIL	39.0	650.0	60.0	1,082.0	74.4	1,349.0
RUBBER/PLASTICS	26.0	N/R	28.0	N/R	31.0	80.0
TRANSPORTATION EQUIPMENT	41.0	250.0	53.0	600.0	67.0	1,100.0
WHOLESALE (CONSUMER GOODS)	40.0	1,250.0	52.0	1,750.0	62.5	2,000.0
OVERALL	**$53.0**	**$1,100.0**	**$63.0**	**$1,750.0**	**$80.0**	**$2,000.0**

FIGURE 64

SALES COMPENSATION AND VOLUME LEVELS — THIRD QUARTILE

ENTRY LEVEL SALES REP

	AVERAGE PERFORMER		BETTER PERFORMER		BEST PERFORMER	
	TOTAL CASH COMP. FOR ALL PLANS COMBINED ($000)	SALES VOLUME ($000)	TOTAL CASH COMP. FOR ALL PLANS COMBINED ($000)	SALES VOLUME ($000)	TOTAL CASH COMP. FOR ALL PLANS COMBINED ($000)	SALES VOLUME ($000)
COMPANY SIZE						
UNDER $5 MILLION	$32.0	$150.0	$39.0	$120.0	$49.0	$200.0
$5MM–$25MM	39.0	700.0	40.0	500.0	50.0	750.0
$25MM–$100MM	43.0	1,300.0	45.0	1,500.0	54.0	1,700.0
$100MM–$250MM	42.0	900.0	40.0	900.0	45.0	1,200.0
OVER $250MM	57.6	1,600.0	66.0	2,000.0	80.0	2,000.0
PRODUCT OR SERVICE						
CONSUMER PRODUCTS	42.0	800.0	50.0	1,000.0	60.0	1,000.0
CONSUMER SERVICES	35.0	800.0	44.0	1,000.0	60.0	1,200.0
INDUSTRIAL PRODUCTS	43.0	800.0	50.0	1,000.0	60.0	1,000.0
INDUSTRIAL SERVICES	45.0	750.0	53.0	1,000.0	61.0	1,800.0
OFFICE PRODUCTS	45.0	600.0	60.0	479.0	70.0	800.0
OFFICE SERVICES	43.0	500.0	60.0	700.0	60.5	800.0
TYPE OF BUYER						
CONSUMERS	40.0	800.0	47.0	900.0	60.0	1,000.0
DISTRIBUTORS	43.0	800.0	60.0	1,000.0	68.0	1,300.0
INDUSTRY	45.0	776.0	53.0	1,000.0	60.0	1,110.0
RETAILERS	40.0	800.0	48.0	900.0	70.0	1,000.0
INDUSTRY						
BANKING	92.0	75.0	144.0	75.0	148.0	3,446.4
BUSINESS SERVICES	45.0	700.0	50.2	800.0	60.0	1,000.0
CHEMICALS	36.4	1,500.0	47.0	2,000.0	55.0	4,000.0
COMMUNICATIONS	45.0	200.0	30.5	212.0	71.0	281.0
CONSTRUCTION	35.5	1,000.0	38.0	1,500.0	42.0	3,000.0
EDUCATIONAL SERVICES	50.0	280.0	60.0	600.0	70.0	800.0
ELECTRONICS	32.0	1,000.0	45.0	2,000.0	50.0	2,500.0
ELECTRONIC COMPONENTS	55.0	500.0	67.0	1,000.0	80.0	2,000.0
FABRICATED METALS	45.0	300.0	50.0	300.0	68.0	1,800.0
HEALTH SERVICES	43.0	400.0	45.0	600.0	50.0	1,200.0
HOTELS AND OTHER LODGING PLACES	29.0	400.0	33.5	800.0	36.0	1,200.0
INSTRUMENTS	28.5	100.0	30.0	150.0	31.7	200.0
INSURANCE	31.3	500.0	35.0	1,600.0	40.0	2,000.0
MACHINERY	55.0	750.0	80.0	40.0	90.0	1,000.0
MANUFACTURING	40.0	N/R	62.4	N/R	67.2	600.0
OFFICE EQUIPMENT	36.0	1,000.0	50.0	479.0	55.0	1,200.0
PAPER AND ALLIED PRODUCTS	N/R	N/R	N/R	N/R	60.0	300.0
PHARMACEUTICALS	46.0	2,000.0	50.0	2,500.0	53.0	3,000.0
PRINTING AND PUBLISHING	36.0	500.0	44.0	750.0	55.0	1,800.0
REAL ESTATE	10.5	677.0	25.0	1,000.0	40.0	1,500.0
RETAIL	30.0	300.0	39.7	300.0	53.0	700.0
RUBBER/PLASTICS	26.0	N/R	29.0	N/R	65.0	65.0
TRANSPORTATION EQUIPMENT	36.0	125.0	44.0	240.0	54.0	3,000.0
WHOLESALE (CONSUMER GOODS)	35.0	900.0	40.0	1,000.0	45.0	1,200.0
OVERALL	**$40.0**	**$800.0**	**$48.0**	**$1,000.0**	**$60.0**	**$1,200.0**

FIGURE 65

NATIONAL/MAJOR ACCOUNT MANAGER

	AVERAGE PERFORMER		BETTER PERFORMER		BEST PERFORMER	
	TOTAL CASH COMP. FOR ALL PLANS COMBINED ($000)	SALES VOLUME* ($000)	TOTAL CASH COMP. FOR ALL PLANS COMBINED ($000)	SALES VOLUME* ($000)	TOTAL CASH COMP. FOR ALL PLANS COMBINED ($000)	SALES VOLUME* ($000)
COMPANY SIZE						
UNDER $5 MILLION	N/R	N/R	N/R	N/R	$70.0	$1,000.0
$5MM–$25MM	85.0	1,600.0	90.0	1,446.4	110.0	3,000.0
$25MM–$100MM	100.0	4,000.0	95.0	3,446.4	135.0	4,500.0
$100MM–$250MM	140.0	1,500.0	140.0	3,000.0	150.0	5,000.0
OVER $250MM	110.0	3,446.4	115.0	4,000.0	142.0	4,464.0
PRODUCT OR SERVICE						
CONSUMER PRODUCTS	100.0	3,446.4	138.0	4,000.0	142.0	4,000.0
CONSUMER SERVICES	98.0	1,500.0	106.0	2,000.0	120.0	2,000.0
INDUSTRIAL PRODUCTS	95.0	3,446.4	110.0	3,446.4	125.0	3,446.4
INDUSTRIAL SERVICES	125.0	2,500.0	146.5	3,446.4	168.0	4,500.0
OFFICE PRODUCTS	110.0	2,000.0	159.0	3,000.0	160.0	3,446.4
OFFICE SERVICES	140.0	2,446.4	160.0	2,000.0	160.0	3,446.4
TYPE OF BUYER						
CONSUMERS	102.5	1,500.0	110.0	2,000.0	125.0	2,000.0
DISTRIBUTORS	100.0	3,000.0	140.0	3,446.4	140.0	3,446.4
INDUSTRY	110.0	3,446.4	135.0	3,446.4	142.0	4,124.8
RETAILERS	102.5	2,000.0	159.0	2,500.0	160.0	3,000.0
INDUSTRY						
BUSINESS SERVICES	140.0	129.0	175.0	150.0	250.0	4,446.4
COMMUNICATIONS	N/R	N/R	N/R	N/R	75.0	446.4
EDUCATIONAL SERVICES	106.0	1,000.0	140.0	1,500.0	140.0	2,000.0
ELECTRONICS	68.0	2,000.0	77.0	4,000.0	87.0	4,000.0
ELECTRONIC COMPONENTS	90.0	5,000.0	105.0	3,446.4	145.0	5,000.0
FOOD PRODUCTS	N/R	N/R	N/R	N/R	80.0	5,339.2
MACHINERY	65.0	1,000.0	85.0	1,500.0	1,000.0	3,000.0
MANUFACTURING	95.0	N/R	105.0	N/R	120.0	5,000.0
OFFICE EQUIPMENT	80.0	1,446.4	125.0	3,446.4	160.0	3,446.4
PHARMACEUTICALS	127.0	300.0	159.0	309.0	174.3	4,400.0
PRINTING AND PUBLISHING	62.0	1,785.6	77.0	4,500.0	100.0	6,000.0
REAL ESTATE	N/R	56.0	N/R	60.0	45.0	80.0
RETAIL	64.0	500.0	78.0	786.0	90.0	1,174.0
RUBBER/PLASTICS	N/R	3,446.4	N/R	4,892.8	100.0	5,000.0
TRANSPORTATION EQUIPMENT	N/R	N/R	N/R	N/R	100.0	1,800.0
WHOLESALE (CONSUMER GOODS)	100.0	2,446.4	110.0	2,803.2	120.0	5,000.0
OVERALL	**$100.0**	**$3,446.4**	**$138.0**	**$3,446.4**	**$142.0**	**$4,000.0**

*SALES VOLUME FIGURES FOR THIS POSITION ARE A MEASURE OF OVERALL JOB RESPONSIBILITY AND DO NOT NECESSARILY REFLECT ACTUAL SALES MADE.

FIGURE 66

SALES COMPENSATION AND VOLUME LEVELS — THIRD QUARTILE

NATIONAL ACCOUNT REP

	AVERAGE PERFORMER		BETTER PERFORMER		BEST PERFORMER	
	TOTAL CASH COMP. FOR ALL PLANS COMBINED ($000)	SALES VOLUME ($000)	TOTAL CASH COMP. FOR ALL PLANS COMBINED ($000)	SALES VOLUME ($000)	TOTAL CASH COMP. FOR ALL PLANS COMBINED ($000)	SALES VOLUME ($000)
COMPANY SIZE						
UNDER $5 MILLION	N/R	N/R	N/R	N/R	$90.0	N/R
$5MM–$25MM	80.0	1,000.0	55.0	400.0	82.0	2,446.4
$25MM–$100MM	72.0	1,800.0	100.0	4,000.0	130.0	4,800.0
$100MM–$250MM	75.0	57.0	85.0	68.5	100.0	6,000.0
OVER $250MM	89.0	2,892.8	98.0	3,000.0	125.0	3,339.2
PRODUCT OR SERVICE						
CONSUMER PRODUCTS	98.0	1,800.0	125.0	2,000.0	125.0	3,000.0
CONSUMER SERVICES	98.0	1,800.0	108.0	2,000.0	120.0	4,000.0
INDUSTRIAL PRODUCTS	95.0	1,900.0	98.0	1,000.0	125.0	2,000.0
INDUSTRIAL SERVICES	98.0	1,800.0	120.0	1,900.0	150.0	3,000.0
OFFICE PRODUCTS	134.0	2,446.4	150.0	1,800.0	157.0	3,785.6
OFFICE SERVICES	98.0	2,446.4	120.0	3,000.0	134.0	4,000.0
TYPE OF BUYER						
CONSUMERS	90.0	2,000.0	98.0	2,892.8	125.0	3,000.0
DISTRIBUTORS	90.0	2,446.4	92.5	3,000.0	120.0	3,000.0
INDUSTRY	98.0	2,500.0	125.0	3,000.0	125.0	3,000.0
RETAILERS	88.0	2,446.4	92.5	2,892.8	120.0	3,000.0
INDUSTRY						
BANKING	165.0	600.0	200.0	700.0	220.0	700.0
BUSINESS SERVICES	72.0	1,200.0	56.0	4,800.0	95.0	5,700.0
ELECTRONICS	87.0	750.0	98.0	446.4	120.0	1,500.0
HEALTH SERVICES	30.0	80.0	30.0	800.0	55.0	800.0
HOTELS AND OTHER LODGING PLACES	52.0	2,892.8	55.0	3,339.2	61.0	4,785.6
PHARMACEUTICALS	89.0	800.0	108.0	2,500.0	125.0	3,000.0
REAL ESTATE	N/R	47.0	N/R	57.0	170.0	68.5
WHOLESALE (CONSUMER GOODS)	80.0	1,800.0	87.0	N/R	95.0	2,446.4
OVERALL	**$95.0**	**$2,500.0**	**$98.0**	**$2,892.8**	**$125.0**	**$3,000.0**

FIGURE 67

SALES COMPENSATION AND VOLUME LEVELS — THIRD QUARTILE

MAJOR (KEY) ACCOUNT REP

	AVERAGE PERFORMER		BETTER PERFORMER		BEST PERFORMER	
	TOTAL CASH COMP. FOR ALL PLANS COMBINED ($000)	SALES VOLUME ($000)	TOTAL CASH COMP. FOR ALL PLANS COMBINED ($000)	SALES VOLUME ($000)	TOTAL CASH COMP. FOR ALL PLANS COMBINED ($000)	SALES VOLUME ($000)
COMPANY SIZE						
UNDER $5 MILLION	N/R	$300.0	N/R	$2,000.0	$50.0	$2,500.0
$5MM–$25MM	60.0	1,500.0	66.0	2,500.0	120.0	3,000.0
$25MM–$100MM	85.0	2,000.0	90.0	3,000.0	110.0	4,000.0
$100MM–$250MM	100.0	2,000.0	230.0	3,785.6	550.0	4,000.0
OVER $250MM	88.0	2,000.0	98.0	4,200.0	125.0	6,000.0
PRODUCT OR SERVICE						
CONSUMER PRODUCTS	88.0	2,000.0	98.0	2,500.0	120.0	3,446.4
CONSUMER SERVICES	87.0	1,000.0	98.0	2,000.0	120.0	3,000.0
INDUSTRIAL PRODUCTS	85.0	3,000.0	95.0	4,000.0	120.0	5,000.0
INDUSTRIAL SERVICES	87.0	2,500.0	98.0	3,000.0	120.0	3,446.4
OFFICE PRODUCTS	98.0	2,000.0	100.0	3,000.0	125.0	4,000.0
OFFICE SERVICES	90.0	2,000.0	105.0	2,500.0	120.0	5,000.0
TYPE OF BUYER						
CONSUMERS	90.0	1,500.0	98.0	2,000.0	120.0	5,000.0
DISTRIBUTORS	88.0	3,000.0	98.0	3,000.0	125.0	5,000.0
INDUSTRY	87.0	3,000.0	97.0	3,000.0	120.0	5,000.0
RETAILERS	85.0	3,000.0	95.0	3,000.0	120.0	5,000.0
INDUSTRY						
BUSINESS SERVICES	45.0	1,000.0	64.5	2,000.0	74.0	4,000.0
CHEMICALS	N/R	N/R	N/R	1,100.0	26.0	3,000.0
ELECTRONICS	87.0	2,500.0	98.0	4,200.0	120.0	6,500.0
ELECTRONIC COMPONENTS	70.0	3,000.0	77.0	4,000.0	85.0	5,000.0
FABRICATED METALS	N/R	N/R	N/R	N/R	75.0	4,000.0
INSURANCE	N/R	100.0	N/R	N/R	26.5	300.0
OFFICE EQUIPMENT	66.0	250.0	58.0	325.0	92.5	400.0
PHARMACEUTICALS	87.0	46.4	97.0	646.4	108.0	946.4
PRINTING AND PUBLISHING	N/R	200.0	N/R	400.0	80.0	500.0
REAL ESTATE	N/R	39.0	N/R	45.0	100.0	60.0
RETAIL	85.0	500.0	105.0	500.0	120.0	500.0
RUBBER/PLASTICS	N/R	1,446.4	N/R	3,446.4	100.0	5,000.0
TRANSPORTATION EQUIPMENT	N/R	N/R	N/R	N/R	16.5	3,400.0
WHOLESALE (CONSUMER GOODS)	46.0	35.0	58.0	3,000.0	140.0	5,000.0
OVERALL	**$85.0**	**$2,500.0**	**$98.0**	**$2,500.0**	**$120.0**	**$3,446.4**

FIGURE 68 — SENIOR SALES REP PRODUCTIVITY

How much more productive, in measurable terms, are top performers compared to average performers? Survey participants were asked to estimate the degree to which top salespeople outperform their average counterparts. **Figure 68** takes a look at these estimates and provides data from our previous survey as well as current data. This data represents that group of salespeople who sell at least more than $1\frac{1}{2}$ times the amount sold by average performers. It's helpful to group the figures in the following way: The top 10 percent (10.57%) of the top-performing senior salespeople in this survey sell $3\frac{1}{2}$ or more times as much as an average salesperson; nearly 55 percent (54.41%) sell from 2 to $3\frac{1}{2}$ times as much as an average salesperson. Thirty-five percent (35.01%) of the salespeople in this survey selling more than the average sell half again as much as an average salesperson. This data can provide further guidance in helping you decide who your better and best performers are and what it is reasonable to expect from them.

FIGURE 68

SENIOR SALES REP PRODUCTIVITY — 1994

BY HOW MUCH DO TOP PERFORMERS
OUTSHINE AVERAGE PERFORMERS?

39.01%	1.5 TIMES AVG.
31.08	2.0 TIMES AVG.
10.23	2.5 TIMES AVG.
8.30	3.0 TIMES AVG.
1.35	3.5 TIMES AVG.
4.05	4.0 TIMES AVG.
2.12	4.5 TIMES AVG.
2.32	5.0 TIMES AVG.
1.54	MORE THAN 5.0 TIMES AVG.

SENIOR SALES REP PRODUCTIVITY — 1996

BY HOW MUCH DO TOP PERFORMERS
OUTSHINE AVERAGE PERFORMERS?

34.86%	1.5 TIMES AVG.
31.81	2.0 TIMES AVG.
10.69	2.5 TIMES AVG.
10.00	3.0 TIMES AVG.
3.06	3.5 TIMES AVG.
4.03	4.0 TIMES AVG.
1.39	4.5 TIMES AVG.
2.36	5.0 TIMES AVG.
1.80	MORE THAN 5.0 TIMES AVG.

SENIOR SALES REP PRODUCTIVITY — 1998

BY HOW MUCH DO TOP PERFORMERS
OUTSHINE AVERAGE PERFORMERS?

35.01%	1.5 TIMES AVG.
33.50	2.0 TIMES AVG.
9.57	2.5 TIMES AVG.
11.34	3.0 TIMES AVG.
1.76	3.5 TIMES AVG.
1.51	4.0 TIMES AVG.
1.51	4.5 TIMES AVG.
3.02	5.0 TIMES AVG.
2.77	MORE THAN 5.0 TIMES AVG.

FIGURE 69 — SENIOR SALES REP PRODUCTIVITY: BETTER AND BEST PERFORMERS

As mentioned previously, the ability to look at similar data in different ways is one of the values of this survey. **Figure 69** takes another look at just how much more annual sales volume is generated by "better" and "best" performers compared with average sales performers. It is interesting to compare this figure with the data presented in Figure 43, which examines the "percentage premium" paid to better and best performers compared to average performers. (The "percentage premium" is the additional compensation paid to better and best performers expressed as a percentage increase over compensation paid to average performers. See Section 5 for a definition of "better" and "best" performer.) In looking at the overall figures, you will note that although the best performers generate, on average, up to 130 percent more sales volume than their average counterparts, they are compensated, overall, at a rate of 95 percent more than average performers.

This suggests that top performers certainly pull their full share of the load, often generating more annual sales volume per dollar paid in compensation. So, although your top performer may be paid at a significantly higher rate than your average senior performer, the sales volume generated more than outweighs the increased sales costs. For comparison purposes, you might want to calculate these ratios in your own company. First determine average sales volume for "median" senior performers in your company. Then determine how much more sales volume your top performers generate as a percentage increase over average performers. Finally, determine the percentage premium paid to top performers in your company. Although these figures and ratios can differ dramatically from company to company, even within the same industry, this exercise does serve to emphasize the importance of nurturing and cultivating top-performing salespeople. Often, two "median" salespeople will cost more and deliver less than one superstar.

FIGURE 69

SENIOR SALES REP PRODUCTIVITY —
BETTER AND BEST PERFORMERS

	BETTER PERFORMER INCREASE OVER AVERAGE PERFORMER (PERCENT)	BEST PERFORMER INCREASE OVER AVERAGE PERFORMER (PERCENT)
COMPANY SIZE		
UNDER $5 MILLION	46.2%	112.8%
$5MM–$25MM	46.7	112.4
$25MM–$100MM	64.9	153.1
$100MM–$250MM	63.4	156.8
OVER $250MM	59.0	135.1
PRODUCT OR SERVICE		
INDUSTRIAL PRODUCTS	57.8	126.7
INDUSTRIAL SERVICES	58.9	125.6
OFFICE PRODUCTS	55.4	140.0
OFFICE SERVICES	47.6	103.5
CONSUMER PRODUCTS	51.4	120.9
CONSUMER SERVICES	53.7	117.4
TYPE OF BUYER		
INDUSTRY	53.8	125.8
RETAILERS	50.5	126.7
CONSUMERS	50.4	128.2
DISTRIBUTORS	60.6	155.2
INDUSTRY		
BANKING	39.9	77.8
BUSINESS SERVICES	36.9	96.4
CHEMICALS	127.2	274.9
COMMUNICATIONS	41.2	117.6
CONSTRUCTION	166.7	316.7
EDUCATIONAL SERVICES	75.0	180.0
ELECTRONICS	40.9	107.9
ELECTRONIC COMPONENTS	36.9	74.7
FABRICATED METALS	36.7	111.9
HEALTH SERVICES	45.6	83.3
HOTELS AND OTHER LODGING PLACES	62.8	154.3
INSTRUMENTS	20.0	68.0
INSURANCE	33.6	124.4
MACHINERY	76.3	100.8
MANUFACTURING	42.9	74.5
OFFICE EQUIPMENT	60.1	104.2
PAPER AND ALLIED PRODUCTS	50.0	100.0
PHARMACEUTICALS	63.4	127.7
PRINTING AND PUBLISHING	51.2	134.3
REAL ESTATE	77.5	138.8
RETAIL	41.3	110.4
TRANSPORTATION EQUIPMENT	171.8	321.4
WHOLESALE (CONSUMER GOODS)	41.6	106.7
OVERALL	**53.7%**	**129.8%**

EXPENSES, BENEFITS, TRAINING

What do we pay to keep our salespeople out in the field selling? Should we pay for lodging and meals? How about car phones and automobiles? How much do we pay in benefits? And what about training? How much time — and money — do we spend getting our new hires up to speed and then keeping them up to speed once they've become the experienced and productive salespeople we've brought along the way?

Section 8 reviews the costs of sales, field expenses, benefits, and training. The data received from survey respondents on the overall costs of sales efforts, field expenses, benefits, and training is presented through the following exhibits:

- Figure 70 examines sales force total cost as a percent of sales.
- Figure 71 takes a look at how much companies are paying out in field expenses. and benefits for senior salespeople.
- Figures 72–85 present pay practices by field expense item.
- Figure 86 lists the specific benefits offered to salespeople.
- Figure 87 looks at the different methods of training used by companies.
- Figure 88 presents data on the cost and length of training for new hires.
- Figure 89 examines the cost, type of training, and number of training hours per year for experienced salespeople.

In a departure from our previous surveys, smaller companies (those under $5 million in annual sales) spend about the same on field expenses as their larger counterparts. Previously, they had spent less. We noted in our 1996 edition of the survey that smaller companies were in the process of increasing (or restoring) their spending in this area. In our current survey, these companies are spending an average of $16,406 on field expenses. Spending on benefits for these smaller firms has not changed significantly. Smaller firms spend $4,299 in benefits per rep annually. (1996 data: $12,239, field expenses; $4,299, benefits. 1994 data: $7,908, field expenses; $3,503, benefits. 1992 data: $8,789, field expenses; $4,575, benefits.)

Companies both large and small are increasing spending on such items as home fax machines and car phones. Although companies aren't increasing spending on other expense items at the rate they did in 1996, they are at least not cutting spending. In 1994, we saw heavy cost-cutting for a wide variety of expense items. (See chart on page 121.)

Companies that have between $5 million and $25 million in annual sales are spending more on training new hires, while larger companies (those over $100 million) have cut spending in this area. Training costs for new hires in companies under $5 million in annual sales are holding steady at $5,500 versus $5,252.9 in our 1996 survey. Training costs for experienced salespeople are also holding steady. Companies now spend, on average, $4,032 per year training an experienced rep. In 1996, this figure was $4,034.

FIGURE 70 — COST OF SELLING

There isn't anything that can't be sold if you have enough money to get the job done. Unfortunately, selling costs can wreak havoc with your bottom line — there are plenty of examples of companies who have seen their sales climb, only to watch profits plummet.

On the other hand, cutting costs to the point of impeding the performance of your salespeople isn't the answer, either. Remember: The ultimate strategy for cutting daily operating expenses is simply to go out of business.

In our last survey, we were happy to report that companies were in the process of restoring spending in those areas that helped reps get the job done. Companies are continuing to fund those areas, as noted elsewhere in this survey.

In our 1994 survey, we suggested that cost-cutting had gone about as far as it could go and that belt-tightening procedures were, in many cases, making it tougher for companies to get the basic job done. Cost-cutting had simply eliminated the resources necessary for continued success and was having a negative impact on the bottom line.

Figure 70 examines the total cost of sales as a percentage of sales. The overall percentage rate in our current survey is 10.0 percent, slightly lower than the 12.2 percent figure reported two years ago.

The figures on the accompanying table should be regarded as an indication of the relative cost of operating a field sales force in a variety of industries. Within individual industries, a wide range of figures was reported. If your cost of sales as a percent of sales varies considerably from figures presented here, bear in mind that your costs may well be on target for your particular company.

Included in these calculations are the cost of sales compensation, cost of benefits provided to a salesperson, and field expenses. Not included are the costs of sales management, overhead, and the like.

FIGURE 70

COST OF SELLING
(AVERAGE OF MEDIAN RANGE)

	SALES FORCE TOTAL COST AS A PERCENT OF SALES
COMPANY SIZE	
UNDER $5 MILLION	12.7%
$5MM–$25MM	14.0
$25MM–$100MM	9.3
$100MM–$250MM	7.4
OVER $250MM	10.1
PRODUCT OR SERVICE	
INDUSTRIAL PRODUCTS	10.4
INDUSTRIAL SERVICES	11.7
OFFICE PRODUCTS	10.8
OFFICE SERVICES	11.1
CONSUMER PRODUCTS	11.3
CONSUMER SERVICES	11.6
TYPE OF BUYER	
INDUSTRY	9.8
RETAILERS	11.1
CONSUMERS	11.2
DISTRIBUTORS	11.0
INDUSTRY	
BANKING	0.9
BUSINESS SERVICES	10.5
CHEMICALS	3.4
COMMUNICATIONS	9.9
CONSTRUCTION	7.1
EDUCATIONAL SERVICES	12.7
ELECTRONICS	12.6
ELECTRONIC COMPONENTS	4.9
FABRICATED METALS	7.2
FOOD PRODUCTS	2.7
HEALTH SERVICES	13.4
HOTELS AND OTHER LODGING PLACES	1.9
INSTRUMENTS	14.8
MACHINERY	11.3
MANUFACTURING	6.6
OFFICE EQUIPMENT	2.4
PAPER AND ALLIED PRODUCTS	8.2
PHARMACEUTICALS	5.6
PRINTING AND PUBLISHING	22.2
REAL ESTATE	2.8
RETAIL	15.3
RUBBER/PLASTICS	3.6
TRANSPORTATION EQUIPMENT	6.2
WHOLESALE (CONSUMER GOODS)	11.2
OVERALL	**10.0%**

FIGURE 71 — COST PER EXPERIENCED SALESPERSON: FIELD EXPENSES AND BENEFITS

The big news is that smaller companies (those under $5 million in annual sales) have boosted field expense spending 34 percent over the last two years. These smaller companies have traditionally spent the least on field expenses. Now they are outspending some of their larger counterparts. The reason: These companies are finally realizing that money spent to increase the productivity of their sales reps flows directly to the bottom line. Companies in the $25 million to $250 million range have cut spending slightly in this area. Six years ago, we reported that companies were spending less on field expenses on a per-salesperson basis than at any time over the previous 10 years.

In our 1994 survey, we said, "Companies have probably cut back about as far as they can; further reductions could start to have a negative impact on productivity." Apparently, companies, faced with stagnant sales four years ago, are investing more in those activities that can have a positive impact on the bottom line, such as supplying their salespeople with productivity-enhancing tools. (See Figures 72–85 for what companies of all sizes are willing to pay for.)

Figure 71 examines the cost of field expenses and cost of benefits per experienced salesperson.

Benefits costs have held steady across all sizes of companies. Our overall average of what companies spend on benefits per rep per year is $7,614. In our previous survey, this figure was $7,548. As can be illustrated in the graphic below, the amount spent on benefits over the years has remained relatively stable.

(For geographic breakouts of this data, please see Section 11.)

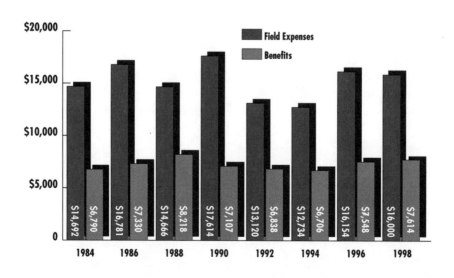

FIGURE 71

COST PER EXPERIENCED SALESPERSON
FIELD EXPENSES AND BENEFITS
(AVERAGE OF MEDIAN RANGE)

	FIELD EXPENSES	BENEFITS
COMPANY SIZE		
UNDER $5 MILLION	$16,406	$4,376
$5MM–$25MM	14,466	7,603
$25MM–$100MM	16,000	9,304
$100MM–$250MM	17,167	13,250
OVER $250MM	20,464	13,625
PRODUCT OR SERVICE		
CONSUMER PRODUCTS	14,425	7,309
CONSUMER SERVICES	11,538	5,468
INDUSTRIAL PRODUCTS	19,140	8,834
INDUSTRIAL SERVICES	16,254	9,011
OFFICE PRODUCTS	14,033	9,499
OFFICE SERVICES	12,702	6,932
TYPE OF BUYER		
CONSUMERS	11,591	5,280
DISTRIBUTORS	17,910	7,469
INDUSTRY	17,432	8,445
RETAILERS	13,288	6,712
INDUSTRY		
BANKING	20,750	8,400
BUSINESS SERVICES	14,238	5,799
CHEMICALS	21,300	13,000
COMMUNICATIONS	12,833	10,714
CONSTRUCTION	12,375	7,250
EDUCATIONAL SERVICES	12,288	6,167
ELECTRONICS	21,591	8,512
ELECTRONIC COMPONENTS	31,060	10,800
FABRICATED METALS	16,625	8,469
HEALTH SERVICES	17,200	6,135
HOTELS AND OTHER LODGING PLACES	21,050	9,000
INSTRUMENTS	32,600	15,520
INSURANCE	13,938	4,288
MACHINERY	30,000	15,500
MANUFACTURING	17,500	6,912
OFFICE EQUIPMENT	13,357	12,833
PHARMACEUTICALS	23,667	13,667
PRINTING AND PUBLISHING	10,929	6,128
REAL ESTATE	10,567	N/R
RETAIL	8,672	4,409
RUBBER/PLASTICS	25,000	21,000
TRANSPORTATION EQUIPMENT	N/R	4,125
WHOLESALE (CONSUMER GOODS)	12,893	6,594
OVERALL	**$16,000**	**$7,614**

FIGURES 72–85 — PERCENTAGE OF COMPANIES THAT PAY FOR ALL OR PART OF EXPENSE ITEMS

Since 1990, we have been tracking what common (and some not so common) expense items companies are willing to pay for. The 14 items on our list include auto — company-owned; auto — company-leased; mileage allowance; other travel reimbursement; lodging; telephone; entertainment; product samples; local promotions; office and/or clerical; home photocopier; home fax machine; car phone; and laptop PC.

Figures 72–85 provide a detailed picture of what companies of all sizes are willing to pay for. Again, these tables are broken out by product, service, type of buyer, and industry.

In 1990, we first reported on what we determined to be a growing trend: the willingness of companies to pay for those items that could lead to an increase in salesperson productivity. These expense items included such things as car phones, home fax machines, laptop PCs, and the like. Interestingly, our survey data showed an even stronger trend to pay for these items than had been previously thought. For example, in 1990, nearly half of responding companies (49%) said they paid 100 percent of the cost of providing home fax machines for their salespeople.

Four years ago, however, only 25 percent of responding companies said they paid 100 percent of this cost. Clearly, companies were cutting back and trying to reduce field expenses. We noted in 1994 that companies may have reached the limit of how much they can scale back spending, and that further reductions could have a negative impact on salesperson productivity — and the bottom line.

The chart on the following page dramatically shows how companies have cut spending in the past and how they are now restoring that spending. We strongly suspect this upward trend will continue, especially as more companies adopt sales automation technology. It is a significant finding of this survey that nearly two-thirds of companies pay 100 percent of the cost of supplying their salespeople with laptops. This certainly sets the stage for further expansion of the use of sales automation.

Percentage of Companies Paying 100% of the Following Expense Items

	1990	1992	1994	1996	1998
Auto — Company-Owned	39%	37%	16%	31%	35%
Auto — Company-Leased	59	34	20	40	31
Mileage Allowance	51	61	37	57	63
Other Travel Reimbursement	88	84	69	79	78
Lodging	94	92	80	87	86
Telephone	94	89	81	86	85
Entertainment	83	83	68	77	75
Product Samples	92	88	63	83	80
Local Promotions	85	84	61	79	80
Office and/or Clerical	88	85	70	82	81
Home Photocopier	39	29	16	41	47
Home Fax Machine	49	46	25	56	53
Car Phone	48	52	38	53	61
Laptop PC	37	44	28	66	65

(For geographic breakouts of selected portions of this data, please see Section 11.)

FIGURE 72

PERCENTAGE OF COMPANIES THAT PAY
FOR ALL OR PART OF EXPENSE ITEMS

AUTO — COMPANY OWNED

	ALL	PART	PART % PAID	NONE
COMPANY SIZE				
UNDER $5 MILLION	34.43%	3.28%	42.50%	62.30%
$5MM–$25MM	39.02	4.88	56.25	56.10
$25MM–$100MM	40.43	6.38	45.00	53.19
$100MM–$250MM	16.67	5.56	90.00	77.78
OVER $250MM	16.67	5.56	90.00	77.78
PRODUCT OR SERVICE				
CONSUMER PRODUCTS	34.21	6.58	70.00	59.21
CONSUMER SERVICES	31.43	10.00	60.71	58.57
INDUSTRIAL PRODUCTS	37.17	4.42	58.00	58.41
INDUSTRIAL SERVICES	36.99	8.22	56.67	54.79
OFFICE PRODUCTS	28.21	5.13	75.00	66.67
OFFICE SERVICES	25.00	7.69	68.75	67.31
TYPE OF BUYER				
CONSUMERS	36.25	8.75	70.71	55.00
DISTRIBUTORS	35.71	9.18	59.44	55.10
INDUSTRY	36.08	3.80	56.67	60.13
RETAILERS	32.88	12.33	53.89	54.79
INDUSTRY				
BANKING	0.00	0.00	0.00	100.00
BUSINESS SERVICES	32.43	2.70	10.00	64.86
CHEMICALS	33.33	0.00	0.00	66.67
COMMUNICATIONS	25.00	0.00	0.00	75.00
CONSTRUCTION	80.00	0.00	0.00	20.00
EDUCATIONAL SERVICES	0.00	0.00	0.00	100.00
ELECTRONICS	30.00	0.00	0.00	70.00
ELECTRONIC COMPONENTS	66.67	16.67	90.00	16.67
FABRICATED METALS	38.46	0.00	0.00	61.54
FOOD PRODUCTS	0.00	0.00	0.00	100.00
HEALTH SERVICES	50.00	0.00	0.00	50.00
HOTELS AND OTHER LODGING PLACES	0.00	0.00	0.00	100.00
INSTRUMENTS	0.00	0.00	0.00	100.00
INSURANCE	0.00	15.38	62.50	84.62
MACHINERY	0.00	20.00	35.00	80.00
MANUFACTURING	30.00	20.00	52.50	50.00
OFFICE EQUIPMENT	50.00	0.00	0.00	50.00
PAPER AND ALLIED PRODUCTS	25.00	0.00	0.00	75.00
PHARMACEUTICALS	20.00	20.00	60.00	60.00
PRINTING AND PUBLISHING	25.00	0.00	0.00	75.00
REAL ESTATE	0.00	0.00	0.00	100.00
RETAIL	64.29	14.29	70.00	21.43
RUBBER/PLASTICS	66.67	0.00	0.00	33.33
TRANSPORTATION EQUIPMENT	60.00	0.00	0.00	40.00
WHOLESALE (CONSUMER GOODS)	36.00	0.00	0.00	64.00
OVERALL	**34.51%**	**4.87%**	**56.82%**	**60.62%**

FIGURE 73

**Percentage of Companies That Pay
For All or Part of Expense Items**

Auto — Company Leased

	All	Part	Part % Paid	None
Company Size				
Under $5 Million	23.64%	3.64%	90.00%	72.73%
$5MM–$25MM	31.65	2.53	92.50	65.82
$25MM–$100MM	31.71	2.44	90.00	65.85
$100MM–$250MM	31.58	5.26	80.00	63.16
Over $250MM	45.00	0.00	0.00	55.00
Product or Service				
Consumer Products	31.34	1.49	80.00	67.16
Consumer Services	23.81	0.00	0.00	76.19
Industrial Products	37.04	4.63	91.00	58.33
Industrial Services	30.26	3.95	91.67	65.79
Office Products	27.50	2.50	90.00	70.00
Office Services	25.93	1.85	90.00	72.22
Type of Buyer				
Consumers	22.86	0.00	0.00	77.14
Distributors	33.33	4.44	88.75	62.22
Industry	33.54	3.80	89.17	62.66
Retailers	28.99	2.90	85.00	68.12
Industry				
Banking	14.29	0.00	0.00	85.71
Business Services	27.78	0.00	0.00	72.22
Chemicals	50.00	0.00	0.00	50.00
Communications	40.00	20.00	90.00	40.00
Construction	0.00	0.00	0.00	100.00
Educational Services	0.00	0.00	0.00	100.00
Electronics	42.86	0.00	0.00	57.14
Electronic Components	50.00	0.00	0.00	50.00
Fabricated Metals	38.46	0.00	0.00	61.54
Food Products	0.00	0.00	0.00	100.00
Health Services	0.00	0.00	0.00	100.00
Hotels and Other Lodging Places	25.00	0.00	0.00	75.00
Instruments	25.00	0.00	0.00	75.00
Insurance	12.50	0.00	0.00	87.50
Machinery	57.14	0.00	0.00	42.86
Manufacturing	50.00	0.00	0.00	50.00
Office Equipment	40.00	0.00	0.00	60.00
Paper and Allied Products	25.00	0.00	0.00	75.00
Pharmaceuticals	66.67	16.67	80.00	16.67
Printing and Publishing	20.00	10.00	90.00	70.00
Real Estate	0.00	0.00	0.00	100.00
Retail	22.22	0.00	0.00	77.78
Rubber/Plastics	100.00	0.00	0.00	0.00
Transportation Equipment	50.00	0.00	0.00	50.00
Wholesale (Consumer Goods)	37.50	12.50	91.67	50.00
Overall	**30.84%**	**2.80%**	**89.17%**	**66.36%**

FIGURE 74

PERCENTAGE OF COMPANIES THAT PAY
FOR ALL OR PART OF EXPENSE ITEMS

MILEAGE ALLOWANCE

	ALL	PART	PART % PAID	NONE
COMPANY SIZE				
UNDER $5 MILLION	65.26%	8.42%	59.75%	26.32%
$5MM–$25MM	65.85	6.50	58.75	27.64
$25MM–$100MM	64.29	14.29	67.00	21.43
$100MM–$250MM	52.63	15.79	36.67	31.58
OVER $250MM	44.44	18.52	53.00	37.04
PRODUCT OR SERVICE				
CONSUMER PRODUCTS	51.58	11.58	60.00	36.84
CONSUMER SERVICES	61.22	8.16	58.75	30.61
INDUSTRIAL PRODUCTS	60.90	12.18	52.37	26.92
INDUSTRIAL SERVICES	69.23	15.38	58.06	15.38
OFFICE PRODUCTS	62.32	14.49	57.50	23.19
OFFICE SERVICES	64.89	13.83	52.54	21.28
TYPE OF BUYER				
CONSUMERS	62.28	7.02	60.00	30.70
DISTRIBUTORS	59.12	12.41	52.06	28.47
INDUSTRY	64.61	11.93	58.55	23.46
RETAILERS	59.09	10.91	54.17	30.00
INDUSTRY				
BANKING	50.00	10.00	50.00	40.00
BUSINESS SERVICES	71.93	10.53	61.33	17.54
CHEMICALS	30.00	20.00	35.00	50.00
COMMUNICATIONS	81.82	9.09	75.00	9.09
CONSTRUCTION	66.67	0.00	0.00	33.33
EDUCATIONAL SERVICES	88.89	11.11	90.00	0.00
ELECTRONICS	76.19	4.76	75.00	19.05
ELECTRONIC COMPONENTS	100.00	0.00	0.00	0.00
FABRICATED METALS	58.82	11.76	70.00	29.41
FOOD PRODUCTS	50.00	50.00	52.50	0.00
HEALTH SERVICES	85.71	0.00	0.00	14.29
HOTELS AND OTHER LODGING PLACES	100.00	0.00	0.00	0.00
INSTRUMENTS	85.71	14.29	5.00	0.00
INSURANCE	66.67	4.76	75.00	28.57
MACHINERY	50.00	20.00	60.00	30.00
MANUFACTURING	57.14	21.43	55.00	21.43
OFFICE EQUIPMENT	66.67	16.67	72.50	16.67
PAPER AND ALLIED PRODUCTS	50.00	0.00	0.00	50.00
PHARMACEUTICALS	25.00	25.00	70.00	50.00
PRINTING AND PUBLISHING	40.00	33.33	47.00	26.67
REAL ESTATE	0.00	0.00	0.00	100.00
RETAIL	56.25	6.25	50.00	37.50
RUBBER/PLASTICS	66.67	0.00	0.00	33.33
TRANSPORTATION EQUIPMENT	80.00	0.00	0.00	20.00
WHOLESALE (CONSUMER GOODS)	50.00	6.67	77.50	43.33
OVERALL	**62.87%**	**10.18%**	**58.62%**	**26.95%**

FIGURE 75

**PERCENTAGE OF COMPANIES THAT PAY
FOR ALL OR PART OF EXPENSE ITEMS**

OTHER TRAVEL REIMBURSEMENT

	ALL	PART	PART % PAID	NONE
COMPANY SIZE				
UNDER $5 MILLION	83.04%	4.46%	47.00%	12.50%
$5MM–$25MM	75.66	4.61	53.57	19.74
$25MM–$100MM	74.68	3.80	40.00	21.52
$100MM–$250MM	95.65	0.00	0.00	4.35
OVER $250MM	63.64	9.09	61.67	27.27
PRODUCT OR SERVICE				
CONSUMER PRODUCTS	66.09	7.83	57.78	26.09
CONSUMER SERVICES	65.79	6.14	61.43	28.07
INDUSTRIAL PRODUCTS	79.58	5.76	45.91	14.66
INDUSTRIAL SERVICES	80.99	8.45	45.83	10.56
OFFICE PRODUCTS	73.75	10.00	41.88	16.25
OFFICE SERVICES	70.30	10.89	45.45	18.81
TYPE OF BUYER				
CONSUMERS	73.72	5.11	57.14	21.17
DISTRIBUTORS	78.57	5.95	42.50	15.48
INDUSTRY	79.39	5.41	49.06	15.20
RETAILERS	73.85	6.92	50.00	19.23
INDUSTRY				
BANKING	50.00	10.00	80.00	40.00
BUSINESS SERVICES	83.05	5.08	53.33	11.86
CHEMICALS	72.73	9.09	20.00	18.18
COMMUNICATIONS	73.33	6.67	10.00	20.00
CONSTRUCTION	62.50	0.00	0.00	37.50
EDUCATIONAL SERVICES	87.50	12.50	80.00	0.00
ELECTRONICS	77.27	0.00	0.00	22.73
ELECTRONIC COMPONENTS	91.67	8.33	80.00	0.00
FABRICATED METALS	90.48	0.00	0.00	9.52
FOOD PRODUCTS	100.00	0.00	0.00	0.00
HEALTH SERVICES	75.00	0.00	0.00	25.00
HOTELS AND OTHER LODGING PLACES	87.50	0.00	0.00	12.50
INSTRUMENTS	88.89	0.00	0.00	11.11
INSURANCE	59.09	0.00	0.00	40.91
MACHINERY	66.67	8.33	10.00	25.00
MANUFACTURING	94.44	5.56	10.00	0.00
OFFICE EQUIPMENT	71.43	14.29	65.00	14.29
PAPER AND ALLIED PRODUCTS	50.00	0.00	0.00	50.00
PHARMACEUTICALS	71.43	14.29	95.00	14.29
PRINTING AND PUBLISHING	68.42	5.26	20.00	26.32
REAL ESTATE	0.00	0.00	0.00	100.00
RETAIL	88.00	4.00	90.00	8.00
RUBBER/PLASTICS	80.00	0.00	0.00	20.00
TRANSPORTATION EQUIPMENT	71.43	0.00	0.00	28.57
WHOLESALE (CONSUMER GOODS)	81.58	5.26	55.00	13.16
OVERALL	**77.69%**	**4.51%**	**50.83%**	**17.79%**

FIGURE 76

**PERCENTAGE OF COMPANIES THAT PAY
FOR ALL OR PART OF EXPENSE ITEMS**

LODGING

	ALL	PART	PART % PAID	NONE
COMPANY SIZE				
UNDER $5 MILLION	87.83%	2.61%	38.33%	9.57%
$5MM–$25MM	85.43	3.97	54.17	10.60
$25MM–$100MM	90.24	2.44	65.00	7.32
$100MM–$250MM	86.96	0.00	0.00	13.04
OVER $250MM	75.76	6.06	10.00	18.18
PRODUCT OR SERVICE				
CONSUMER PRODUCTS	80.83	5.00	42.50	14.17
CONSUMER SERVICES	76.92	4.27	41.00	18.80
INDUSTRIAL PRODUCTS	88.14	4.12	45.62	7.73
INDUSTRIAL SERVICES	89.58	4.86	40.71	5.56
OFFICE PRODUCTS	79.27	7.32	50.83	13.41
OFFICE SERVICES	80.39	6.86	44.29	12.75
TYPE OF BUYER				
CONSUMERS	78.99	4.35	42.50	16.67
DISTRIBUTORS	85.21	4.14	55.00	10.65
INDUSTRY	88.59	3.69	45.45	7.72
RETAILERS	79.26	5.93	56.88	14.81
INDUSTRY				
BANKING	63.64	0.00	0.00	36.36
BUSINESS SERVICES	93.33	3.33	45.00	3.33
CHEMICALS	81.82	9.09	60.00	9.09
COMMUNICATIONS	86.67	6.67	10.00	6.67
CONSTRUCTION	87.50	0.00	0.00	12.50
EDUCATIONAL SERVICES	87.50	12.50	80.00	0.00
ELECTRONICS	95.45	0.00	0.00	4.55
ELECTRONIC COMPONENTS	100.00	0.00	0.00	0.00
FABRICATED METALS	95.45	0.00	0.00	4.55
FOOD PRODUCTS	100.00	0.00	0.00	0.00
HEALTH SERVICES	87.50	0.00	0.00	12.50
HOTELS AND OTHER LODGING PLACES	100.00	0.00	0.00	0.00
INSTRUMENTS	100.00	0.00	0.00	0.00
INSURANCE	63.64	4.55	10.00	31.82
MACHINERY	83.33	8.33	50.00	8.33
MANUFACTURING	82.35	17.65	46.67	0.00
OFFICE EQUIPMENT	92.86	0.00	0.00	7.14
PAPER AND ALLIED PRODUCTS	75.00	0.00	0.00	25.00
PHARMACEUTICALS	100.00	0.00	0.00	0.00
PRINTING AND PUBLISHING	78.95	0.00	0.00	21.05
REAL ESTATE	0.00	0.00	0.00	100.00
RETAIL	92.31	0.00	0.00	7.69
RUBBER/PLASTICS	100.00	0.00	0.00	0.00
TRANSPORTATION EQUIPMENT	71.43	0.00	0.00	28.57
WHOLESALE (CONSUMER GOODS)	82.05	5.13	65.00	12.82
OVERALL	**86.39%**	**3.22%**	**45.38%**	**10.40%**

FIGURE 77

PERCENTAGE OF COMPANIES THAT PAY
FOR ALL OR PART OF EXPENSE ITEMS

TELEPHONE

	ALL	PART	PART % PAID	NONE
COMPANY SIZE				
UNDER $5 MILLION	88.14%	5.08%	40.83%	6.78%
$5MM–$25MM	84.97	7.84	65.42	7.19
$25MM–$100MM	85.71	4.76	60.00	9.52
$100MM–$250MM	86.96	4.35	50.00	8.70
OVER $250MM	75.76	6.06	15.00	18.18
PRODUCT OR SERVICE				
CONSUMER PRODUCTS	79.51	8.20	51.50	12.30
CONSUMER SERVICES	78.51	9.09	51.36	12.40
INDUSTRIAL PRODUCTS	86.50	6.50	48.46	7.00
INDUSTRIAL SERVICES	86.75	7.28	45.45	5.96
OFFICE PRODUCTS	74.39	12.20	53.50	13.41
OFFICE SERVICES	75.49	9.80	45.00	14.71
TYPE OF BUYER				
CONSUMERS	79.86	7.91	55.45	12.23
DISTRIBUTORS	83.72	7.56	49.62	8.72
INDUSTRY	87.54	5.25	47.50	7.21
RETAILERS	80.43	10.14	55.36	9.42
INDUSTRY				
BANKING	63.64	9.09	20.00	27.27
BUSINESS SERVICES	87.50	7.81	54.00	4.69
CHEMICALS	72.73	9.09	5.00	18.18
COMMUNICATIONS	87.50	12.50	30.00	0.00
CONSTRUCTION	88.89	0.00	0.00	11.11
EDUCATIONAL SERVICES	88.89	11.11	50.00	0.00
ELECTRONICS	90.91	4.55	75.00	4.55
ELECTRONIC COMPONENTS	100.00	0.00	0.00	0.00
FABRICATED METALS	81.82	9.09	87.50	9.09
FOOD PRODUCTS	100.00	0.00	0.00	0.00
HEALTH SERVICES	100.00	0.00	0.00	0.00
HOTELS AND OTHER LODGING PLACES	85.71	14.29	25.00	0.00
INSTRUMENTS	100.00	0.00	0.00	0.00
INSURANCE	75.00	5.00	75.00	20.00
MACHINERY	91.67	8.33	25.00	0.00
MANUFACTURING	83.33	16.67	46.67	0.00
OFFICE EQUIPMENT	93.33	0.00	0.00	6.67
PAPER AND ALLIED PRODUCTS	100.00	0.00	0.00	0.00
PHARMACEUTICALS	100.00	0.00	0.00	0.00
PRINTING AND PUBLISHING	84.21	0.00	0.00	15.79
REAL ESTATE	0.00	20.00	50.00	80.00
RETAIL	83.33	4.17	90.00	12.50
RUBBER/PLASTICS	100.00	0.00	0.00	0.00
TRANSPORTATION EQUIPMENT	71.43	14.29	50.00	14.29
WHOLESALE (CONSUMER GOODS)	82.93	2.44	90.00	14.63
OVERALL	**85.40%**	**6.08%**	**54.00%**	**8.52%**

FIGURE 78

PERCENTAGE OF COMPANIES THAT PAY
FOR ALL OR PART OF EXPENSE ITEMS

ENTERTAINMENT

	ALL	PART	PART % PAID	NONE
COMPANY SIZE				
UNDER $5 MILLION	70.87%	8.74%	56.67%	20.39%
$5MM–$25MM	75.18	11.35	45.31	13.48
$25MM–$100MM	82.72	8.64	27.14	8.64
$100MM–$250MM	82.61	4.35	90.00	13.04
OVER $250MM	64.52	12.90	32.50	22.58
PRODUCT OR SERVICE				
CONSUMER PRODUCTS	66.07	12.50	44.29	21.43
CONSUMER SERVICES	62.62	11.21	45.00	26.17
INDUSTRIAL PRODUCTS	80.00	8.11	39.67	11.89
INDUSTRIAL SERVICES	76.60	11.35	46.25	12.06
OFFICE PRODUCTS	66.67	16.00	37.92	17.33
OFFICE SERVICES	62.37	18.28	45.88	19.35
TYPE OF BUYER				
CONSUMERS	58.91	14.73	44.21	26.36
DISTRIBUTORS	73.68	15.13	42.61	11.18
INDUSTRY	79.00	8.54	44.38	12.46
RETAILERS	67.48	15.45	46.84	17.07
INDUSTRY				
BANKING	63.64	9.09	50.00	27.27
BUSINESS SERVICES	79.31	13.79	51.25	6.90
CHEMICALS	80.00	0.00	0.00	20.00
COMMUNICATIONS	75.00	0.00	0.00	25.00
CONSTRUCTION	66.67	11.11	20.00	22.22
EDUCATIONAL SERVICES	71.43	14.29	10.00	14.29
ELECTRONICS	90.48	4.76	50.00	4.76
ELECTRONIC COMPONENTS	87.50	12.50	80.00	0.00
FABRICATED METALS	81.82	4.55	50.00	13.64
FOOD PRODUCTS	100.00	0.00	0.00	0.00
HEALTH SERVICES	100.00	0.00	0.00	0.00
HOTELS AND OTHER LODGING PLACES	100.00	0.00	0.00	0.00
INSTRUMENTS	90.00	0.00	0.00	10.00
INSURANCE	31.82	27.27	50.00	40.91
MACHINERY	75.00	16.67	25.00	8.33
MANUFACTURING	82.35	11.76	37.50	5.88
OFFICE EQUIPMENT	85.71	7.14	30.00	7.14
PAPER AND ALLIED PRODUCTS	75.00	25.00	50.00	0.00
PHARMACEUTICALS	57.14	42.86	63.33	0.00
PRINTING AND PUBLISHING	56.25	12.50	47.50	31.25
REAL ESTATE	0.00	0.00	0.00	100.00
RETAIL	61.90	9.52	37.50	28.57
RUBBER/PLASTICS	100.00	0.00	0.00	0.00
TRANSPORTATION EQUIPMENT	71.43	14.29	10.00	14.29
WHOLESALE (CONSUMER GOODS)	80.56	5.56	40.00	13.89
OVERALL	**75.20%**	**9.76%**	**44.46%**	**15.04%**

FIGURE 79

	ALL	PART	PART % PAID	NONE
COMPANY SIZE				
UNDER $5 MILLION	80.46%	2.30%	65.00%	17.24%
$5MM–$25MM	76.27	3.39	63.00	20.34
$25MM–$100MM	90.62	1.56	2.00	7.81
$100MM–$250MM	85.71	0.00	0.00	14.29
OVER $250MM	68.18	13.64	47.67	18.18
PRODUCT OR SERVICE				
CONSUMER PRODUCTS	75.00	5.21	50.80	19.79
CONSUMER SERVICES	62.96	3.70	41.33	33.33
INDUSTRIAL PRODUCTS	85.38	4.68	49.62	9.94
INDUSTRIAL SERVICES	84.07	5.31	45.67	10.62
OFFICE PRODUCTS	79.37	7.94	65.40	12.70
OFFICE SERVICES	76.39	4.17	57.33	19.44
TYPE OF BUYER				
CONSUMERS	67.31	2.88	57.33	29.81
DISTRIBUTORS	82.98	5.67	59.12	11.35
INDUSTRY	85.46	3.96	49.67	10.57
RETAILERS	77.57	6.54	61.71	15.89
INDUSTRY				
BANKING	25.00	25.00	50.00	50.00
BUSINESS SERVICES	89.74	0.00	0.00	10.26
CHEMICALS	88.89	11.11	4.00	0.00
COMMUNICATIONS	75.00	0.00	0.00	25.00
CONSTRUCTION	100.00	0.00	0.00	0.00
EDUCATIONAL SERVICES	100.00	0.00	0.00	0.00
ELECTRONICS	81.25	0.00	0.00	18.75
ELECTRONIC COMPONENTS	100.00	0.00	0.00	0.00
FABRICATED METALS	94.74	0.00	0.00	5.26
FOOD PRODUCTS	100.00	0.00	0.00	0.00
HEALTH SERVICES	83.33	0.00	0.00	16.67
HOTELS AND OTHER LODGING PLACES	80.00	0.00	0.00	20.00
INSTRUMENTS	100.00	0.00	0.00	0.00
INSURANCE	26.67	0.00	0.00	73.33
MACHINERY	80.00	0.00	0.00	20.00
MANUFACTURING	73.33	20.00	35.67	6.67
OFFICE EQUIPMENT	100.00	0.00	0.00	0.00
PAPER AND ALLIED PRODUCTS	100.00	0.00	0.00	0.00
PHARMACEUTICALS	100.00	0.00	0.00	0.00
PRINTING AND PUBLISHING	76.47	0.00	0.00	23.53
REAL ESTATE	0.00	0.00	0.00	100.00
RETAIL	76.47	0.00	0.00	23.53
RUBBER/PLASTICS	100.00	0.00	0.00	0.00
TRANSPORTATION EQUIPMENT	80.00	0.00	0.00	20.00
WHOLESALE (CONSUMER GOODS)	83.33	8.33	71.33	8.33
OVERALL	**80.45%**	**3.21%**	**52.70%**	**16.35%**

FIGURE 80

**PERCENTAGE OF COMPANIES THAT PAY
FOR ALL OR PART OF EXPENSE ITEMS**

LOCAL PROMOTIONS

	ALL	PART	PART % PAID	NONE
COMPANY SIZE				
UNDER $5 MILLION	83.00%	2.00%	62.50%	15.00%
$5MM–$25MM	74.42	6.20	40.62	19.38
$25MM–$100MM	85.29	2.94	70.00	11.76
$100MM–$250MM	85.71	4.76	50.00	9.52
OVER $250MM	80.77	3.85	50.00	15.38
PRODUCT OR SERVICE				
CONSUMER PRODUCTS	79.25	4.72	54.00	16.04
CONSUMER SERVICES	71.72	6.06	50.00	22.22
INDUSTRIAL PRODUCTS	83.14	4.07	39.29	12.79
INDUSTRIAL SERVICES	88.89	3.97	34.00	7.14
OFFICE PRODUCTS	82.61	4.35	50.00	13.04
OFFICE SERVICES	79.27	4.88	50.00	15.85
TYPE OF BUYER				
CONSUMERS	72.13	6.56	45.00	21.31
DISTRIBUTORS	84.93	5.48	48.75	9.59
INDUSTRY	85.02	3.24	40.62	11.74
RETAILERS	81.51	5.88	53.57	12.61
INDUSTRY				
BANKING	71.43	0.00	0.00	28.57
BUSINESS SERVICES	88.68	3.77	50.00	7.55
CHEMICALS	77.78	0.00	0.00	22.22
COMMUNICATIONS	80.00	0.00	0.00	20.00
CONSTRUCTION	60.00	0.00	0.00	40.00
EDUCATIONAL SERVICES	83.33	16.67	50.00	0.00
ELECTRONICS	82.35	0.00	0.00	17.65
ELECTRONIC COMPONENTS	80.00	10.00	55.00	10.00
FABRICATED METALS	73.33	6.67	50.00	20.00
FOOD PRODUCTS	100.00	0.00	0.00	0.00
HEALTH SERVICES	83.33	0.00	0.00	16.67
HOTELS AND OTHER LODGING PLACES	100.00	0.00	0.00	0.00
INSTRUMENTS	100.00	0.00	0.00	0.00
INSURANCE	37.50	6.25	75.00	56.25
MACHINERY	90.91	0.00	0.00	9.09
MANUFACTURING	75.00	12.50	10.00	12.50
OFFICE EQUIPMENT	100.00	0.00	0.00	0.00
PAPER AND ALLIED PRODUCTS	100.00	0.00	0.00	0.00
PHARMACEUTICALS	100.00	0.00	0.00	0.00
PRINTING AND PUBLISHING	70.59	0.00	0.00	29.41
REAL ESTATE	0.00	40.00	50.00	60.00
RETAIL	84.00	4.00	50.00	12.00
RUBBER/PLASTICS	100.00	0.00	0.00	0.00
TRANSPORTATION EQUIPMENT	66.67	0.00	0.00	33.33
WHOLESALE (CONSUMER GOODS)	81.58	5.26	82.50	13.16
OVERALL	**80.23%**	**4.07%**	**49.29%**	**15.70%**

FIGURE 81

**PERCENTAGE OF COMPANIES THAT PAY
FOR ALL OR PART OF EXPENSE ITEMS**

OFFICE AND/OR CLERICAL

	ALL	PART	PART % PAID	NONE
COMPANY SIZE				
UNDER $5 MILLION	81.90%	3.81%	10.25%	14.29%
$5MM–$25MM	81.20	0.75	25.00	18.05
$25MM–$100MM	83.82	4.41	55.67	11.76
$100MM–$250MM	85.71	4.76	20.00	9.52
OVER $250MM	66.67	3.70	90.00	29.63
PRODUCT OR SERVICE				
CONSUMER PRODUCTS	77.36	3.77	52.50	18.87
CONSUMER SERVICES	78.10	0.95	25.00	20.95
INDUSTRIAL PRODUCTS	83.93	2.98	29.60	13.10
INDUSTRIAL SERVICES	83.21	4.58	28.83	12.21
OFFICE PRODUCTS	84.93	2.74	27.50	12.33
OFFICE SERVICES	80.43	3.26	13.33	16.30
TYPE OF BUYER				
CONSUMERS	79.55	0.76	25.00	19.70
DISTRIBUTORS	84.62	2.56	25.00	12.82
INDUSTRY	85.00	3.08	34.12	11.92
RETAILERS	83.06	2.42	33.33	14.52
INDUSTRY				
BANKING	57.14	0.00	0.00	42.86
BUSINESS SERVICES	89.09	3.64	17.50	7.27
CHEMICALS	66.67	11.11	5.00	22.22
COMMUNICATIONS	84.62	0.00	0.00	15.38
CONSTRUCTION	87.50	0.00	0.00	12.50
EDUCATIONAL SERVICES	85.71	0.00	0.00	14.29
ELECTRONICS	88.89	0.00	0.00	11.11
ELECTRONIC COMPONENTS	100.00	0.00	0.00	0.00
FABRICATED METALS	82.35	0.00	0.00	17.65
FOOD PRODUCTS	75.00	25.00	20.00	0.00
HEALTH SERVICES	71.43	0.00	0.00	28.57
HOTELS AND OTHER LODGING PLACES	100.00	0.00	0.00	0.00
INSTRUMENTS	100.00	0.00	0.00	0.00
INSURANCE	52.63	0.00	0.00	47.37
MACHINERY	83.33	0.00	0.00	16.67
MANUFACTURING	84.62	7.69	25.00	7.69
OFFICE EQUIPMENT	92.31	7.69	1.00	0.00
PAPER AND ALLIED PRODUCTS	100.00	0.00	0.00	0.00
PHARMACEUTICALS	66.67	16.67	90.00	16.67
PRINTING AND PUBLISHING	57.14	7.14	67.00	35.71
REAL ESTATE	20.00	0.00	0.00	80.00
RETAIL	88.46	0.00	0.00	11.54
RUBBER/PLASTICS	80.00	20.00	50.00	0.00
TRANSPORTATION EQUIPMENT	83.33	0.00	0.00	16.67
WHOLESALE (CONSUMER GOODS)	72.73	3.03	50.00	24.24
OVERALL	**81.07%**	**2.82%**	**34.30%**	**16.10%**

FIGURE 82

PERCENTAGE OF COMPANIES THAT PAY
FOR ALL OR PART OF EXPENSE ITEMS

HOME PHOTOCOPIER

	ALL	PART	PART % PAID	NONE
COMPANY SIZE				
UNDER $5 MILLION	35.85%	1.89%	75.00%	62.26%
$5MM–$25MM	45.68	2.47	37.50	51.85
$25MM–$100MM	59.09	0.00	0.00	40.91
$100MM–$250MM	71.43	0.00	0.00	28.57
OVER $250MM	35.00	5.00	90.00	60.00
PRODUCT OR SERVICE				
CONSUMER PRODUCTS	39.34	3.28	70.00	57.38
CONSUMER SERVICES	40.32	0.00	0.00	59.68
INDUSTRIAL PRODUCTS	50.98	2.94	50.00	46.08
INDUSTRIAL SERVICES	43.84	2.74	50.00	53.42
OFFICE PRODUCTS	44.44	0.00	0.00	55.56
OFFICE SERVICES	34.00	0.00	0.00	66.00
TYPE OF BUYER				
CONSUMERS	38.03	0.00	0.00	61.97
DISTRIBUTORS	47.19	2.25	37.50	50.56
INDUSTRY	47.97	2.70	60.00	49.32
RETAILERS	41.79	1.49	25.00	56.72
INDUSTRY				
BANKING	57.14	0.00	0.00	42.86
BUSINESS SERVICES	51.85	0.00	0.00	48.15
CHEMICALS	66.67	0.00	0.00	33.33
COMMUNICATIONS	42.86	0.00	0.00	57.14
CONSTRUCTION	33.33	0.00	0.00	66.67
EDUCATIONAL SERVICES	0.00	0.00	0.00	100.00
ELECTRONICS	78.57	0.00	0.00	21.43
ELECTRONIC COMPONENTS	60.00	20.00	50.00	20.00
FABRICATED METALS	55.56	0.00	0.00	44.44
FOOD PRODUCTS	100.00	0.00	0.00	0.00
HEALTH SERVICES	50.00	0.00	0.00	50.00
HOTELS AND OTHER LODGING PLACES	50.00	0.00	0.00	50.00
INSTRUMENTS	66.67	0.00	0.00	33.33
INSURANCE	6.67	0.00	0.00	93.33
MACHINERY	71.43	0.00	0.00	28.57
MANUFACTURING	25.00	12.50	25.00	62.50
OFFICE EQUIPMENT	50.00	10.00	75.00	40.00
PAPER AND ALLIED PRODUCTS	100.00	0.00	0.00	0.00
PHARMACEUTICALS	25.00	25.00	90.00	50.00
PRINTING AND PUBLISHING	35.71	0.00	0.00	64.29
REAL ESTATE	0.00	0.00	0.00	100.00
RETAIL	50.00	0.00	0.00	50.00
RUBBER/PLASTICS	66.67	0.00	0.00	33.33
TRANSPORTATION EQUIPMENT	25.00	0.00	0.00	75.00
WHOLESALE (CONSUMER GOODS)	41.18	0.00	0.00	58.82
OVERALL	**46.70%**	**1.89%**	**60.00%**	**51.42%**

FIGURE 83

PERCENTAGE OF COMPANIES THAT PAY
FOR ALL OR PART OF EXPENSE ITEMS

HOME FAX MACHINE

	ALL	PART	PART % PAID	NONE
COMPANY SIZE				
UNDER $5 MILLION	46.77%	3.23%	26.50%	50.00%
$5MM–$25MM	45.24	5.95	45.00	48.81
$25MM–$100MM	69.39	0.00	0.00	30.61
$100MM–$250MM	77.78	0.00	0.00	22.22
OVER $250MM	45.45	0.00	0.00	54.55
PRODUCT OR SERVICE				
CONSUMER PRODUCTS	52.94	2.94	50.00	44.12
CONSUMER SERVICES	43.08	3.08	50.00	53.85
INDUSTRIAL PRODUCTS	56.41	3.42	43.75	40.17
INDUSTRIAL SERVICES	54.88	3.66	41.67	41.46
OFFICE PRODUCTS	53.66	4.88	50.00	41.46
OFFICE SERVICES	41.51	3.77	26.50	54.72
TYPE OF BUYER				
CONSUMERS	39.73	2.74	50.00	57.53
DISTRIBUTORS	51.55	4.12	43.75	44.33
INDUSTRY	55.15	3.03	35.60	41.82
RETAILERS	50.00	2.63	37.50	47.37
INDUSTRY				
BANKING	62.50	0.00	0.00	37.50
BUSINESS SERVICES	58.82	11.76	38.25	29.41
CHEMICALS	71.43	0.00	0.00	28.57
COMMUNICATIONS	33.33	0.00	0.00	66.67
CONSTRUCTION	66.67	0.00	0.00	33.33
EDUCATIONAL SERVICES	0.00	0.00	0.00	100.00
ELECTRONICS	73.33	0.00	0.00	26.67
ELECTRONIC COMPONENTS	60.00	20.00	50.00	20.00
FABRICATED METALS	72.73	9.09	50.00	18.18
FOOD PRODUCTS	100.00	0.00	0.00	0.00
HEALTH SERVICES	50.00	0.00	0.00	50.00
HOTELS AND OTHER LODGING PLACES	66.67	0.00	0.00	33.33
INSTRUMENTS	71.43	0.00	0.00	28.57
INSURANCE	6.67	0.00	0.00	93.33
MACHINERY	77.78	0.00	0.00	22.22
MANUFACTURING	44.44	11.11	25.00	44.44
OFFICE EQUIPMENT	54.55	0.00	0.00	45.45
PAPER AND ALLIED PRODUCTS	100.00	0.00	0.00	0.00
PHARMACEUTICALS	50.00	0.00	0.00	50.00
PRINTING AND PUBLISHING	53.33	0.00	0.00	46.67
REAL ESTATE	0.00	0.00	0.00	100.00
RETAIL	45.45	0.00	0.00	54.55
RUBBER/PLASTICS	66.67	0.00	0.00	33.33
TRANSPORTATION EQUIPMENT	25.00	0.00	0.00	75.00
WHOLESALE (CONSUMER GOODS)	47.62	0.00	0.00	52.38
OVERALL	**53.19%**	**2.98%**	**39.71%**	**43.83%**

FIGURE 84

PERCENTAGE OF COMPANIES THAT PAY
FOR ALL OR PART OF EXPENSE ITEMS

CAR PHONE

	ALL	PART	PART % PAID	NONE
COMPANY SIZE				
UNDER $5 MILLION	65.48%	9.52%	48.75%	25.00%
$5MM–$25MM	53.97	20.63	54.04	25.40
$25MM–$100MM	73.91	11.59	70.00	14.49
$100MM–$250MM	63.64	9.09	62.50	27.27
OVER $250MM	48.39	12.90	62.50	38.71
PRODUCT OR SERVICE				
CONSUMER PRODUCTS	45.56	20.00	54.44	34.44
CONSUMER SERVICES	55.67	14.43	59.64	29.90
INDUSTRIAL PRODUCTS	61.54	15.98	57.59	22.49
INDUSTRIAL SERVICES	66.67	18.25	61.09	15.08
OFFICE PRODUCTS	50.00	22.86	55.62	27.14
OFFICE SERVICES	62.22	14.44	54.23	23.33
TYPE OF BUYER				
CONSUMERS	54.78	13.91	60.31	31.30
DISTRIBUTORS	57.97	18.84	55.96	23.19
INDUSTRY	65.85	13.82	58.82	20.33
RETAILERS	53.40	18.45	55.53	28.16
INDUSTRY				
BANKING	60.00	0.00	0.00	40.00
BUSINESS SERVICES	71.70	18.87	61.00	9.43
CHEMICALS	77.78	0.00	0.00	22.22
COMMUNICATIONS	64.29	14.29	45.00	21.43
CONSTRUCTION	66.67	16.67	50.00	16.67
EDUCATIONAL SERVICES	40.00	20.00	50.00	40.00
ELECTRONICS	83.33	5.56	50.00	11.11
ELECTRONIC COMPONENTS	71.43	28.57	70.00	0.00
FABRICATED METALS	61.11	16.67	56.67	22.22
FOOD PRODUCTS	100.00	0.00	0.00	0.00
HEALTH SERVICES	87.50	12.50	50.00	0.00
HOTELS AND OTHER LODGING PLACES	40.00	20.00	50.00	40.00
INSTRUMENTS	87.50	0.00	0.00	12.50
INSURANCE	27.78	16.67	61.67	55.56
MACHINERY	88.89	11.11	50.00	0.00
MANUFACTURING	56.25	18.75	23.33	25.00
OFFICE EQUIPMENT	50.00	14.29	62.50	35.71
PAPER AND ALLIED PRODUCTS	0.00	100.00	58.33	0.00
PHARMACEUTICALS	60.00	20.00	50.00	20.00
PRINTING AND PUBLISHING	61.11	5.56	80.00	33.33
REAL ESTATE	0.00	0.00	0.00	100.00
RETAIL	43.75	18.75	63.33	37.50
RUBBER/PLASTICS	80.00	0.00	0.00	20.00
TRANSPORTATION EQUIPMENT	40.00	0.00	0.00	60.00
WHOLESALE (CONSUMER GOODS)	50.00	20.00	61.67	30.00
OVERALL	**61.14%**	**14.46%**	**56.88%**	**24.40%**

FIGURE 85

**PERCENTAGE OF COMPANIES THAT PAY
FOR ALL OR PART OF EXPENSE ITEMS**

LAPTOP PC

	ALL	PART	PART % PAID	NONE
COMPANY SIZE				
UNDER $5 MILLION	55.70%	5.06%	35.00%	39.24%
$5MM–$25MM	61.61	6.25	47.14	32.14
$25MM–$100MM	73.13	1.49	50.00	25.37
$100MM–$250MM	85.00	0.00	0.00	15.00
OVER $250MM	71.88	3.12	50.00	25.00
PRODUCT OR SERVICE				
CONSUMER PRODUCTS	56.47	7.06	43.33	36.47
CONSUMER SERVICES	54.12	3.53	50.00	42.35
INDUSTRIAL PRODUCTS	66.03	4.49	37.14	29.49
INDUSTRIAL SERVICES	66.38	6.03	44.29	27.59
OFFICE PRODUCTS	67.16	7.46	48.00	25.37
OFFICE SERVICES	60.24	8.43	42.14	31.33
TYPE OF BUYER				
CONSUMERS	56.07	2.80	60.00	41.12
DISTRIBUTORS	66.41	3.91	45.00	29.69
INDUSTRY	68.40	5.19	40.83	26.41
RETAILERS	63.44	2.15	37.50	34.41
INDUSTRY				
BANKING	66.67	0.00	0.00	33.33
BUSINESS SERVICES	68.09	8.51	35.00	23.40
CHEMICALS	77.78	0.00	0.00	22.22
COMMUNICATIONS	77.78	0.00	0.00	22.22
CONSTRUCTION	62.50	12.50	50.00	25.00
EDUCATIONAL SERVICES	50.00	16.67	50.00	33.33
ELECTRONICS	78.95	5.26	50.00	15.79
ELECTRONIC COMPONENTS	85.71	14.29	50.00	0.00
FABRICATED METALS	81.25	0.00	0.00	18.75
FOOD PRODUCTS	100.00	0.00	0.00	0.00
HEALTH SERVICES	87.50	0.00	0.00	12.50
HOTELS AND OTHER LODGING PLACES	66.67	0.00	0.00	33.33
INSTRUMENTS	90.00	0.00	0.00	10.00
INSURANCE	35.29	0.00	0.00	64.71
MACHINERY	90.00	0.00	0.00	10.00
MANUFACTURING	63.64	9.09	25.00	27.27
OFFICE EQUIPMENT	73.33	0.00	0.00	26.67
PAPER AND ALLIED PRODUCTS	100.00	0.00	0.00	0.00
PHARMACEUTICALS	100.00	0.00	0.00	0.00
PRINTING AND PUBLISHING	46.67	6.67	50.00	46.67
REAL ESTATE	0.00	0.00	0.00	100.00
RETAIL	56.25	0.00	0.00	43.75
RUBBER/PLASTICS	33.33	0.00	0.00	66.67
TRANSPORTATION EQUIPMENT	40.00	20.00	50.00	40.00
WHOLESALE (CONSUMER GOODS)	50.00	3.85	25.00	46.15
OVERALL	**65.16%**	**4.19%**	**43.85%**	**30.65%**

FIGURE 86 — PERCENTAGE OF COMPANIES OFFERING SPECIFIC BENEFITS

Although nearly 100 percent of survey respondents offer their salespeople some sort of medical plan, less than one-quarter (21%) offer an Employee Stock Option Plan (ESOP). This data **(Figure 86)** is essentially unchanged from our last survey period. As noted earlier in this survey, the amount of dollars companies allot to benefits has remained relatively stable over the years. In comparing this year's data with data gathered two years ago, companies are also allocating these dollars in much the same way as they have in the past. In short, there have been no dramatic changes in either the specific benefits companies are offering or the amount they are spending on those benefits.

Previous Dartnell surveys have commented on the fact that smaller firms traditionally provide fewer benefits in short- and long-term disability, dental, and pension plans, which reduces their overall cost of benefits. Companies under $5 million in annual sales continue to spend the least on benefits (see Figure 71).

FIGURE 86

**PERCENTAGE OF COMPANIES
OFFERING SPECIFIC BENEFITS**

	GROUP LIFE	L-T DISAB.	MEDICAL PLAN	S-T DISAB.	DENTAL PLAN	PROFIT SHARING	PENSION PLAN	ESOP	THRIFT SAVINGS PLAN
COMPANY SIZE									
UNDER $5 MILLION	56%	40%	90%	33%	53%	38%	41%	13	11%
$5MM–$25MM	79	55	98	47	69	44	53	20	19
$25MM–$100MM	89	70	99	59	80	42	65	17	31
$100MM–$250MM	83	57	96	65	87	52	48	17	39
OVER $250MM	97	81	100	75	81	59	88	62	41
PRODUCT OR SERVICE									
CONSUMER PRODUCTS	76	54	95	47	70	43	59	23	20
CONSUMER SERVICES	75	50	97	41	67	39	61	20	24
INDUSTRIAL PRODUCTS	81	63	97	58	69	51	55	25	25
INDUSTRIAL SERVICES	78	62	96	55	68	47	59	25	28
OFFICE PRODUCTS	77	59	95	47	64	48	47	26	25
OFFICE SERVICES	72	56	95	45	65	49	50	24	24
TYPE OF BUYER									
CONSUMERS	75	48	97	43	65	37	56	19	23
DISTRIBUTORS	79	58	97	53	70	42	56	23	25
INDUSTRY	78	60	96	54	68	49	54	23	24
RETAILERS	76	50	97	47	65	42	53	19	24
INDUSTRY									
AGRICULTURE, FORESTRY, AND FISHING	100	100	100	100	100	0	0	0	0
BANKING	92	67	100	50	67	50	58	33	58
BUSINESS SERVICES	68	57	95	43	65	48	44	16	21
CHEMICALS	89	78	100	56	89	33	78	44	33
COMMUNICATIONS	69	62	94	50	69	31	38	19	25
CONSTRUCTION	50	25	100	12	38	88	62	25	25
EDUCATIONAL SERVICES	62	50	100	62	75	38	62	0	12
ELECTRONICS	76	57	95	43	76	48	38	33	19
ELECTRONIC COMPONENTS	100	73	91	73	91	45	55	36	36
FABRICATED METALS	90	76	95	76	67	62	67	10	29
FOOD PRODUCTS	33	67	100	33	100	33	33	33	0
FURNITURE AND FIXTURES	100	50	100	50	100	50	100	50	0
HEALTH SERVICES	88	62	100	38	62	12	88	25	12
HOTELS AND OTHER LODGING PLACES	100	38	100	50	100	25	38	25	25
INSTRUMENTS	80	70	100	80	80	50	40	40	20
INSURANCE	78	56	100	50	50	28	78	11	22
MACHINERY	88	75	100	62	62	25	62	38	25
MANUFACTURING	76	53	100	53	47	41	59	24	12
OFFICE EQUIPMENT	87	73	100	53	73	40	47	27	27
PAPER AND ALLIED PRODUCTS	100	67	100	33	67	33	67	0	33
PHARMACEUTICALS	71	71	100	86	100	29	71	14	14
PRINTING AND PUBLISHING	88	50	100	56	81	44	75	25	19
REAL ESTATE	0	0	0	0	0	100	0	0	0
RETAIL	68	23	90	19	58	35	39	10	13
RUBBER/PLASTICS	50	50	83	50	50	50	83	0	33
TRANSPORTATION BY AIR	100	33	100	33	100	67	100	33	0
TRANSPORTATION EQUIPMENT	86	57	100	29	71	71	43	14	29
TRUCKING AND WAREHOUSING	100	67	100	67	67	33	67	0	33
WHOLESALE (CONSUMER GOODS)	71	45	90	48	67	55	50	19	17
OVERALL	**77%**	**56%**	**96%**	**49%**	**69%**	**44%**	**55%**	**21%**	**22%**

How effective our salespeople ultimately will be depends, in large part, on their training. Figures 87–89 take an in-depth look at the training methods companies use to train their reps, how much time and money are invested in bringing new hires up to speed, and how much time and money are invested in keeping experienced reps as good as they can be.

But, although training has always been an important aspect of sales management, the overriding concern of sales force effectiveness is becoming more and more critical in these supercompetitive times.

One area that can have a dramatic effect on how effective a sales force ultimately will be revolves around recruitment and selection of the salespeople — putting the right people in the job to begin with. Over the years, sales managers have debated who makes the best sales candidate: an entry level rep, or a rep with experience. This survey examines this problem and presents its findings in Figure 99.

However, because this issue is both a training issue and a sales force effectiveness issue, we'll highlight some of the findings here.

When asked what level of experience they prefer in a newly hired sales rep, 49.7 percent of the sales managers said they prefer intermediate level reps — those with one to three years of experience. Another 39.9 percent of sales managers said they prefer senior level reps — those with more than three years of experience. Just 10.4 percent of managers said they prefer to hire entry level people.

Here are some general observations:

Sales managers preferring less than one year of experience say they want to train new people themselves. A moldable person is best, they say. Another consideration: lower salaries. Initiative and "being hungry" were other factors deemed important.

Sales managers preferring one to three years of experience say it is clear these individuals are good at sales but not stuck in their ways. Hiring trained people also reduces training costs. Additionally, these people have an existing customer base — a big plus, these managers say. Another advantage: These individuals know that they like sales.

Sales managers preferring more than three years of experience say they want maturity, stability, and experience in the people they hire. Other considerations: These individuals already are trained, so the company doesn't have to spend money on training. Furthermore, these individuals can hit the ground running and only have to learn about the company's products. Many sales managers who say they prefer an experienced salesperson also say the company has no sales training program. Another recurring reason for preferring a senior rep: Many companies have specialized product lines or are in highly technical, complex industries.

Selected comments from survey respondents:

Entry level (less than one year of experience) preferred:

"Train in our way of selling. No bad habits."

"Very specialized market. Very few experienced people locally available."

"Want to train in our system, not retrain from other's."

"Not many bad habits to break. We like to train."

"Selling techniques are very specific to our industry. We prefer training from scratch, not teaching old dogs new tricks."

"Easier to train without developed habits and preconceived attitudes."

"Grow your own."

"Very specific market. Prefer to train reps on how we do business."

"This is a new deregulated industry. No one has experience in this field."

"Gives us the opportunity to train in our system without resistance to old ways. Also, most good reps with experience don't move from company to company."

"We like to train our way."

Intermediate level (one to three years of experience) preferred:

"This experience level gives the rep confidence plus an open mind to learn new concepts of selling."

"We think that at least a year's experience is sufficient, and this has proven valid."

"We like selling experience, but want to allow room to develop new habits."

"We don't have time to train an inexperienced person."

"Our products are pretty basic. We like to train."

"A new hire needs some experience in our complex industry."

"We want some knowledge of industry, but budgets prevent us from hiring 'seasoned' salespeople."

"We have a very specific product, so we are just looking for general sales experience."

"Some outside experience helps to let us know he or she wants to sell and has the ability to go out and get the business. The person is hungry and knows what it takes to sell."

"Not fresh, but not set in their ways, either."

"Needs some experience, but must be able to adapt to our situation."

"Our product is a very specific sell. If you've done it before, you have a huge head start."

"Some experience makes the transition to the position easier. Too much experience would require too much initial salary."

"Income at the start is best-suited for someone in this group."

Senior level (three or more years of experience) preferred:

"We look for as much experience as possible."

"It takes at least three years to gain the technical knowledge to sell our product."

"A person with long industry experience already knows the downside and is more apt to stay."

"They know what to expect."

"I can train for product knowledge. I can't train for sales savvy or experience."

"Less experienced people have been less successful, resulting in more turnover."

"We want someone who has already learned the basics of selling and proved that they can sell."

"Better results quicker."

"May bring established accounts and relationships to us."

"Don't have resources to do training."

"We only have eight total employees. Everyone must be advanced in their abilities and skills."

"We are the highest-priced leader in our industry. Reps average 29 years of experience."

"When we get to a point of need, we need productivity immediately. This, in my opinion, is poor planning."

"Need pros!!!!!!"

"I don't want to have to teach them how to sell. I only want to have to teach them about our product and industry."

FIGURE 87 — TRAINING METHODS

On-the-job training continues to be the most prevalent method of training salespeople and is used by nearly 85 percent of responding companies, close to the percentage reported in our 1996 survey (82.3%). External seminars, used by 71.0 percent of responding companies, and individual instruction, used by 69.8 percent of responding companies, are again among the "top three picks" of survey participants. As a training method, "home assignments" are least favored and are used by just 17.7 percent of respondents. These figures have remained relatively stable throughout the last several survey periods. (Total exceeds 100 percent due to multiple responses.)

Over the past eight years, the number of companies using external seminars has been steadily moving upward, stabilizing at around 70 percent. In 1990, 59 percent of responding companies said they used this training method for their salespeople. This percentage increased to 69 percent in 1992 and reached 72 percent of responding companies in 1994.

FIGURE 87

TRAINING METHODS — PERCENTAGE OF COMPANIES USING:

	INDIVIDUAL INSTRUCTION	HOME ASSIGNMENTS	IN-HOUSE CLASS	ON THE JOB	EXTERNAL SEMINARS	OTHER
COMPANY SIZE						
UNDER $5 MILLION	72.3%	13.1%	43.1%	78.5%	59.2%	6.2%
$5MM–$25MM	71.2	16.9	64.4	85.0	72.5	8.8
$25MM–$100MM	65.1	17.4	69.8	87.2	80.2	7.0
$100MM–$250MM	54.2	20.8	75.0	91.7	79.2	4.2
OVER $250MM	76.5	38.2	79.4	91.2	79.4	0.0
PRODUCT OR SERVICE						
CONSUMER PRODUCTS	75.7	21.3	61.8	89.7	72.1	6.6
CONSUMER SERVICES	74.3	16.9	62.5	85.3	69.1	7.4
INDUSTRIAL PRODUCTS	66.0	20.0	62.5	83.0	71.5	6.5
INDUSTRIAL SERVICES	66.9	18.2	60.4	79.2	76.0	7.8
OFFICE PRODUCTS	70.9	25.6	65.1	93.0	74.4	4.7
OFFICE SERVICES	69.0	19.5	62.8	88.5	71.7	7.1
TYPE OF BUYER						
CONSUMERS	73.6	18.2	56.6	87.4	69.8	6.3
DISTRIBUTORS	69.6	18.7	62.6	85.4	74.9	5.8
INDUSTRY	69.7	18.1	62.3	83.2	72.6	7.1
RETAILERS	72.4	20.0	60.0	91.0	71.7	7.6
INDUSTRY						
AGRICULTURE, FORESTRY, AND FISHING	66.7	0.0	66.7	66.7	66.7	0.0
BANKING	83.3	33.3	33.3	100.0	66.7	8.3
BUSINESS SERVICES	75.4	10.1	63.8	79.7	72.5	10.1
CHEMICALS	81.8	27.3	63.6	90.9	72.7	0.0
COMMUNICATIONS	66.7	22.2	61.1	88.9	72.2	16.7
CONSTRUCTION	80.0	10.0	50.0	70.0	70.0	0.0
EDUCATIONAL SERVICES	50.0	0.0	87.5	100.0	87.5	0.0
ELECTRONICS	66.7	28.6	66.7	85.7	52.4	0.0
ELECTRONIC COMPONENTS	58.3	0.0	66.7	75.0	66.7	0.0
FABRICATED METALS	69.6	4.3	52.2	78.3	69.6	4.3
FOOD PRODUCTS	75.0	0.0	0.0	100.0	50.0	0.0
FURNITURE AND FIXTURES	100.0	66.7	66.7	100.0	100.0	0.0
HEALTH SERVICES	33.3	0.0	55.6	66.7	100.0	0.0
HOTELS AND OTHER LODGING PLACES	62.5	25.0	87.5	75.0	87.5	0.0
INSTRUMENTS	40.0	30.0	60.0	80.0	90.0	10.0
INSURANCE	73.9	13.0	43.5	87.0	60.9	0.0
MACHINERY	66.7	33.3	58.3	75.0	58.3	16.7
MANUFACTURING	66.7	22.2	55.6	77.8	77.8	0.0
OFFICE EQUIPMENT	62.5	18.8	56.2	93.8	56.2	6.2
PAPER AND ALLIED PRODUCTS	100.0	0.0	0.0	100.0	100.0	0.0
PHARMACEUTICALS	50.0	50.0	100.0	100.0	100.0	0.0
PRINTING AND PUBLISHING	58.8	17.6	70.6	88.2	76.5	0.0
REAL ESTATE	100.0	33.3	83.3	66.7	83.3	16.7
RETAIL	73.5	20.6	73.5	88.2	58.8	2.9
RUBBER/PLASTICS	80.0	20.0	80.0	100.0	60.0	0.0
TRANSPORTATION BY AIR	66.7	0.0	66.7	100.0	66.7	0.0
TRANSPORTATION EQUIPMENT	85.7	14.3	57.1	85.7	28.6	0.0
TRUCKING AND WAREHOUSING	100.0	33.3	33.3	100.0	100.0	66.7
WHOLESALE (CONSUMER GOODS)	76.7	14.0	58.1	86.0	83.7	11.6
OVERALL	**69.8%**	**17.7%**	**60.8%**	**84.3%**	**71.0%**	**6.7%**

FIGURE 88 — TRAINING NEW HIRES

Average spending across all companies to train a newly hired sales rep is down approximately 11 percent from levels of two years ago, standing now at $7,079 compared with $7,937 in 1996. (See pages 138–139 for data on experience level preferred in newly hired sales reps.) The decline in our overall average figure resulted primarily from declines in spending among companies with more than $100 million in annual sales.

Compared with data from two years ago, smaller companies (those under $5 million in annual sales) have increased spending modestly. These smaller companies today are spending, on average, $5,500 per year on training new hires, up 4.5 percent over 1996 data, when these companies spent $5,252 per rep. In 1994, these companies spent just $3,688 to train a newly hired sales rep. These fluctuations indicate a continuing commitment to a well-trained sales force. Companies are beginning to realize that cutting costs on training can end up costing more than it saves.

The length of training for new hires in these smaller companies has increased from 3.5 months in 1996 to 4.4 months in the current survey. This increase also reflects a commitment to spend the time necessary to bring new hires up to speed. These companies realize that only the best-trained sales forces can hope to compete effectively in today's increasingly complex marketplace.

(For geographic breakouts of this data, please see Section 11.)

TRAINING PERIOD AND TRAINING COSTS FOR NEW HIRES 1990–1998 — TOTAL RANGE OF RESPONSES

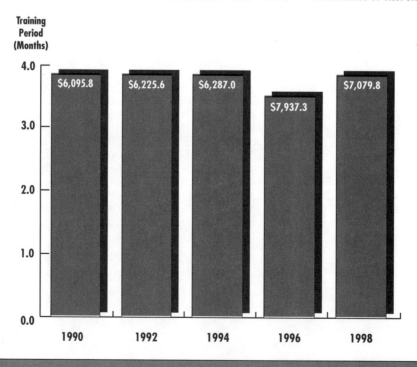

FIGURE 88

TRAINING NEW HIRES
(AVERAGE OF MEDIAN RANGE)

	TRAINING PERIOD FOR NEW HIRES (MONTHS)	COST
COMPANY SIZE		
UNDER $5 MILLION	4.4	$5,500.0
$5MM–$25MM	4.2	8,141.1
$25MM–$100MM	3.7	8,090.9
$100MM–$250MM	1.7	7,400.0
OVER $250MM	3.6	7,000.0
PRODUCT OR SERVICE		
CONSUMER PRODUCTS	3.4	5,354.2
CONSUMER SERVICES	3.3	4,537.3
INDUSTRIAL PRODUCTS	4.8	9,893.5
INDUSTRIAL SERVICES	4.8	9,060.5
OFFICE PRODUCTS	3.8	6,269.4
OFFICE SERVICES	3.2	6,200.0
TYPE OF BUYER		
CONSUMERS	3.3	4,220.6
DISTRIBUTORS	3.9	7,256.5
INDUSTRY	4.3	8,234.2
RETAILERS	3.2	6,711.0
INDUSTRY		
AGRICULTURE, FORESTRY, AND FISHING	9.0	5,333.3
BANKING	5.0	4,300.0
BUSINESS SERVICES	3.6	7,172.0
CHEMICALS	6.3	17,666.7
COMMUNICATIONS	2.7	8,500.0
CONSTRUCTION	7.2	11,125.0
EDUCATIONAL SERVICES	1.2	2,850.0
ELECTRONICS	4.4	10,950.0
ELECTRONIC COMPONENTS	6.2	12,500.0
FABRICATED METALS	4.3	9,040.0
FOOD PRODUCTS	4.5	12,500.0
HEALTH SERVICES	1.2	3,250.0
HOTELS AND OTHER LODGING PLACES	3.0	4,250.0
INSTRUMENTS	3.3	10,666.7
INSURANCE	5.0	3,875.0
MACHINERY	3.8	16,500.0
MANUFACTURING	4.2	6,687.5
OFFICE EQUIPMENT	2.8	5,833.3
PHARMACEUTICALS	5.0	16,000.0
PRINTING AND PUBLISHING	3.0	7,437.5
REAL ESTATE	3.7	1,433.3
RETAIL	2.6	3,725.0
RUBBER/PLASTICS	3.3	6,166.7
TRANSPORTATION EQUIPMENT	4.0	7,666.7
TRUCKING AND WAREHOUSING	5.7	10,000.0
WHOLESALE (CONSUMER GOODS)	4.8	10,312.5
OVERALL	**3.9**	**$ 7,079.8**

FIGURE 89 — TRAINING EXPERIENCED REPS

Once you have experienced salespeople in the field, you need to keep them up and running. Experienced sales reps in our current survey are given, on average, 32.5 hours of ongoing training per year, at a cost of $4,032 per rep. This compares with 33.9 hours of training, at a cost of $4,034 per rep, in 1996. Eight years ago, experienced reps received just 27 hours of training per year.

The fact that experienced reps continue to receive a significant amount of training reflects a continuing commitment on the part of management to provide ongoing learning opportunities for their senior salespeople. Quite simply, companies realize that training is, by and large, an inexpensive way to protect their investments in their sales forces.

Companies continue to spend an increasing amount of time on product training and less on training in selling skills as a percentage of total training time spent. In editions of this survey from several years ago, the "split" was about equal.

(For geographic breakouts of this data, please see Section 11.)

FIGURE 89

TRAINING EXPERIENCED REPS

	HOURS PER YEAR OF ONGOING TRAINING	TYPE OF TRAINING SELLING SKILLS(%)	PRODUCT(%)	COST
COMPANY SIZE				
UNDER $5 MILLION	30.1	40.7%	60.0%	$3,752
$5MM–$25MM	36.1	44.6	53.3	3,947
$25MM–$100MM	31.0	45.4	47.6	3,902
$100MM–$250MM	25.2	43.4	56.9	5,365
OVER $250MM	38.0	44.2	51.3	4,824
PRODUCT OR SERVICE				
CONSUMER PRODUCTS	35.8	44.1	50.1	4,039
CONSUMER SERVICES	33.9	49.3	47.5	3,623
INDUSTRIAL PRODUCTS	31.6	37.1	58.9	5,149
INDUSTRIAL SERVICES	30.8	41.8	53.9	4,867
OFFICE PRODUCTS	41.8	38.0	59.0	4,261
OFFICE SERVICES	33.3	45.2	56.0	3,470
TYPE OF BUYER				
CONSUMERS	36.2	45.3	53.4	3,142
DISTRIBUTORS	35.7	40.2	55.1	4,168
INDUSTRY	31.5	43.2	55.2	4,605
RETAILERS	32.9	43.7	51.9	4,181
INDUSTRY				
AGRICULTURE, FORESTRY, AND FISHING	86.7	15.0	48.3	2,833
BANKING	24.3	51.8	50.0	6,705
BUSINESS SERVICES	33.7	52.7	51.5	3,810
CHEMICALS	21.7	42.3	41.4	5,920
COMMUNICATIONS	40.9	45.9	49.1	4,549
CONSTRUCTION	46.7	58.5	36.5	2,244
EDUCATIONAL SERVICES	12.8	54.3	51.2	1,964
ELECTRONICS	28.1	36.8	58.8	7,084
ELECTRONIC COMPONENTS	46.0	37.5	65.0	4,329
FABRICATED METALS	20.5	37.9	60.9	3,061
FOOD PRODUCTS	35.0	37.5	42.5	3,167
FURNITURE AND FIXTURES	48.7	18.3	76.7	1,333
HEALTH SERVICES	24.8	52.5	51.4	1,536
HOTELS AND OTHER LODGING PLACES	42.0	79.3	21.0	1,798
INSTRUMENTS	32.5	30.6	67.8	4,500
INSURANCE	26.6	44.0	55.4	2,691
MACHINERY	32.3	29.5	61.0	6,781
MANUFACTURING	25.2	46.3	57.9	1,915
OFFICE EQUIPMENT	34.0	32.4	66.8	4,077
PHARMACEUTICALS	50.0	36.0	63.3	7,917
PRINTING AND PUBLISHING	28.8	48.6	41.2	6,350
REAL ESTATE	35.0	65.0	43.8	350
RETAIL	37.3	36.0	55.7	2,411
RUBBER/PLASTICS	20.0	41.0	53.0	5,500
TRANSPORTATION EQUIPMENT	26.0	38.3	42.1	5,800
WHOLESALE (CONSUMER GOODS)	37.8	36.2	62.0	2,562
OVERALL	**32.5**	**43.6%**	**54.0%**	**$4,032**

INCENTIVE PLAN DESIGN PRACTICES

How we design our sales compensation plans can have a tremendous effect on their overall success. This section reviews the typical incentive plan design practices of survey participants. In reviewing the data in this section, it is helpful to keep in mind that how you pay your sales force can have a dramatic effect on directing the overall behavior of your salespeople. Enlightened companies are now coming to view sales compensation as a real tool for generating profits, rather than as a "necessary evil" or just another expense item to justify.

In reviewing your compensation plan, ask yourself this question: "Am I getting what I'm paying for?" If you feel you're not getting all you're paying for, determine how you can make your compensation dollars work harder for you.

The tables in this section examine the relationship between incentive pay and performance:

- Figures 90–93 examine the relationship between activities sales managers regard as critically important and whether these performance measures are included in their companies' compensation plan designs. Specific performance measures looked at include selling to major accounts, retaining existing customers, finding new accounts, and reducing selling costs.
- Figure 94 examines the importance of profit contribution vs. sales rep and sales manager incentives.
- Figures 95–97 focus on the degree of sales force effectiveness and include an examination of how effectively sales forces perform the tasks that sales managers say are important.
- Figure 98 provides a breakout of when senior rep incentives are earned — from first dollar sold or when threshold is reached.
- Figure 99 shows the experience level preferred in newly-hired sales reps.

It's worth noting that independent Dartnell studies show that motivating the sales force is one of the prime concerns of sales managers. Yet, often, little thought is given to designing the compensation plan so that salespeople are motivated to do what the company wants them to do.

Here's an example: Let's say that the XYZ Company, a midsize manufacturer, has determined that company survival depends on dramatically increasing its customer base. Although its current customer base is a good source of steady income, these accounts don't have significant growth potential. The word goes out to the sales force: "We need new business, and it's up to you to do the job! We're all counting on you, and we know you can do it!" Sound farfetched? Although there's nothing wrong with a good old-fashioned pep talk, more enlightened companies look to their compensation plans to do the motivating.

Our hypothetical XYZ Company, like many companies, uses a combination (salary plus incentive) compensation plan. Salaries are modest to keep fixed costs down; commissions are based on a percentage of total sales volume achieved to keep the administration costs of the plan low. When the plan was set up, a major concern of the top marketing executive was to keep the plan easy to understand and fair to all concerned.

The important point to remember is that the XYZ Company is rewarding all sales the same (i.e., a standard commission rate is paid based on the total dollar amount of the sale made). Whether salary represents 5 percent — or 75 percent — of total compensation received, the incentive value of sales made never varies: All sales are rewarded on the same basis, regardless of the difficulty of the sale or whether the sale helps the company reach its overall marketing objectives.

Remember, money motivates and salespeople are motivated by money. They are also very focused on maximizing their earnings. If "easy" sales are compensated at the same rate as hard-to-make sales, is it likely that your salespeople will spend a significant amount of time going after those tough sales? It's not likely at all. But what if your salespeople earned more — far more — for making those tough sales? Now you're talking their language!

Let's go back to our XYZ Company. Now let's suppose its compensation plan paid a significantly higher commission rate on all sales representing new business. In that scenario, you'd find your salespeople going after those accounts because it was now in their best monetary interests to do so.

There's nothing magic going on here. What we're doing is taking a look at what we need our salespeople to do, and paying them more to do those specific things. If opening new accounts is important for your salespeople to do, pay them more for opening new accounts. For example, you might consider paying your salespeople twice their standard commission rate on all sales representing new business. This new rate would apply to all sales placed by the new account for a period of six months — or some other predetermined time period — at which point the new account would be reclassified as established business.

To further encourage your salespeople to actively seek new business, you also might pay a flat fee for appointments secured at selected accounts — whether or not the appointment results in a sale. In this case, we are specifically rewarding those activities that can ultimately lead to additional sales in the future.

The more effectively your compensation plan links pay to performance, the more effectively it will influence the behavior of your salespeople.

In looking at the overall design of your compensation plan, determine if you are:
- Overpaying for low-priority salesperson activities;
- Underpaying for high-priority salesperson activities;
- Not distinguishing between high-priority and low-priority salesperson activities.

To rephrase that old cliché, you get what you pay for.

FIGURES 90–93 — IMPORTANCE OF SALES TASKS VERSUS SALES REP INCENTIVES

The right incentive program can be the engine that drives your salespeople to success. Or, put another way, the lack of an effective incentive program can derail your best-intentioned sales efforts. Human nature being what it is, salespeople are much more likely to behave in certain ways when there is "something in it for them." There is nothing new here. But what may be new is to realize that many compensation programs are not designed to specifically reward those sales activities that the company believes are important. The data on the following tables looks at this potential problem in detail.

Figures 90–93 focus on the importance of sales tasks vs. sales rep incentives. Sales tasks examined include: selling to major accounts, retaining existing customers, finding new accounts, and reducing selling costs. We asked sales managers how they rated these tasks: very important, important, somewhat important, or not important. We then asked sales managers whether their current sales compensation plans specifically included an incentive for performing these particular tasks. The results are displayed on the following four tables. In looking at Figure 90, for example, we can see that the overwhelming majority of responding companies (92.1%) consider selling to major accounts to be an important sales task, yet less than 30 percent (28.6%) of responding companies have an incentive that would reward that activity.

It is no secret that salespeople more readily and willingly perform those tasks when there is "something in it for them." It is often a mistake to regard these important-rated activities as "just part of the sales job." The demands on a salesperson's time are immense, and the individual frequently has to decide which task of many he or she should concentrate his or her efforts on. Often a conflict arises.

For example, finding new accounts may be regarded as a very important activity by the company, but, by the same token, this particular activity requires a greater expenditure of the salesperson's time than is spent securing additional business from long-established existing accounts.

Here's the point: If your salesperson sees the major portion of the job as one of making quota, where is it most likely that those sales will come from? Clearly, the easiest sales to secure are those from existing accounts. Consequently, finding new accounts, although it may be regarded as part of the job, often is neglected.

As you look through these tables, ask yourself whether better results could be obtained from your salespeople if these important-rated activities were included in your overall incentive picture, rather than just being regarded as "part of the job." The question you need to answer is: "How important are these activities *really*."

Interestingly, our *overall figures* for the last five survey periods (1990–1998) have remained virtually unchanged, an indication that companies are slow to move in this area of sales compensation planning.

FIGURE 90

IMPORTANCE OF SALES TASKS VS. SALES REP INCENTIVES/SELLING TO MAJOR ACCOUNTS

	PERCENTAGE WHO CONSIDER IMPORTANT	PERCENTAGE WITH SENIOR SALESPERSON INCENTIVE	GAP (%)
COMPANY SIZE			
UNDER $5 MILLION	90.2%	21.3%	68.8%
$5MM–$25MM	92.7	27.4	65.2
$25MM–$100MM	94.2	30.2	64.0
$100MM–$250MM	88.5	41.7	46.8
OVER $250MM	94.3	47.1	47.2
PRODUCT OR SERVICE			
CONSUMER PRODUCTS	86.8	35.6	51.2
CONSUMER SERVICES	87.2	29.6	57.6
INDUSTRIAL PRODUCTS	95.6	31.1	64.5
INDUSTRIAL SERVICES	95.0	31.1	63.8
OFFICE PRODUCTS	94.5	28.1	66.4
OFFICE SERVICES	94.8	32.7	62.0
TYPE OF BUYER			
CONSUMERS	86.8	30.1	56.7
DISTRIBUTORS	92.7	34.9	57.8
INDUSTRY	95.6	30.9	64.7
RETAILERS	93.2	36.8	56.4
INDUSTRY			
AGRICULTURE, FORESTRY, AND FISHING	100.0	66.7	33.3
BANKING	91.7	27.3	64.4
BUSINESS SERVICES	95.8	23.6	72.2
CHEMICALS	100.0	54.5	45.5
COMMUNICATIONS	94.4	41.2	53.3
CONSTRUCTION	77.8	0.0	77.8
EDUCATIONAL SERVICES	77.8	71.4	6.3
ELECTRONICS	95.5	14.3	81.2
ELECTRONIC COMPONENTS	100.0	33.3	66.7
FABRICATED METALS	95.7	19.0	76.6
FOOD PRODUCTS	100.0	0.0	100.0
FURNITURE AND FIXTURES	100.0	33.3	66.7
HEALTH SERVICES	100.0	33.3	66.7
HOTELS AND OTHER LODGING PLACES	87.5	37.5	50.0
INSTRUMENTS	90.0	10.0	80.0
INSURANCE	77.3	28.6	48.7
MACHINERY	100.0	16.7	83.3
MANUFACTURING	100.0	26.3	73.7
OFFICE EQUIPMENT	93.8	40.0	53.8
PAPER AND ALLIED PRODUCTS	75.0	25.0	50.0
PHARMACEUTICALS	85.7	50.0	35.7
PRINTING AND PUBLISHING	100.0	33.3	66.7
REAL ESTATE	71.4	0.0	71.4
RETAIL	78.8	21.2	57.6
RUBBER/PLASTICS	100.0	60.0	40.0
TRANSPORTATION BY AIR	100.0	33.3	66.7
TRANSPORTATION EQUIPMENT	83.3	42.9	40.5
TRUCKING AND WAREHOUSING	33.3	33.3	0.0
WHOLESALE (CONSUMER GOODS)	97.6	36.6	61.0
OVERALL	**92.1%**	**28.6%**	**63.5%**

FIGURE 91

Importance of Sales Tasks vs. Sales Rep Incentives/Retaining Existing Customers

	Percentage Who Consider Important	Percentage with Senior Salesperson Incentive	Gap (%)
Company Size			
Under $5 Million	99.3%	30.3%	68.9%
$5MM–$25MM	97.5	29.9	67.7
$25MM–$100MM	97.7	33.7	64.0
$100MM–$250MM	100.0	33.3	66.7
Over $250MM	94.3	38.2	56.1
Product or Service			
Consumer Products	96.4	37.8	58.6
Consumer Services	96.4	35.6	60.8
Industrial Products	98.6	33.2	65.4
Industrial Services	98.1	33.8	64.3
Office Products	96.7	27.0	69.7
Office Services	98.2	31.0	67.3
Type of Buyer			
Consumers	95.7	33.3	62.4
Distributors	97.8	35.5	62.2
Industry	98.8	33.9	64.9
Retailers	95.9	38.9	57.0
Industry			
Agriculture, Forestry, and Fishing	100.0	0.0	100.0
Banking	83.3	9.1	74.2
Business Services	100.0	30.6	69.4
Chemicals	100.0	54.5	45.5
Communications	100.0	52.9	47.1
Construction	90.0	0.0	90.0
Educational Services	88.9	57.1	31.7
Electronics	95.5	19.0	76.4
Electronic Components	100.0	33.3	66.7
Fabricated Metals	100.0	23.8	76.2
Food Products	100.0	0.0	100.0
Furniture and Fixtures	100.0	33.3	66.7
Health Services	88.9	22.2	66.7
Hotels and Other Lodging Places	100.0	50.0	50.0
Instruments	100.0	10.0	90.0
Insurance	100.0	47.6	52.4
Machinery	100.0	16.7	83.3
Manufacturing	94.7	26.3	68.4
Office Equipment	93.8	33.3	60.4
Paper and Allied Products	100.0	25.0	75.0
Pharmaceuticals	100.0	50.0	50.0
Printing and Publishing	100.0	16.7	83.3
Real Estate	100.0	14.3	85.7
Retail	100.0	30.3	69.7
Rubber/Plastics	100.0	80.0	20.0
Transportation by Air	100.0	66.7	33.3
Transportation Equipment	100.0	28.6	71.4
Trucking and Warehousing	100.0	100.0	0.0
Wholesale (Consumer Goods)	100.0	41.5	58.5
Overall	**98.0%**	**31.6%**	**66.4%**

FIGURE 92

IMPORTANCE OF SALES TASKS VS. SALES REP INCENTIVES/FINDING NEW ACCOUNTS

	PERCENTAGE WHO CONSIDER IMPORTANT	PERCENTAGE WITH SENIOR SALESPERSON INCENTIVE	GAP (%)
COMPANY SIZE			
UNDER $5 MILLION	97.0%	33.6%	63.4%
$5MM–$25MM	94.5	37.8	56.7
$25MM–$100MM	86.2	38.4	47.8
$100MM–$250MM	76.9	45.8	31.1
OVER $250MM	85.7	55.9	29.8
PRODUCT OR SERVICE			
CONSUMER PRODUCTS	92.1	45.9	46.2
CONSUMER SERVICES	95.7	45.9	49.7
INDUSTRIAL PRODUCTS	91.7	42.3	49.4
INDUSTRIAL SERVICES	93.1	43.0	50.0
OFFICE PRODUCTS	91.2	39.3	51.9
OFFICE SERVICES	93.9	42.5	51.4
TYPE OF BUYER			
CONSUMERS	95.7	43.6	52.1
DISTRIBUTORS	91.6	46.7	44.8
INDUSTRY	92.2	41.8	50.4
RETAILERS	89.9	45.8	44.0
INDUSTRY			
AGRICULTURE, FORESTRY, AND FISHING	100.0	0.0	100.0
BANKING	83.3	36.4	47.0
BUSINESS SERVICES	98.6	38.9	59.7
CHEMICALS	91.7	63.6	28.0
COMMUNICATIONS	94.4	64.7	29.7
CONSTRUCTION	100.0	10.0	90.0
EDUCATIONAL SERVICES	88.9	57.1	31.7
ELECTRONICS	95.5	28.6	66.9
ELECTRONIC COMPONENTS	91.7	44.4	47.2
FABRICATED METALS	78.3	38.1	40.2
FOOD PRODUCTS	100.0	0.0	100.0
FURNITURE AND FIXTURES	100.0	33.3	66.7
HEALTH SERVICES	100.0	33.3	66.7
HOTELS AND OTHER LODGING PLACES	100.0	50.0	50.0
INSTRUMENTS	100.0	20.0	80.0
INSURANCE	87.0	61.9	25.1
MACHINERY	66.7	16.7	50.0
MANUFACTURING	100.0	26.3	73.7
OFFICE EQUIPMENT	100.0	46.7	53.3
PAPER AND ALLIED PRODUCTS	100.0	25.0	75.0
PHARMACEUTICALS	57.1	16.7	40.5
PRINTING AND PUBLISHING	84.2	38.9	45.3
REAL ESTATE	100.0	14.3	85.7
RETAIL	93.9	39.4	54.5
RUBBER/PLASTICS	100.0	60.0	40.0
TRANSPORTATION BY AIR	100.0	66.7	33.3
TRANSPORTATION EQUIPMENT	83.3	57.1	26.2
TRUCKING AND WAREHOUSING	100.0	100.0	0.0
WHOLESALE (CONSUMER GOODS)	88.4	39.0	49.3
OVERALL	**92.0%**	**38.6%**	**53.4%**

FIGURE 93

IMPORTANCE OF SALES TASKS VS. SALES REP INCENTIVES/REDUCING SELLING COSTS

	PERCENTAGE WHO CONSIDER IMPORTANT	PERCENTAGE WITH SENIOR SALESPERSON INCENTIVE	GAP (%)
COMPANY SIZE			
UNDER $5 MILLION	58.1%	9.8%	48.3%
$5MM–$25MM	60.0	15.9	44.1
$25MM–$100MM	60.2	23.3	37.0
$100MM–$250MM	61.5	20.8	40.7
OVER $250MM	68.6	29.4	39.2
PRODUCT OR SERVICE			
CONSUMER PRODUCTS	70.5	22.2	48.3
CONSUMER SERVICES	68.6	16.3	52.3
INDUSTRIAL PRODUCTS	60.2	19.4	40.8
INDUSTRIAL SERVICES	54.8	22.5	32.3
OFFICE PRODUCTS	64.0	16.9	47.2
OFFICE SERVICES	54.9	15.0	39.8
TYPE OF BUYER			
CONSUMERS	67.5	15.4	52.1
DISTRIBUTORS	63.7	18.9	44.8
INDUSTRY	58.1	18.8	39.4
RETAILERS	62.6	20.1	42.4
INDUSTRY			
AGRICULTURE, FORESTRY, AND FISHING	100.0	0.0	100.0
BANKING	50.0	27.3	22.7
BUSINESS SERVICES	55.1	11.1	44.0
CHEMICALS	66.7	18.2	48.5
COMMUNICATIONS	77.8	5.9	71.9
CONSTRUCTION	70.0	10.0	60.0
EDUCATIONAL SERVICES	44.4	28.6	15.9
ELECTRONICS	45.5	4.8	40.7
ELECTRONIC COMPONENTS	50.0	22.2	27.8
FABRICATED METALS	50.0	23.8	26.2
FOOD PRODUCTS	100.0	0.0	100.0
FURNITURE AND FIXTURES	100.0	33.3	66.7
HEALTH SERVICES	50.0	22.2	27.8
HOTELS AND OTHER LODGING PLACES	75.0	12.5	62.5
INSTRUMENTS	50.0	10.0	40.0
INSURANCE	60.9	19.0	41.8
MACHINERY	33.3	8.3	25.0
MANUFACTURING	57.9	21.1	36.8
OFFICE EQUIPMENT	56.2	26.7	29.6
PAPER AND ALLIED PRODUCTS	25.0	0.0	25.0
PHARMACEUTICALS	33.3	66.7	–33.3
PRINTING AND PUBLISHING	36.8	22.2	14.6
REAL ESTATE	85.7	0.0	85.7
RETAIL	69.7	18.2	51.5
RUBBER/PLASTICS	83.3	40.0	43.3
TRANSPORTATION BY AIR	100.0	0.0	100.0
TRANSPORTATION EQUIPMENT	85.7	0.0	85.7
TRUCKING AND WAREHOUSING	33.3	66.7	–33.3
WHOLESALE (CONSUMER GOODS)	76.7	19.5	57.2
OVERALL	**60.3%**	**17.0%**	**43.3%**

FIGURE 94 — IMPORTANCE OF PROFIT CONTRIBUTION VS. USE OF INCENTIVES

With companies paying increasingly more attention to bottom-line matters, it is more and more important to examine the role that sales incentives play in the overall profit picture.

Every company's ultimate objective is profitability, and **Figure 94** addresses the bottom-line profitability issue head-on. The data on this table examines the importance of profit contribution vs. the use of incentives. Again, it is in the company's best interest to have salespeople sell its products and services to those important large accounts that will contribute the most to the bottom line. Yet, just more than half of the responding companies (51.6%) said they provide an incentive that would specifically reward more profitable sales. This figure has not changed significantly since we first started tracking this data in 1990. In 1990, 48.9 percent of responding companies provided a salesperson incentive based on profitability of the sale; in 1992, 45.8 percent of responding companies said they provided such an incentive, and in 1994, 48.8% provided an incentive based on sales profitability. In 1996, 53.1 percent provided this incentive.

Interestingly, companies appear to be more inclined to offer an incentive to *sales management* for securing more profitable sales. In our current survey, 64.9 percent of responding companies offer such an incentive to their sales managers, about the same as two years ago, when the figure was 66.9 percent. In 1992, 45.3 percent of companies offered an incentive to sales management based on profitability of sales. One possible reason companies are slow to include salespeople: Companies are still reluctant to share sensitive financial information with their salespeople, preferring instead to leave final responsibility for profitable sales with sales management.

(See Figure 98 — "How Commissions Are Determined" — for related data on this important topic.)

FIGURE 94

IMPORTANCE OF PROFIT CONTRIBUTION VS. USE OF INCENTIVES

	PERCENTAGE WHO CONSIDER IMPORTANT	PERCENTAGE WITH SALESPERSON INCENTIVE	GAP (%)	PERCENTAGE WITH SALES MANAGER INCENTIVE	GAP (%)
COMPANY SIZE					
UNDER $5 MILLION	84.0%	39.3%	44.6%	45.1%	38.9%
$5MM–$25MM	88.8	57.3	31.5	70.1	18.7
$25MM–$100MM	90.9	53.5	37.4	74.4	16.5
$100MM–$250MM	84.6	50.0	34.6	70.8	13.8
OVER $250MM	85.7	64.7	21.0	82.4	3.4
PRODUCT OR SERVICE					
CONSUMER PRODUCTS	90.6	60.7	29.9	69.6	21.0
CONSUMER SERVICES	87.4	47.4	40.0	57.8	29.6
INDUSTRIAL PRODUCTS	86.3	62.8	23.6	70.4	15.9
INDUSTRIAL SERVICES	90.4	56.3	34.2	66.9	23.6
OFFICE PRODUCTS	90.0	62.9	27.1	70.8	19.2
OFFICE SERVICES	88.4	47.8	40.6	66.4	22.0
TYPE OF BUYER					
CONSUMERS	88.1	50.6	37.5	57.1	31.1
DISTRIBUTORS	87.0	54.4	32.6	65.7	21.3
INDUSTRY	87.7	54.6	33.1	68.4	19.3
RETAILERS	87.0	55.6	31.4	68.8	18.2
INDUSTRY					
AGRICULTURE, FORESTRY, AND FISHING	100.0	100.0	0.0	66.7	33.3
BANKING	66.7	72.7	–6.1	90.9	–24.2
BUSINESS SERVICES	90.0	43.1	46.9	68.1	21.9
CHEMICALS	83.3	36.4	47.0	81.8	1.5
COMMUNICATIONS	94.4	47.1	47.4	58.8	35.6
CONSTRUCTION	100.0	30.0	70.0	60.0	40.0
EDUCATIONAL SERVICES	77.8	42.9	34.9	71.4	6.3
ELECTRONICS	72.7	38.1	34.6	66.7	6.1
ELECTRONIC COMPONENTS	83.3	66.7	16.7	88.9	–5.6
FABRICATED METALS	90.9	42.9	48.1	52.4	38.5
FOOD PRODUCTS	100.0	25.0	75.0	75.0	25.0
FURNITURE AND FIXTURES	100.0	100.0	0.0	100.0	0.0
HEALTH SERVICES	62.5	22.2	40.3	44.4	18.1
HOTELS AND OTHER LODGING PLACES	100.0	37.5	62.5	25.0	75.0
INSTRUMENTS	55.6	10.0	45.6	70.0	–14.4
INSURANCE	77.3	23.8	53.5	28.6	48.7
MACHINERY	91.7	50.0	41.7	50.0	41.7
MANUFACTURING	94.7	73.7	21.1	57.9	36.8
OFFICE EQUIPMENT	75.0	66.7	8.3	66.7	8.3
PAPER AND ALLIED PRODUCTS	100.0	50.0	50.0	75.0	25.0
PHARMACEUTICALS	100.0	83.3	16.7	83.3	16.7
PRINTING AND PUBLISHING	88.9	50.0	38.9	88.9	0.0
REAL ESTATE	85.7	28.6	57.1	57.1	28.6
RETAIL	90.9	66.7	24.2	54.5	36.4
RUBBER/PLASTICS	83.3	20.0	63.3	40.0	43.3
TRANSPORTATION BY AIR	100.0	66.7	33.3	100.0	0.0
TRANSPORTATION EQUIPMENT	100.0	85.7	14.3	57.1	42.9
TRUCKING AND WAREHOUSING	100.0	100.0	0.0	33.3	66.7
WHOLESALE (CONSUMER GOODS)	93.0	78.0	15.0	80.5	12.5
OVERALL	**87.3%**	**51.6%**	**35.7%**	**64.9%**	**22.4%**

FIGURE 95 — DEGREE OF SALES FORCE EFFECTIVENESS

Just how effective are today's salespeople in the eyes of their sales managers? Although such measurements can be subjective, they nonetheless can be enlightening.

Figure 95 takes a look at the degree of overall sales force effectiveness as perceived by sales managers. We asked survey participants to (1) rate the relative importance of a variety of selling tasks, and then (2) rate how well their salespeople performed those tasks. The "gap" is the difference between the importance of the task and how well salespeople perform the task. (For more complete breakouts of this data, see Figure 97.)

Tasks rated included selling to major accounts, finding new accounts, selling new products, integrating new technology, reducing selling costs, retaining existing customers, and improving profit contribution. With the exception of finding new accounts, salespeople are generally perceived as less effective in performing less important tasks. This may be a bias on the part of the sales managers. After all, one is less likely to appreciate how well a task is being done if the overall merit of performing the task in the first place is in question.

Dartnell has been collecting sales force effectiveness data since 1990. Since that time, salespeople have been judged to be most effective at retaining existing customers and least effective at finding new accounts.

If your salespeople have been encountering difficulties in securing new business, now may be the time to take a fresh look at your incentive plan. It's worth repeating that salespeople are less likely to perform well those activities they are not specifically rewarded to perform. Making sure that your compensation plan rewards the activities you deem important is one of the keys to boosting sales force effectiveness. Readers interested in further exploring the relationship between incentive pay and performance are encouraged to compare the data in Figures 90–93 with the data in Figures 95 and 97. Alert readers will note that there appears to be a strong correlation between lack of incentive pay and lack of performance.

FIGURE 95

DEGREE OF SALES FORCE EFFECTIVENESS

SALES TASK	IMPORTANCE	EFFECTIVENESS	GAP
RETAINING EXISTING CUSTOMERS	98.0%	81.8%	16.2%
SELLING TO MAJOR ACCOUNTS	92.1	60.9	31.2
FINDING NEW ACCOUNTS	92.0	53.8	38.2
IMPROVING PROFIT CONTRIBUTION	87.3	53.1	34.2
SELLING NEW PRODUCTS	68.1	55.0	13.1
INTEGRATING NEW TECHNOLOGY	62.1	42.1	20.0
REDUCING SELLING COSTS	60.3	43.1	17.2

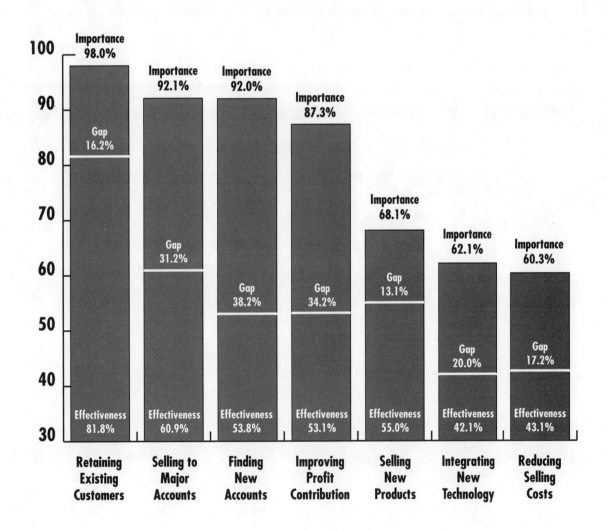

FIGURE 96 — DEGREE OF SALES FORCE EFFECTIVENESS: PERCENTAGE OF FIRMS INDICATING THEIR SALES FORCE IS EFFECTIVE IN PERFORMING TASKS RATED IMPORTANT

In our current survey, 75.7 percent of responding companies say their sales forces are effective in performing tasks rated important. This is a significant improvement over 1990 data, when just 59 percent of the companies gave high marks to their sales forces. Two years ago, 77.6 percent of companies participating in the survey said their sales forces were effective in performing tasks rated important. Although this data is based on subjective measures, it does seem to indicate that today's salespeople are holding their own in key task areas.

(For geographic breakouts of this data, please see Section 11.)

FIGURE 96

DEGREE OF SALES FORCE EFFECTIVENESS

	PERCENTAGE OF FIRMS INDICATING THEIR SALES FORCES ARE EFFECTIVE IN PERFORMING TASKS RATED IMPORTANT
COMPANY SIZE	
UNDER $5 MILLION	80.9%
$5MM–$25MM	75.3
$25MM–$100MM	68.4
$100MM–$250MM	77.7
OVER $250MM	75.3
PRODUCT OR SERVICE	
CONSUMER PRODUCTS	70.5
CONSUMER SERVICES	71.9
INDUSTRIAL PRODUCTS	73.9
INDUSTRIAL SERVICES	75.7
OFFICE PRODUCTS	70.1
OFFICE SERVICES	71.5
TYPE OF BUYER	
CONSUMERS	73.9
DISTRIBUTORS	72.6
INDUSTRY	76.1
RETAILERS	72.5
INDUSTRY	
AGRICULTURE, FORESTRY, AND FISHING	28.6
BANKING	87.9
BUSINESS SERVICES	79.7
CHEMICALS	72.6
COMMUNICATIONS	65.1
CONSTRUCTION	84.0
EDUCATIONAL SERVICES	73.6
ELECTRONICS	73.2
ELECTRONIC COMPONENTS	89.0
FABRICATED METALS	76.6
FOOD PRODUCTS	84.5
FURNITURE AND FIXTURES	61.9
HEALTH SERVICES	78.1
HOTELS AND OTHER LODGING PLACES	76.8
INSTRUMENTS	77.3
INSURANCE	84.9
MACHINERY	86.1
MANUFACTURING	75.2
OFFICE EQUIPMENT	73.2
PAPER AND ALLIED PRODUCTS	89.3
PHARMACEUTICALS	97.3
PRINTING AND PUBLISHING	62.3
REAL ESTATE	76.2
RETAIL	68.9
RUBBER/PLASTICS	62.9
TRANSPORTATION BY AIR	42.9
TRANSPORTATION EQUIPMENT	68.0
TRUCKING AND WAREHOUSING	71.4
WHOLESALE (CONSUMER GOODS)	73.5
OVERALL	**75.7%**

FIGURE 97 — IMPROVING OVERALL COMPANY EFFECTIVENESS

The data contained in **Figure 97** is a further breakout of the data presented in Figure 95. The data for Figure 95 was generated by combining the percentage of respondents who rated a particular sales task as either "very important" or "important," and comparing the resulting number with the percentage of respondents rating their sales forces either "very effective" or "effective" in performing the task.

Over the last four survey periods, reps did not score well in the "very effective" column, with the possible exception of "retaining existing customers." As noted in our 1992 survey, the task of retaining existing customers is one of the easier tasks to perform simply because it is easier to obtain business from existing customers than to gain business from new prospects. However, in any economic climate, one important way to ensure the growth of a company is to expand the number of its customers. The data here indicates that this is one area where companies need to do a better job.

FIGURE 97

**IMPROVING OVERALL COMPANY EFFECTIVENESS
(ALL RESPONDENTS)**

	IMPORTANCE TO IMPROVING PERFORMANCE			
	VERY IMPORTANT	IMPORTANT	SOMEWHAT IMPORTANT	NOT IMPORTANT
SALES TASK				
SELLING TO MAJOR ACCOUNTS	68.8%	23.3%	4.5%	3.4%
FINDING NEW ACCOUNTS	68.1	23.9	7.1	0.9
SELLING NEW PRODUCTS	32.9	35.2	22.9	9.0
INTEGRATING NEW TECHNOLOGY	28.7	33.3	27.8	10.1
REDUCING SELLING COSTS	23.9	36.3	28.9	10.8
RETAINING EXISTING CUSTOMERS	83.6	14.3	2.0	0.0
IMPROVING PROFIT CONTRIBUTION	52.4	34.9	10.4	2.3

	CURRENT EFFECTIVENESS OF SALES FORCE			
	VERY EFFECTIVE	EFFECTIVE	SOMEWHAT EFFECTIVE	NOT EFFECTIVE
SALES TASK				
SELLING TO MAJOR ACCOUNTS	19.3%	41.6%	33.1%	6.0%
FINDING NEW ACCOUNTS	10.6	43.2	38.7	7.5
SELLING NEW PRODUCTS	10.6	44.5	37.0	7.9
INTEGRATING NEW TECHNOLOGY	10.5	31.5	43.5	14.5
REDUCING SELLING COSTS	9.4	33.7	46.1	10.8
RETAINING EXISTING CUSTOMERS	32.7	49.1	17.0	1.1
IMPROVING PROFIT CONTRIBUTION	8.7	44.4	40.9	6.0

FIGURE 98 — HOW COMMISSIONS ARE DETERMINED

With all the emphasis on bottom-line results (also see Figure 94), we thought it might be interesting to find out how many companies consider the *profitability* of the sale when calculating sales commissions. The data table on the right tells the story.

Although nearly half the companies (46.25 percent) continue to determine commission on the basis of sales volume only, a growing number of companies are looking at the profitability of the sale in determining their compensation programs. When the number of companies paying commissions on the "Profitability of Sale Only" category are added to the category of those who pay commissions on "Sales Volume *and* Profitability of Sale," we see that nearly 49 percent of responding companies give thought to profitability issues when they determine sales commissions.

Respondents checking the "Other" category did so in many cases to indicate that they do not pay sales commissions.

FIGURE 98

HOW COMMISSIONS ARE DETERMINED

<u>PERCENTAGE OF COMPANIES PAYING COMMISSIONS BASED ON</u>

	SALES VOLUME ONLY	PROFITABILITY OF SALE ONLY	COMBINATION OF SALES VOLUME AND PROFITABILITY OF SALE	OTHER
COMPANY SIZE				
UNDER $5 MILLION	53.45%	11.21%	29.31%	6.03%
$5MM–$25MM	37.82	22.44	35.26	4.49
$25MM–$100MM	48.19	14.46	31.33	6.02
$100MM–$250MM	56.00	8.00	28.00	8.00
OVER $250MM	48.48	6.06	42.42	3.03
PRODUCT OR SERVICE				
CONSUMER PRODUCTS	43.28	10.45	38.06	8.21
CONSUMER SERVICES	49.61	10.08	32.56	7.75
INDUSTRIAL PRODUCTS	40.53	18.42	37.89	3.16
INDUSTRIAL SERVICES	39.73	15.75	41.78	2.74
OFFICE PRODUCTS	43.82	20.22	33.71	2.25
OFFICE SERVICES	45.95	16.22	35.14	2.70
TYPE OF BUYER				
CONSUMERS	47.95	14.38	32.19	5.48
DISTRIBUTORS	49.38	11.11	35.80	3.70
INDUSTRY	43.49	17.81	35.27	3.42
RETAILERS	48.94	9.93	36.88	4.26
INDUSTRY				
BANKING	50.00	8.33	33.33	8.33
BUSINESS SERVICES	41.43	10.00	45.71	2.86
CHEMICALS	55.56	11.11	11.11	22.22
COMMUNICATIONS	52.94	11.76	29.41	5.88
EDUCATIONAL SERVICES	25.00	12.50	25.00	37.50
FABRICATED METALS	47.37	10.53	31.58	10.53
INSURANCE	66.67	9.52	19.05	4.76
MANUFACTURING	55.56	22.22	11.11	11.11
RETAIL	34.38	25.00	34.38	6.25
WHOLESALE (CONSUMER GOODS)	23.81	35.71	33.33	7.14
OVERALL	**46.25%**	**15.50%**	**32.93%**	**5.33%**

FIGURE 99 — EXPERIENCE LEVEL PREFERRED IN NEWLY HIRED SALESPEOPLE

Figure 99 presents full data on the experience level preferred in newly hired salespeople. With just more than 10 percent (10.43%) of survey respondents saying they prefer to hire entry-level candidates, the implication may well be that it is getting harder to break into the field of sales. However, as the data suggests, there are a significant number of industries that entry level reps might investigate for first-time employment to gain the experience they need.

(See pages 138–139 for a further discussion of this topic as well as comments from sales managers as to why they prefer a particular level of experience in a sales candidate.)

FIGURE 99

EXPERIENCE LEVEL PREFERRED IN NEWLY HIRED SALESPEOPLE
(BY PERCENTAGE OF RESPONDENTS)

	ENTRY LEVEL REP (LESS THAN 1 YEAR OF EXPERIENCE)	INTERMEDIATE REP (1–3 YEARS OF EXPERIENCE)	SENIOR REP (MORE THAN 3 YEARS OF EXPERIENCE)
COMPANY SIZE			
UNDER $5 MILLION	16.92%	49.23%	33.85%
$5MM-$25MM	7.93	48.78	43.29
$25MM-$100MM	9.30	52.33	38.37
$100MM-$250MM	3.85	50.00	46.15
OVER $250MM	5.71	48.57	45.71
PRODUCT OR SERVICES			
CONSUMER PRODUCTS	11.43	50.71	37.86
CONSUMER SERVICES	15.22	54.35	30.43
INDUSTRIAL PRODUCTS	9.31	47.55	43.14
INDUSTRIAL SERVICES	10.39	45.45	44.16
OFFICE PRODUCTS	12.09	43.96	43.96
OFFICE SERVICES	13.04	49.57	37.39
TYPE OF BUYER			
CONSUMERS	17.90	50.00	32.10
DISTRIBUTORS	11.49	47.70	40.80
INDUSTRY	9.52	49.84	40.63
RETAILERS	8.90	49.32	41.78
INDUSTRY			
BUSINESS SERVICES	8.57	57.14	34.29
EDUCATIONAL SERVICES	25.00	37.50	37.50
FABRICATED METALS	4.35	52.17	43.48
HEALTH SERVICES	12.50	50.00	37.50
INSTRUMENTS	10.00	20.00	70.00
INSURANCE	30.43	52.17	17.39
MACHINERY	27.27	36.36	36.36
MANUFACTURING	5.26	52.63	42.11
OFFICE EQUIPMENT	18.75	50.00	31.25
PRINTING AND PUBLISHING	5.26	47.37	47.37
REAL ESTATE	28.57	57.14	14.29
RETAIL	29.41	47.06	23.53
WHOLESALE (CONSUMER GOODS)	4.65	60.47	34.88
OVERALL	**10.43%**	**49.66%**	**39.91%**

A PORTRAIT OF TODAY'S SALES FORCE

This section focuses on today's sales force as a unit. Over the years, the dynamics of the typical sales force and the environment it operates in have brought about dramatic changes. These changes are examined through the following exhibits:

- Figure 100 looks at the percentage of women in the sales force and the percentage of women in sales management positions.
- Figure 101 examines the educational level achieved by sales professionals.
- Figure 102 provides a look at the typical spans of control — that is, the average number of salespeople a sales manager is responsible for in varying sizes of companies and varying industries.
- Figure 103 looks at the amount of time salespeople spend on selling and non-selling activities during a typical week. How many hours they spend on a variety of activities is broken out by company size, product or service sold, type of buyer, and industry.
- Figure 104 looks at face-to-face selling and provides data on the average number of calls per day, along with the average number of calls required to close the sale, broken out by company size, product or service sold, type of buyer, and industry.
- Figure 105 shows how many companies are increasing or decreasing the overall size of their sales forces, as well as the number of companies that are maintaining the status quo.
- Figure 106 looks at sales force turnover. Turnover data is provided for size of company, product or service sold, type of buyer, and industry. In addition, turnover is examined from the various factors that cause it: resignations, terminations, retirements, and corporate restructuring.
- Figure 107 provides data on how many companies use manufacturers' representatives to augment the activities of their direct sales forces and also reports the average commission paid.

In reviewing this data, bear in mind that these figures provide indications of general trends and may or may not exactly match the profile of your particular sales force. However, over the years, our survey data has consistently provided sales executives with a comprehensive look at what may be happening "down the road."

FIGURE 100 — WOMEN IN THE SALES FORCE

One of the most profound changes in the selling profession over the past 16 years has been the relatively steady influx of women into what had been traditionally male-dominated territory. In 1982, the year Dartnell began tracking the number of women in the sales force, less than 7 percent of the total number of salespeople were women. This figure now stands at 24.3 percent — nearly unchanged from 24.1 percent reported in our 1996 survey. In 1992, we reported an all-time high of 26 percent women in the sales force.

A word of caution in drawing conclusions from our survey data: Percentages can, at times, be deceiving. Smaller sales forces can often give a distorted view of the picture when percentage figures only are considered. For example, a company employing four salespeople would have 25 percent women on its sales force, even if just one member of the sales force was a woman. Thus, use judgment when trying to compare the percentage of women your company employs with the percentages shown in our survey **(Figure 100)**.

The data in **Figure 100** also provides an indication of those industries that tend to hire significant numbers of women in sales positions.

The reasons for the influx of women into the ranks of salespeople are varied. Here are some of these reasons, reprinted from our previous edition and listed in no particular order:

- Women are good at sales — in many cases, better than men. Companies that originally may have recruited women as the "politically correct" thing to do found, perhaps to their surprise, that women were a vast untapped resource who could have a significant positive impact on the bottom line.

- Economic pressures creating dual-earner households forced many women to look for work. Sales is one of the two professions (teaching is the other) where inequality of pay is less likely to exist — all salespeople on a particular pay plan are paid equally for equivalent work. Further, earnings opportunities in sales are much greater than in many other careers — selling provides women the opportunity to maximize earnings faster.

- Women face different responsibilities — taking care of the house, children, and so on. There are many part-time sales opportunities that allow time for these other tasks. Even full-time sales jobs provide enough freedom of movement to attend to domestic emergencies.

- As the sales job has become more professional, opportunities for women have increased. Sales is no longer an "old boys network." Buyers, too, are more professional and don't throw the business to a friend who just shows them a good time on the town.

- Sales managers are younger and have grown up with the women's movement. Many of these younger managers who "took a chance on a woman" found her outproducing men. In view of these positive results, more women were hired. (One Chicago company, for example, had traditionally hired men. For several years now, women have represented this company's top producers. What's more, men who were working in losing territories were replaced by women who succeeded in turning these same territories around.)

Although we tend to take these changes for granted today, they didn't come easily. In talking with sales managers 14 years ago, the idea of hiring women in sales was a pretty alien concept. Here are some of those "old-time concerns," again, listed in no particular order:

- "What would my sales*men* think? How would they react?"

- "Sales involves a lot of travel — I'd feel uncomfortable subjecting a woman to that. What if something happened — would the company be liable?"

- "I need to spend a lot of time with my people in the field — sometimes overnight. That just wouldn't work with a woman. Besides, what would my wife think?"

- "Some of the people we call on have reputations for womanizing. I couldn't subject one of our employees to that kind of thing."

- "I'm not sure exactly how I'd manage a woman if I did hire one. I'd feel uncomfortable."

Although all this was going on before the current awareness of sexual harassment, these gender considerations were an important, if not overriding, factor in the reluctance to recruit women into the sales force. It was more "a fear of the unknown" than anything else, frankly. For decades, sales forces had been dominated by men doing "men" things. Women just wouldn't fit into this type of environment without causing a fundamental change in how the men conducted themselves and, indeed, how business was conducted in general.

(For geographic breakouts of this data, please see Section 11.)

PERCENTAGE OF WOMEN IN THE SALES FORCE 1982–1998

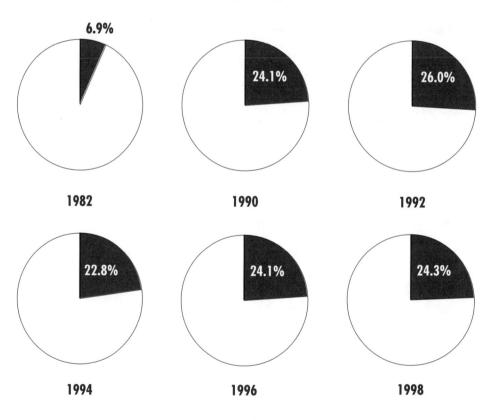

FIGURE 100

WOMEN IN THE SALES FORCE

	PERCENT OF SALES REPS	PERCENT OF SALES MANAGERS
COMPANY SIZE		
UNDER $5 MILLION	23.0%	9.8%
$5MM–$25MM	23.2	15.0
$25MM–$100MM	24.4	15.3
$100MM–$250MM	24.3	12.5
OVER $250MM	34.5	28.2
PRODUCT OR SERVICE		
CONSUMER PRODUCTS	25.5	16.2
CONSUMER SERVICES	33.3	20.9
INDUSTRIAL PRODUCTS	15.9	9.6
INDUSTRIAL SERVICES	19.7	12.0
OFFICE PRODUCTS	23.9	14.7
OFFICE SERVICES	27.9	16.6
TYPE OF BUYER		
CONSUMERS	31.1	20.8
DISTRIBUTORS	22.8	15.5
INDUSTRY	22.6	13.7
RETAILERS	28.3	16.4
INDUSTRY		
AGRICULTURE, FORESTRY, AND FISHING	4.7	0.0
BANKING	24.7	23.3
BUSINESS SERVICES	30.3	21.5
CHEMICALS	9.1	5.7
COMMUNICATIONS	34.7	15.3
CONSTRUCTION	20.0	20.0
EDUCATIONAL SERVICES	50.4	37.8
ELECTRONICS	19.6	5.4
ELECTRONIC COMPONENTS	10.8	14.2
FABRICATED METALS	5.9	10.3
FOOD PRODUCTS	28.5	43.8
FURNITURE AND FIXTURES	44.3	25.7
HEALTH SERVICES	45.1	6.8
HOTELS AND OTHER LODGING PLACES	83.0	73.6
INSTRUMENTS	10.7	8.2
INSURANCE	27.4	14.0
MACHINERY	8.2	3.8
MANUFACTURING	17.6	6.8
OFFICE EQUIPMENT	24.1	7.4
PAPER AND ALLIED PRODUCTS	1.8	12.5
PHARMACEUTICALS	31.0	17.4
PRINTING AND PUBLISHING	38.9	23.2
REAL ESTATE	50.0	22.0
RETAIL	20.0	5.6
RUBBER/PLASTICS	17.7	20.8
TRANSPORTATION BY AIR	21.7	24.3
TRANSPORTATION EQUIPMENT	23.9	14.3
TRUCKING AND WAREHOUSING	0.0	0.0
WHOLESALE (CONSUMER GOODS)	19.5	4.8
OVERALL	**24.3%**	**14.3%**

FIGURE 101 — SALES FORCE EDUCATION LEVEL

As the data in **Figure 101** illustrates, the educational level of today's salesperson has never been higher. Currently, nearly 66 percent (65.6%) of salespeople have a college degree, a dramatic increase over our findings of 14 years ago. In 1982, just 20 percent of U.S. salespeople had attained a college degree.

What's more, the number of salespeople holding postgraduate degrees has increased as well. Of today's sales professionals, 6.5 percent have educational credentials that extend beyond college, compared with just 3 percent eight years ago.

The higher educational level of today's salespeople enables this group to maintain a higher earnings level and standard of living than many, if not most, of the nation's workers.

(For geographic breakouts of this data, please see Section 11.)

FIGURE 101

SALES FORCE EDUCATION LEVEL

	HIGH SCHOOL	SOME COLLEGE	COLLEGE DEGREE	POST-GRAD	TECHNICAL TRAINING
COMPANY SIZE					
UNDER $5 MILLION	33.3%	40.7%	53.3%	5.2%	16.3%
$5MM–$25MM	36.1	40.4	68.1	9.6	24.7
$25MM–$100MM	44.8	36.8	73.6	4.6	19.5
$100MM–$250MM	29.2	20.8	87.5	0.0	20.8
OVER $250MM	42.4	39.4	66.7	6.1	18.2
PRODUCT OR SERVICE					
CONSUMER PRODUCTS	50.0	42.9	56.4	5.0	18.6
CONSUMER SERVICES	48.6	40.6	57.2	6.5	16.7
INDUSTRIAL PRODUCTS	35.5	39.4	66.5	7.9	28.6
INDUSTRIAL SERVICES	33.5	38.7	63.2	10.3	31.0
OFFICE PRODUCTS	32.2	37.8	77.8	11.1	23.3
OFFICE SERVICES	31.3	40.9	73.9	10.4	18.3
TYPE OF BUYER					
CONSUMERS	48.8	45.1	57.9	4.9	18.9
DISTRIBUTORS	36.0	40.4	70.2	6.7	24.7
INDUSTRY	31.5	38.2	69.4	7.9	25.6
RETAILERS	48.3	45.6	61.7	6.7	20.1
INDUSTRY					
AGRICULTURE, FORESTRY, AND FISHING	33.3	33.3	66.7	0.0	0.0
BANKING	27.3	36.4	45.5	9.1	9.1
BUSINESS SERVICES	28.2	31.0	71.8	8.5	15.5
CHEMICALS	36.4	36.4	72.7	18.2	36.4
COMMUNICATIONS	44.4	61.1	55.6	5.6	33.3
CONSTRUCTION	40.0	50.0	40.0	0.0	10.0
EDUCATIONAL SERVICES	55.6	55.6	66.7	11.1	22.2
ELECTRONICS	18.2	36.4	77.3	22.7	31.8
ELECTRONIC COMPONENTS	25.0	33.3	66.7	8.3	50.0
FABRICATED METALS	43.5	39.1	60.9	0.0	30.4
FOOD PRODUCTS	0.0	25.0	75.0	0.0	25.0
FURNITURE AND FIXTURES	0.0	0.0	100.0	33.3	0.0
HEALTH SERVICES	12.5	12.5	100.0	0.0	25.0
HOTELS AND OTHER LODGING PLACES	50.0	62.5	75.0	0.0	0.0
INSTRUMENTS	20.0	30.0	70.0	0.0	10.0
INSURANCE	37.5	41.7	75.0	4.2	20.8
MACHINERY	33.3	16.7	75.0	0.0	0.0
MANUFACTURING	38.9	38.9	77.8	5.6	44.4
OFFICE EQUIPMENT	37.5	43.8	68.8	18.8	31.2
PAPER AND ALLIED PRODUCTS	25.0	25.0	75.0	0.0	0.0
PHARMACEUTICALS	57.1	28.6	100.0	0.0	14.3
PRINTING AND PUBLISHING	26.3	31.6	84.2	5.3	10.5
REAL ESTATE	66.7	16.7	33.3	0.0	0.0
RETAIL	73.5	44.1	29.4	0.0	11.8
RUBBER/PLASTICS	16.7	0.0	83.3	0.0	33.3
TRANSPORTATION BY AIR	100.0	66.7	100.0	0.0	33.3
TRANSPORTATION EQUIPMENT	57.1	57.1	28.6	14.3	28.6
TRUCKING AND WAREHOUSING	66.7	66.7	33.3	0.0	0.0
WHOLESALE (CONSUMER GOODS)	31.0	52.4	61.9	7.1	19.0
OVERALL*	**37.1%**	**38.7%**	**65.6%**	**6.5%**	**20.4%**

*FIGURES TOTAL MORE THAN 100% DUE TO MULTIPLE RESPONSES.

FIGURE 102 — TYPICAL SPANS OF CONTROL

How many salespeople does the average sales manager supervise? According to current survey results, a typical sales manager oversees the activities of approximately eight salespeople. **Figure 102** examines the typical spans of control (i.e., the average number of salespeople reporting to a single sales manager). Not surprisingly, the ratio of sales managers to salespeople in smaller companies is lower than in larger companies. This makes sense when you realize that a small company may employ just three salespeople, yet also have a need to employ someone to direct sales activities.

FIGURE 102

TYPICAL SPANS OF CONTROL

	TOTAL NUMBER OF SALESPEOPLE	NUMBER OF SALES MANAGERS	SPAN OF CONTROL (RATIO)
COMPANY SIZE			
UNDER $5 MILLION	6,121	912	4.4:1
$5MM–$25MM	10,838	1,600	6.0:1
$25MM–$100MM	6,521	940	7.8:1
$100MM–$250MM	5,558	652	11.5:1
OVER $250MM	27,126	2,179	29.4:1
PRODUCT OR SERVICE			
CONSUMER PRODUCTS	30,544	3,075	9.5:1
CONSUMER SERVICES	26,870	2,643	10.5:1
INDUSTRIAL PRODUCTS	25,478	4,080	8.2:1
INDUSTRIAL SERVICES	19,440	3,516	6.3:1
OFFICE PRODUCTS	13,798	2,390	8.6:1
OFFICE SERVICES	12,588	2,208	7.5:1
TYPE OF BUYER			
CONSUMERS	24,518	1,728	9.8:1
DISTRIBUTORS	23,446	4,022	6.8:1
INDUSTRY	37,081	5,308	7.2:1
RETAILERS	21,936	3,715	7.6:1
INDUSTRY			
AGRICULTURE, FORESTRY, AND FISHING	73	25	7.7:1
BANKING	2,902	137	17.2:1
BUSINESS SERVICES	3,292	451	5.9:1
CHEMICALS	3,280	294	26.0:1
COMMUNICATIONS	387	92	4.9:1
CONSTRUCTION	208	35	5.3:1
EDUCATIONAL SERVICES	1,232	320	8.3:1
ELECTRONICS	2,163	272	6.9:1
ELECTRONIC COMPONENTS	1,292	268	5.9:1
FABRICATED METALS	896	105	8.2:1
FOOD PRODUCTS	80	28	3.2:1
FURNITURE AND FIXTURES	502	80	6.0:1
HEALTH SERVICES	608	54	9.0:1
HOTELS AND OTHER LODGING PLACES	572	128	5.6:1
INSTRUMENTS	252	80	4.4:1
INSURANCE	11,190	425	18.8:1
MACHINERY	720	99	5.7:1
MANUFACTURING	5,196	969	5.2:1
OFFICE EQUIPMENT	4,006	1,193	5.0:1
PAPER AND ALLIED PRODUCTS	83	12	5.0:1
PHARMACEUTICALS	5,200	307	5.7:1
PRINTING AND PUBLISHING	2,604	316	8.1:1
REAL ESTATE	1,993	83	23.8:1
RETAIL	2,361	243	8.6:1
RUBBER/PLASTICS	169	38	5.2:1
TRANSPORTATION BY AIR	131	28	4.3:1
TRANSPORTATION EQUIPMENT	1,449	192	5.9:1
TRUCKING AND WAREHOUSING	41	9	4.3:1
WHOLESALE (CONSUMER GOODS)	2,352	316	7.1:1
OVERALL	**55,234**	**6,599**	**8.0:1**

FIGURE 103 — SELLING AND NONSELLING WORK ACTIVITIES
(IN HOURS PER WEEK)

Today's sales professional, on average, works a total of 48.2 hours per week — up from the 46.9 hours reported two years ago. Here's how reps spend their time now. Data from previous surveys is included for comparison purposes.

Sales Reps and Their Use of Time — 1998

Task	Percent of Weekly Time
• Selling face-to-face	28.8% (13.9 hours)
• Selling over the phone	25.1% (12.1 hours)
• Administrative tasks	16% (7.7 hours)
• Waiting/traveling	17.4% (8.4 hours)
• Service calls	12.7% (6.1 hours)

Sales Reps and Their Use of Time — 1996

Task	Percent of Weekly Time
• Selling face-to-face	31% (14.3 hours)
• Selling over the phone	25% (11.6 hours)
• Administrative tasks	15% (7.2 hours)
• Waiting/traveling	18% (8.5 hours)
• Service calls	11% (5.3 hours)

Sales Reps and Their Use of Time — 1994

Task	Percent of Weekly Time
• Selling face-to-face	30% (13.9 hours)
• Selling over the phone	25% (11.5 hours)
• Administrative tasks	15% (7.0 hours)
• Waiting/traveling	18% (8.5 hours)
• Service calls	12% (5.6 hours)

Sales Reps and Their Use of Time — 1992

Task	Percent of Weekly Time
• Selling face-to-face	30% (13.8 hours)
• Selling over the phone	21% (9.5 hours)
• Administrative tasks	17% (7.7 hours)
• Waiting/traveling	20% (9.0 hours)
• Service calls	12% (5.5 hours)

Sales Reps and Their Use of Time — 1990

Task	Percent of Weekly Time
• Selling face-to-face	31.1% (14.6 hours)
• Selling over the phone	20% (9.4 hours)
• Administrative tasks	13.4% (6.3 hours)
• Waiting/traveling	22% (10.4 hours)
• Service calls	13.5% (6.3 hours)

Figures for the last five survey periods have been relatively consistent.

In looking at the 1998 split between hours per week, on average, spent on selling activities (26 hours or 53.9 percent) and nonselling activities (22.2 hours or 46.1 percent), we see that today's salespeople continue to spend a greater percentage of total working hours on direct selling activities. This wasn't always the case. In survey periods as recent as six years ago, salespeople divided their time about equally between selling and nonselling activities. In 1990, the split was dead even, with 50 percent of the time spent on selling activities and 50 percent of the time spent on nonselling activities. In 1992, 51 percent of the time was spent on selling activities vs. 49 percent on nonselling activities.

As noted in our 1992 survey edition, if one considers that service calls are part of the selling process — and it is feasible — then we have 32 hours of selling time vs. approximately 16 hours of nonselling time. In working with this data, feel free to consider the figures in a variety of different ways.

Assuming most salespeople work a five-day week, you can generate additional findings from this table:

• Dividing the total number of hours per week spent face-to-face by five gives us the number of hours per day spent in direct contact with customers and prospects — a little less than three hours. By the same token, a little more than two hours is spent on the phone on a daily basis.

• Following the same mathematical procedure — and including service calls as a part of the selling process — we find that our "average" salesperson spends a little more than six hours a day in some form of sales activity. Even if we don't include service calls, our average salesperson still spends five hours a day in selling-related activities. This really isn't too bad when you stop to think about it.

- If we divide the total amount of time spent per week on travel by five, we find that the average salesperson spends less than two hours a day (1.68 hours) traveling, an indication of good territory planning and coverage.

You can follow this same procedure to generate figures for your own industry and size of company.

It should be noted that these time estimates of how salespeople spent their time were made by sales managers. We thought it only fair to ask salespeople the same question. Details of that survey are presented in Section 12. We'll mention here, however, that salespeople say they're working longer than managers think: 55 hours, or nearly seven hours more a week. One explanation: Reps appear to be spending more time surfing the Internet in search of customer and product information. In any event, reps are not putting much of this extra time into face-to-face selling: They say they spend 15.4 hours in front of prospects and customers. That's just 1½ hours more than sales managers estimate. To our way of thinking, it's time spent in front of buyers that is most likely to translate into sales. If salespeople are, in fact, putting in more time than managers are aware of, they should be using that time more productively.

(For geographic breakouts of this data, please see Section 11.)

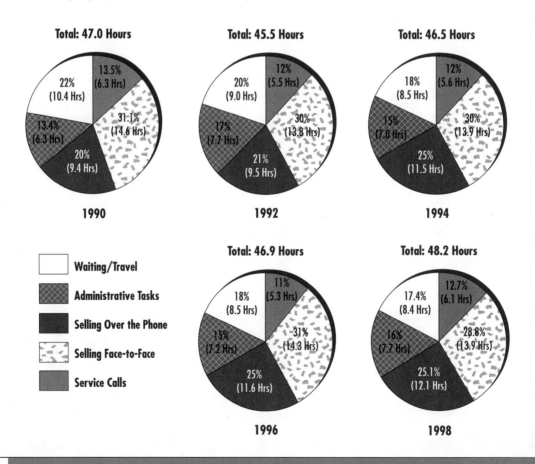

FIGURE 103

SELLING AND NONSELLING WORK ACTIVITIES
(IN HOURS PER WEEK)

	TOTAL WORK HOURS PER WEEK	TIME SPENT SELLING	SELLING TIME SPENT:		TIME SPENT NON-SELLING	NONSELLING TIME SPENT:		
			FACE-TO-FACE	ON THE PHONE		ADMIN.	TRAVEL	SERVICE CALLS
COMPANY SIZE								
UNDER $5 MILLION	46.8	26.0	12.9	13.1	20.7	7.9	6.5	6.3
$5MM–$25MM	49.2	27.1	13.7	13.4	22.1	7.3	8.9	6.0
$25MM–$100MM	47.2	25.6	15.1	10.5	21.6	7.8	8.6	5.2
$100MM–$250MM	45.0	21.9	12.8	9.0	23.2	6.9	9.5	6.8
OVER $250MM	54.5	25.0	17.2	7.9	29.5	9.6	12.3	7.5
PRODUCT OR SERVICE								
CONSUMER PRODUCTS	48.9	27.3	17.2	10.1	21.6	7.5	8.6	5.6
CONSUMER SERVICES	48.7	26.2	15.3	10.9	22.5	7.9	6.8	7.7
INDUSTRIAL PRODUCTS	48.3	26.2	14.1	12.1	22.1	6.9	9.3	5.8
INDUSTRIAL SERVICES	47.4	25.4	13.6	11.8	22.0	7.8	8.6	5.7
OFFICE PRODUCTS	45.8	25.4	13.1	12.3	20.4	7.1	8.2	5.1
OFFICE SERVICES	44.3	24.3	11.4	12.9	20.0	7.6	7.2	5.3
TYPE OF BUYER								
CONSUMERS	49.3	27.2	15.0	12.2	22.1	8.3	6.9	6.8
DISTRIBUTORS	48.4	25.5	12.4	13.0	22.9	8.2	8.5	6.2
INDUSTRY	47.4	26.1	12.8	13.3	21.3	7.3	8.2	5.7
RETAILERS	49.0	26.2	14.9	11.2	22.8	7.7	8.6	6.5
INDUSTRY								
AGRICULTURE, FORESTRY, AND FISHING	39.7	15.0	8.3	6.7	24.7	6.7	15.0	3.0
BANKING	59.0	27.4	16.6	10.8	31.6	12.1	6.4	13.0
BUSINESS SERVICES	44.4	26.5	11.0	15.5	17.9	6.7	6.6	4.6
CHEMICALS	47.5	22.1	15.7	6.4	25.5	6.8	11.5	7.1
COMMUNICATIONS	48.0	25.9	14.1	11.8	22.1	6.9	6.5	8.6
CONSTRUCTION	47.0	27.2	21.4	5.8	19.8	8.8	6.9	4.1
EDUCATIONAL SERVICES	47.9	24.0	10.3	13.7	23.9	11.3	5.3	7.2
ELECTRONICS	45.8	25.9	13.6	12.3	19.9	7.8	9.2	3.0
ELECTRONIC COMPONENTS	59.6	31.2	13.5	17.8	28.4	10.1	6.8	11.5
FABRICATED METALS	47.5	26.6	14.6	12.0	20.9	7.2	9.2	4.5
FOOD PRODUCTS	40.5	16.2	8.0	8.2	24.2	8.8	12.5	3.0
FURNITURE AND FIXTURES	46.0	19.7	14.0	5.7	26.3	14.0	5.0	7.3
HEALTH SERVICES	53.9	23.1	10.7	12.4	30.8	9.1	9.0	12.6
HOTELS AND OTHER LODGING PLACES	44.9	28.0	9.4	18.6	16.9	7.6	4.6	4.6
INSTRUMENTS	49.1	28.2	13.2	15.0	20.9	6.5	10.0	4.4
INSURANCE	48.5	22.1	11.7	10.3	26.4	7.5	8.6	10.3
MACHINERY	52.8	21.5	12.2	9.2	31.3	9.3	14.2	7.8
MANUFACTURING	51.1	27.5	12.9	14.6	23.6	8.9	8.0	6.6
OFFICE EQUIPMENT	42.3	25.9	11.0	14.9	16.4	5.6	8.2	2.6
PAPER AND ALLIED PRODUCTS	45.0	29.5	15.5	14.0	15.5	3.2	5.0	7.2
PHARMACEUTICALS	52.1	23.6	17.1	6.4	28.6	12.3	10.9	5.4
PRINTING AND PUBLISHING	43.8	22.2	11.8	10.3	21.6	9.2	8.4	4.0
REAL ESTATE	51.6	19.2	11.8	7.5	32.4	10.6	8.8	13.0
RETAIL	48.8	28.9	20.2	8.6	19.9	7.9	8.4	3.6
RUBBER/PLASTICS	53.0	28.2	18.2	10.0	24.8	9.0	9.2	6.7
TRANSPORTATION BY AIR	63.0	41.3	18.0	23.3	21.7	5.0	10.0	6.7
TRANSPORTATION EQUIPMENT	49.3	30.3	13.7	16.6	19.0	7.6	6.9	4.6
TRUCKING AND WAREHOUSING	51.7	26.0	18.3	7.7	25.7	12.3	4.3	9.0
WHOLESALE (CONSUMER GOODS)	52.1	28.3	15.9	12.4	23.8	5.5	10.9	7.4
OVERALL	**48.2**	**26.0**	**13.9**	**12.1**	**22.2**	**7.7**	**8.4**	**6.1**

FIGURE 104 — FACE-TO-FACE SELLING

The average number of sales calls typically needed to close a sale and the average number of sales calls made per day have remained relatively stable over the last few survey periods. The average number of sales calls per day, 3.0, has changed insignificantly over the last three survey periods. In 1982, however, salespeople made an average of six sales calls per day. Can we infer from this that today's sales professional is less effective? No — and here's why: Sixteen years ago, it was common for sales managers to set a minimum number of sales calls that their salespeople had to make in any given day. Over the years, sales managers began to realize that the *quality* of the sales calls made was more important than the overall *quantity*. Today's salespeople now go into sales calls much better-prepared than they were in the past.

The average number of calls to close a sale, 3.8, is relatively unchanged from the 4.0 figure reported two years ago. This change is insignificant. Fourteen years ago, it took an average of five calls to close the sale — an indication that today's sales professional has greatly improved his or her efficiency.

(For geographic breakouts of this data, please see Section 11.)

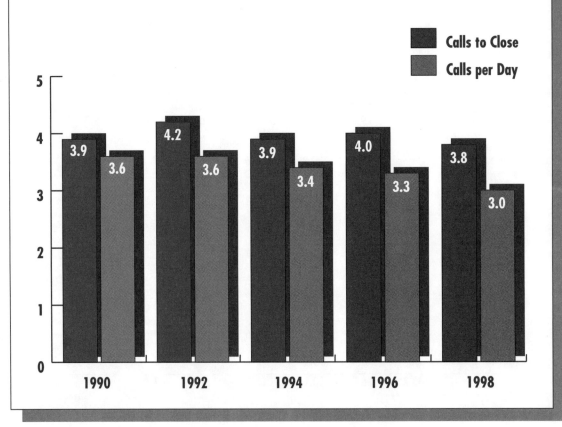

FIGURE 104

FACE-TO-FACE SELLING

	AVERAGE NUMBER OF CALLS TO CLOSE SALE	NUMBER OF CALLS PER DAY
COMPANY SIZE		
UNDER $5 MILLION	3.4	3.0
$5MM–$25MM	3.9	3.1
$25MM–$100MM	4.2	2.9
$100MM–$250MM	4.4	2.6
OVER $250MM	3.9	2.6
PRODUCT OR SERVICE		
CONSUMER PRODUCTS	3.2	3.4
CONSUMER SERVICES	3.5	3.2
INDUSTRIAL PRODUCTS	3.9	2.9
INDUSTRIAL SERVICES	4.2	2.5
OFFICE PRODUCTS	4.2	3.1
OFFICE SERVICES	4.1	2.4
TYPE OF BUYER		
CONSUMERS	3.3	3.1
DISTRIBUTORS	3.8	2.9
INDUSTRY	4.0	2.8
RETAILERS	3.6	3.2
INDUSTRY		
BANKING	3.5	2.5
BUSINESS SERVICES	4.2	2.2
CHEMICALS	5.4	3.2
COMMUNICATIONS	4.0	3.1
CONSTRUCTION	6.2	2.2
EDUCATIONAL SERVICES	5.0	1.8
ELECTRONICS	5.0	2.5
ELECTRONIC COMPONENTS	5.0	2.6
FABRICATED METALS	3.7	2.5
FOOD PRODUCTS	2.3	2.3
HEALTH SERVICES	4.0	3.5
HOTELS AND OTHER LODGING PLACES	3.8	2.8
INSTRUMENTS	4.6	2.8
INSURANCE	2.8	3.1
MACHINERY	4.0	2.6
MANUFACTURING	3.5	2.9
OFFICE EQUIPMENT	3.8	2.7
PAPER AND ALLIED PRODUCTS	0.0	4.0
PHARMACEUTICALS	4.2	4.0
PRINTING AND PUBLISHING	4.9	2.5
REAL ESTATE	3.8	2.7
RETAIL	3.5	4.2
RUBBER/PLASTICS	3.8	3.5
TRANSPORTATION BY AIR	4.7	0.0
TRANSPORTATION EQUIPMENT	4.0	3.2
TRUCKING AND WAREHOUSING	6.0	4.0
WHOLESALE (CONSUMER GOODS)	2.6	3.9
OVERALL	**3.8**	**3.0**

FIGURE 105 — THE CHANGING SIZE OF THE SALES FORCE

In our current survey, 12.1 percent of responding companies said the size of their sales forces decreased over the past year. Nearly 43 percent (42.9%) of responding companies are increasing the size of their sales forces in anticipation of expanding markets and additional growth opportunities. Nearly half of the companies in the survey (44.9%) say the size of their sales forces is expected to remain constant — about the same percentage as reported two years ago.

(For geographic breakouts of this data, please see Section 11.)

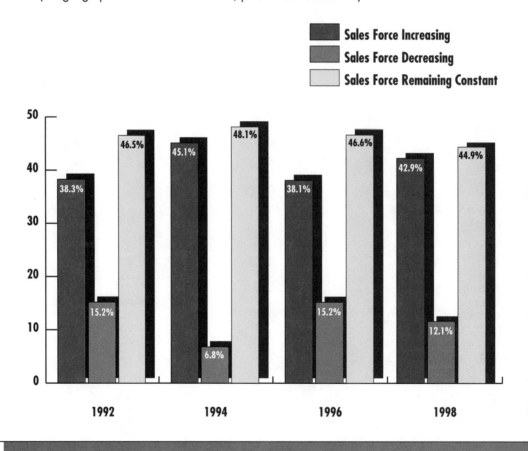

FIGURE 105

CHANGING SIZE OF SALES FORCE

	SALES FORCE INCREASING		SALES FORCE DECREASING		SALES FORCE REMAINING CONSTANT
	PERCENT OF FIRMS	AVERAGE SIZE OF INCREASE	PERCENT OF FIRMS	AVERAGE SIZE OF DECREASE	PERCENT OF FIRMS
COMPANY SIZE					
UNDER $5 MILLION	34.1%	4	8.9%	19	57.0%
$5MM–$25MM	44.2	4	12.1	2	43.6
$25MM–$100MM	47.1	4	16.1	5	36.8
$100MM–$250MM	68.0	8	8.0	2	24.0
OVER $250MM	42.4	16	18.2	25	39.4
PRODUCT OR SERVICE					
CONSUMER PRODUCTS	42.1	7	11.4	22	46.4
CONSUMER SERVICES	38.7	8	16.1	17	45.3
INDUSTRIAL PRODUCTS	41.9	4	12.3	7	45.8
INDUSTRIAL SERVICES	39.1	4	12.2	6	48.7
OFFICE PRODUCTS	36.7	6	16.7	6	46.7
OFFICE SERVICES	42.6	5	16.5	4	40.9
TYPE OF BUYER					
CONSUMERS	39.9	8	9.8	18	50.3
DISTRIBUTORS	42.1	5	13.5	9	44.4
INDUSTRY	41.8	4	14.5	10	43.7
RETAILERS	46.3	6	9.4	6	44.3
INDUSTRY					
AGRICULTURE, FORESTRY, AND FISHING	100.0	3	0.0	0	0.0
BANKING	45.5	12	9.1	1	45.5
BUSINESS SERVICES	51.4	5	13.9	2	34.7
CHEMICALS	36.4	7	0.0	0	63.6
COMMUNICATIONS	27.8	1	27.8	5	44.4
CONSTRUCTION	60.0	2	0.0	0	40.0
EDUCATIONAL SERVICES	44.4	3	11.1	1	44.4
ELECTRONICS	57.1	3	4.8	1	38.1
ELECTRONIC COMPONENTS	41.7	12	16.7	2	41.7
FABRICATED METALS	34.8	3	13.0	2	52.2
FOOD PRODUCTS	100.0	3	0.0	0	0.0
FURNITURE AND FIXTURES	33.3	8	33.3	1	33.3
HEALTH SERVICES	28.6	6	14.3	8	57.1
HOTELS AND OTHER LODGING PLACES	50.0	10	12.5	1	37.5
INSTRUMENTS	20.0	2	30.0	1	50.0
INSURANCE	20.8	5	8.3	100	70.8
MACHINERY	50.0	4	0.0	0	50.0
MANUFACTURING	33.3	2	11.1	2	55.6
OFFICE EQUIPMENT	43.8	6	18.8	10	37.5
PAPER AND ALLIED PRODUCTS	50.0	2	0.0	0	50.0
PHARMACEUTICALS	28.6	28	14.3	3	57.1
PRINTING AND PUBLISHING	47.4	4	31.6	4	21.1
REAL ESTATE	50.0	12	16.7	15	33.3
RETAIL	32.4	12	5.9	7	61.8
RUBBER/PLASTICS	33.3	2	0.0	0	66.7
TRANSPORTATION BY AIR	0.0	0	0.0	0	100.0
TRANSPORTATION EQUIPMENT	57.1	2	14.3	50	28.6
TRUCKING AND WAREHOUSING	100.0	2	0.0	0	0.0
WHOLESALE (CONSUMER GOODS)	44.2	2	11.6	18	44.2
OVERALL	**42.9%**	**5**	**12.1%**	**9**	**44.9%**

FIGURE 106 — SALES FORCE TURNOVER

Figure 106 examines sales force turnover and reports an average turnover rate of 15.2 percent, up slightly from the 14.1 percent turnover figure reported two years ago. Turnover rates seem to have stabilized from 1990, when poor job prospects kept a significant number of reps from leaving their current employers.

Regardless of the numbers, turnover can be a problem at some companies. Here's what respondents told us about turnover at their companies. Reading these comments also can provide insights into the dynamics of the companies in our survey.

REASONS GIVEN FOR *LOWER* TURNOVER THAN USUAL

"Good morale."

"New sales management team, training program, and new hire compensation plan."

"Changed profile of recruit."

"Good compensation plan."

"Business good."

"Growing organization."

"Great recruiting and great working conditions."

"We have good, dedicated, motivated people."

"Better pay scale."

"Happy salespeople, good earnings."

"Great new programs."

"Better compensation system; more responsive to salespeople's needs."

"Choose more carefully when hired."

"Good chemistry in company."

"Strong company in a growing industry."

"Stable environment."

"Good products and more educated sales force."

"Compensation has improved."

"Guaranteed commission program."

"Working harder with sales force and upper management to define focus."

"People like what they do."

"Company growth, and everybody was hitting quota and making what they expected."

"New technology and better comp plan."

"Good pay, exciting job."

"Initial sales training."

"Good working atmosphere."

REASONS GIVEN FOR *NORMAL* TURNOVER

"Improved hiring practices."

"Industry growth and availability of better personnel. We can upgrade for no more cost."

"Some departures to competitors, and some people who weren't making the cut."

"Down to normal because we have a good working environment and a very fair commission structure."

"Pay or opportunity too low."

"We hire people who are qualified."

"We have a good understanding of a person who fits our company and our industry better."

"Good incentive program, fringe benefits, and recognition."

"Great economy. Money was great for most."

"We have an excellent comp/benefit package, we are the leader in our industry, and salespeople are largely autonomous and output-based."

"Increased competition."

"Lack of good management and the top exec's ability to lead the company in a successful direction."

"We try to create a good business environment for our company."

"Competition is targeting our sales force with more attractive compensation plans."

"Turnover is common in this industry."

REASONS GIVEN FOR *HIGHER* THAN NORMAL TURNOVER

"Lack of results in sales."

"Corporate change."

"Likely poor choices when hired."

"Previous manager ineffective, created animosity with reps."

"Soft years in sales, high pressure on team."

"Change in commissions and salary. Lower salary, higher commission."

"Poor hiring."

"Field reorganization. Although most salespeople were retained, the jobs changed and many left because they did not like their new jobs."

"Corporate refocus."

"I am cleaning out 'deadwood' and bringing in my own team."

"Implemented standards for performance."

"Corporate change, better outside offers."

"Competitors targeting our sales force for recruiting."

"Most were hired away by other companies."

"Change in recruiting practices."

"Left for better opportunities."

"New branch manager came in and cleaned house."

"Sales management team driving toward a higher level of professionalism in the field. Terminations were all poor performers who could not meet the new challenge."

"Weeding out troublemakers."

"Management change created communication breakdowns and frustration."

"Poor compensation and salary."

"Lack of sales and direction by previous sales managers. We've had two managers in one year."

Sales force turnover as a percentage of total salespeople employed has remained relatively stable over the last 16 years, according to Dartnell studies. Better-educated, career-minded salespeople are certainly a factor in this trend. But other factors, largely under the direct control of the sales organization, are making an impact, too.

(For geographic breakouts of this data, please see Section 11.)

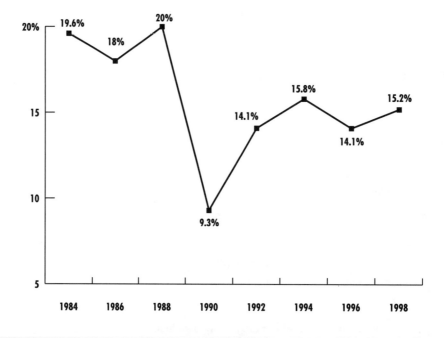

FIGURE 106

SALES FORCE TURNOVER

	SALESPEOPLE	RESIGNATIONS	TERMINATIONS	RETIREMENT	CORP. RESTRUC- TURING	TOTAL TURNOVER (%)
COMPANY SIZE						
UNDER $5 MILLION	6,121	256	12	422	57	12.2%
$5MM–$25MM	10,838	1,155	169	950	115	22.1
$25MM–$100MM	6,521	1,046	28	473	204	26.9
$100MM–$250MM	5,558	544	38	409	86	19.4
OVER $250MM	27,126	1,673	211	358	320	9.4
PRODUCT OR SERVICE						
CONSUMER PRODUCTS	30,544	2,704	256	1,491	361	15.8
CONSUMER SERVICES	26,870	1,945	176	1,120	304	13.3
INDUSTRIAL PRODUCTS	25,478	2,550	355	857	518	18.1
INDUSTRIAL SERVICES	19,440	1,836	288	643	352	16.0
OFFICE PRODUCTS	13,798	1,878	140	1,084	246	26.6
OFFICE SERVICES	12,588	1,833	99	694	256	22.9
TYPE OF BUYER						
CONSUMERS	24,518	1,401	96	1,113	224	11.6
DISTRIBUTORS	23,446	2,176	316	835	531	16.5
INDUSTRY	37,081	3,440	400	1,600	627	16.4
RETAILERS	21,936	2,480	240	1,308	352	20.0
INDUSTRY						
AGRICULTURE, FORESTRY, AND FISHING	73	19	9	0	0	26.1
BANKING	2,902	22	22	76	3	4.3
BUSINESS SERVICES	3,292	524	6	310	22	26.2
CHEMICALS	3,280	310	6	41	9	11.2
COMMUNICATIONS	387	60	9	44	48	41.3
CONSTRUCTION	208	12	0	16	0	13.8
EDUCATIONAL SERVICES	1,232	230	0	102	64	32.2
ELECTRONICS	2,163	99	38	83	83	14.1
ELECTRONIC COMPONENTS	1,292	105	22	51	9	13.4
FABRICATED METALS	896	44	16	19	6	10.0
FOOD PRODUCTS	80	9	0	0	0	12.0
FURNITURE AND FIXTURES	502	35	6	6	0	9.6
HEALTH SERVICES	608	70	3	57	25	25.8
HOTELS AND OTHER LODGING PLACES	572	80	19	60	6	29.1
INSTRUMENTS	252	22	0	19	0	19.0
INSURANCE	11,190	70	6	0	0	0.8
MACHINERY	720	64	3	16	12	13.3
MANUFACTURING	5,196	83	83	60	48	5.4
OFFICE EQUIPMENT	4,006	1,193	67	620	0	47.0
PAPER AND ALLIED PRODUCTS	83	6	0	6	0	15.4
PHARMACEUTICALS	5,200	345	28	57	0	8.3
PRINTING AND PUBLISHING	2,604	243	12	160	54	18.1
REAL ESTATE	1,993	38	0	198	0	11.9
RETAIL	2,361	684	16	412	96	51.2
RUBBER/PLASTICS	169	32	0	9	0	24.5
TRANSPORTATION BY AIR	131	22	0	3	6	24.4
TRANSPORTATION EQUIPMENT	1,449	60	80	19	64	15.5
TRUCKING AND WAREHOUSING	41	3	0	0	0	7.7
WHOLESALE (CONSUMER GOODS)	2,352	115	25	96	198	18.5
OVERALL	**55,234**	**4,599**	**476**	**2,540**	**753**	**15.2%**

FIGURE 107 — USE OF MANUFACTURERS' REPRESENTATIVES

Approximately 26 percent of companies participating in this survey use manufacturers' representatives to augment the efforts of their direct sales forces. In last year's survey, 27 percent of responding companies used manufacturers' reps. The average commission rate paid in the last survey period was 10.7 percent — consistent with this year's figure of 12.1 percent.

FIGURE 107

USE OF MANUFACTURERS' REPRESENTATIVES

	PERCENT USING MANUFACTURERS' REPS	AVERAGE COMMISSION (PERCENT OF SALES)
COMPANY SIZE		
UNDER $5 MILLION	26.3%	13.3%
$5MM–$25MM	29.9	10.7
$25MM–$100MM	29.5	9.8
$100MM–$250MM	7.7	29.5
OVER $250MM	11.4	24.8
PRODUCT OR SERVICE		
CONSUMER PRODUCTS	29.1	13.4
CONSUMER SERVICES	14.9	16.5
INDUSTRIAL PRODUCTS	38.2	11.6
INDUSTRIAL SERVICES	28.9	13.3
OFFICE PRODUCTS	23.1	20.2
OFFICE SERVICES	10.3	25.2
TYPE OF BUYER		
CONSUMERS	18.0	16.6
DISTRIBUTORS	32.6	12.0
INDUSTRY	27.6	12.5
RETAILERS	25.8	14.8
INDUSTRY		
AGRICULTURE, FORESTRY, AND FISHING	100.0	9.3
BANKING	16.7	30.0
BUSINESS SERVICES	12.3	17.9
CHEMICALS	25.0	12.0
COMMUNICATIONS	11.1	11.5
CONSTRUCTION	20.0	2.5
ELECTRONICS	40.9	12.6
ELECTRONIC COMPONENTS	58.3	7.9
FABRICATED METALS	47.8	7.0
FOOD PRODUCTS	75.0	5.0
HEALTH SERVICES	22.2	29.5
HOTELS AND OTHER LODGING PLACES	12.5	6.5
INSTRUMENTS	50.0	10.4
INSURANCE	16.7	7.9
MACHINERY	41.7	16.2
MANUFACTURING	47.4	9.3
OFFICE EQUIPMENT	18.8	18.3
PAPER AND ALLIED PRODUCTS	25.0	5.0
PHARMACEUTICALS	28.6	22.5
PRINTING AND PUBLISHING	15.8	15.3
REAL ESTATE	14.3	55.0
RETAIL	8.8	8.7
RUBBER/PLASTICS	66.7	10.5
TRANSPORTATION BY AIR	33.3	20.0
TRANSPORTATION EQUIPMENT	28.6	5.8
WHOLESALE (CONSUMER GOODS)	37.2	11.6
OVERALL	**26.0**	**12.1%**

GEOGRAPHIC BREAKOUTS

D ue to the extremely high participation level in this survey edition, we are again able to take a look at selected data for the nine major geographic regions that comprise the United States. Specific breakouts include the following regions and states:

New England Region
Connecticut
Maine
Massachusetts
New Hampshire
Rhode Island
Vermont

Mid-Atlantic Region
New Jersey
New York
Pennsylvania

East North Central Region
Illinois
Indiana
Michigan
Ohio
Wisconsin

West North Central Region
Iowa
Kansas
Minnesota
Missouri
Nebraska
North Dakota
South Dakota

South Atlantic Region
Delaware
Florida
Georgia
Maryland
North Carolina
South Carolina
Virginia
Washington, D.C.
West Virginia

East South Central Region
Alabama
Kentucky
Mississippi
Tennessee

West South Central Region
Arkansas
Louisiana
Oklahoma
Texas

Mountain States Region
Arizona
Colorado
Idaho
Montana
Nevada
New Mexico
Utah
Wyoming

Pacific States Region
Alaska
California
Hawaii
Oregon
Washington

Geographic data breakouts include percentage of companies anticipating higher senior salesperson earnings in 1999; percentage of companies anticipating lower senior salesperson earnings in 1999; average percent merit increase; total cash compensation for senior, intermediate, and entry-level salespeople; total cost of field expenses and benefits; percentage of companies paying the entire cost of the following expense items: home photocopier, home fax machine, car phone, laptop computer; length of training and cost of training for new hires; time spent on ongoing training and cost of training for experienced salespeople; degree of sales force effectiveness; women in the sales force; salesperson educational level; how salespeople spend their time — total work hours per week, total hours per week spent on selling activities, total hours per week spent selling face-to-face; number of calls to close a sale; number of sales calls per day; the changing size of sales forces; and salesperson turnover rates. This data is illustrated through the following graphics:

Regional Breakout for Figures 3 and 4 — Projected Salesperson Earnings*

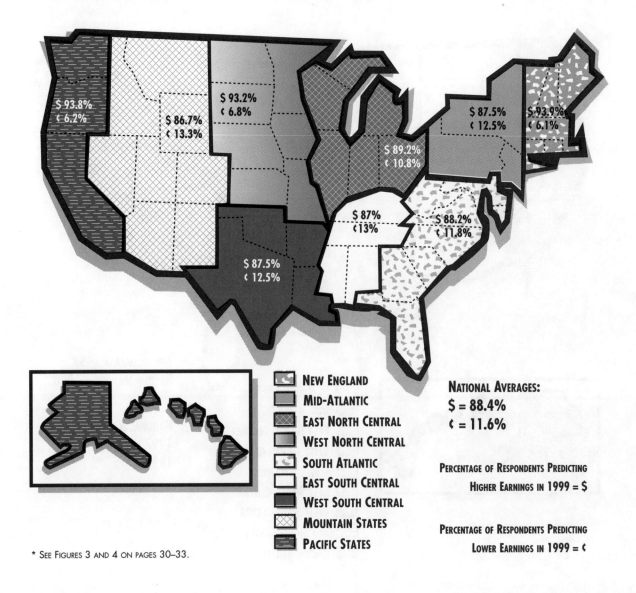

$ 93.8%
¢ 6.2%

$ 86.7%
¢ 13.3%

$ 93.2%
¢ 6.8%

$ 87.5%
¢ 12.5%

$ 93.9%
¢ 6.1%

$ 89.2%
¢ 10.8%

$ 87%
¢ 13%

$ 88.2%
¢ 11.8%

$ 87.5%
¢ 12.5%

New England
Mid-Atlantic
East North Central
West North Central
South Atlantic
East South Central
West South Central
Mountain States
Pacific States

National Averages:
$ = 88.4%
¢ = 11.6%

Percentage of Respondents Predicting
Higher Earnings in 1999 = $

Percentage of Respondents Predicting
Lower Earnings in 1999 = ¢

* See Figures 3 and 4 on pages 30–33.

REGIONAL BREAKOUT FOR FIGURE 5 — AVERAGE PERCENT MERIT INCREASE*

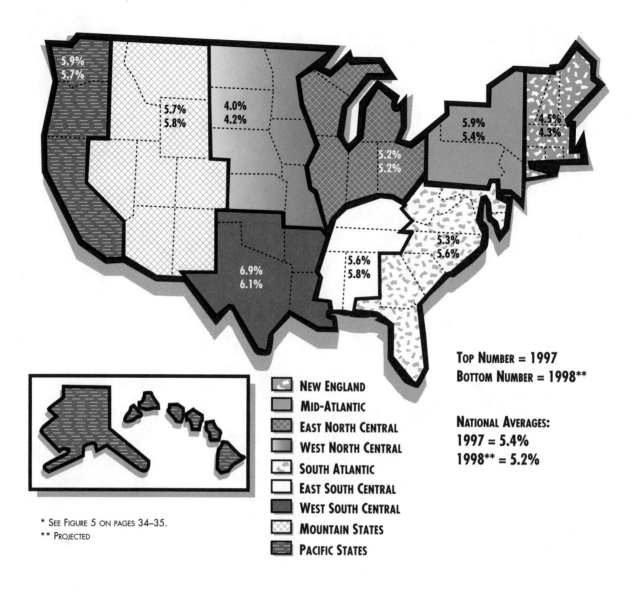

TOP NUMBER = 1997
BOTTOM NUMBER = 1998**

NATIONAL AVERAGES:
1997 = 5.4%
1998** = 5.2%

◻ NEW ENGLAND
◻ MID-ATLANTIC
◻ EAST NORTH CENTRAL
◻ WEST NORTH CENTRAL
◻ SOUTH ATLANTIC
◻ EAST SOUTH CENTRAL
◻ WEST SOUTH CENTRAL
◻ MOUNTAIN STATES
◻ PACIFIC STATES

* SEE FIGURE 5 ON PAGES 34–35.
** PROJECTED

REGIONAL BREAKOUT FOR FIGURES 14, 15, AND 16 — TOTAL CASH COMPENSATION*
(IN THOUSANDS OF DOLLARS — ALL PLANS COMBINED)

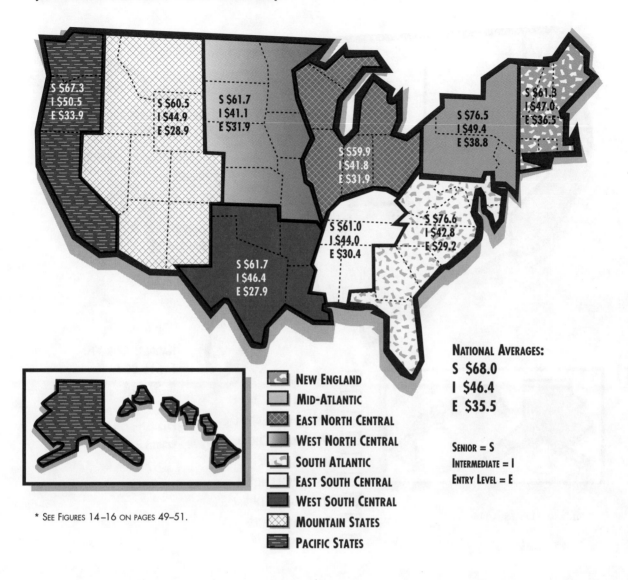

NATIONAL AVERAGES:
S $68.0
I $46.4
E $35.5

SENIOR = S
INTERMEDIATE = I
ENTRY LEVEL = E

Legend:
- NEW ENGLAND
- MID-ATLANTIC
- EAST NORTH CENTRAL
- WEST NORTH CENTRAL
- SOUTH ATLANTIC
- EAST SOUTH CENTRAL
- WEST SOUTH CENTRAL
- MOUNTAIN STATES
- PACIFIC STATES

Map values:
- S $67.3 / I $50.5 / E $33.9
- S $60.5 / I $44.9 / E $28.9
- S $61.7 / I $41.1 / E $31.9
- S $59.9 / I $41.8 / E $31.9
- S $76.5 / I $49.4 / E $38.8
- S $61.3 / I $47.0 / E $36.5
- S $61.0 / I $44.0 / E $30.4
- S $76.6 / I $42.8 / E $29.2
- S $61.7 / I $46.4 / E $27.9

* SEE FIGURES 14–16 ON PAGES 49–51.

REGIONAL BREAKOUT FOR FIGURE 71 — FIELD EXPENSES AND BENEFITS*

F $11,976
B $4,222

F $11,918
B $4,720

F $10,838
B $6,778

F $18,318
B $9,017

F $18,143
B $8,507

F $14,682
B $8,017

F $14,389
B $5,009

F $21,028
B $6,744

F $12,667
B $6,117

NEW ENGLAND
MID-ATLANTIC
EAST NORTH CENTRAL
WEST NORTH CENTRAL
SOUTH ATLANTIC
EAST SOUTH CENTRAL
WEST SOUTH CENTRAL
MOUNTAIN STATES
PACIFIC STATES

NATIONAL AVERAGES:
F $16,000
B $7,614

FIELD EXPENSES = F
BENEFITS = B

* SEE FIGURE 71 ON PAGES 118–119.

REGIONAL BREAKOUT FOR FIGURES 82, 83, 84, AND 85 — PERCENTAGE OF RESPONDING COMPANIES PAYING 100% OF FOLLOWING EXPENSE ITEMS*

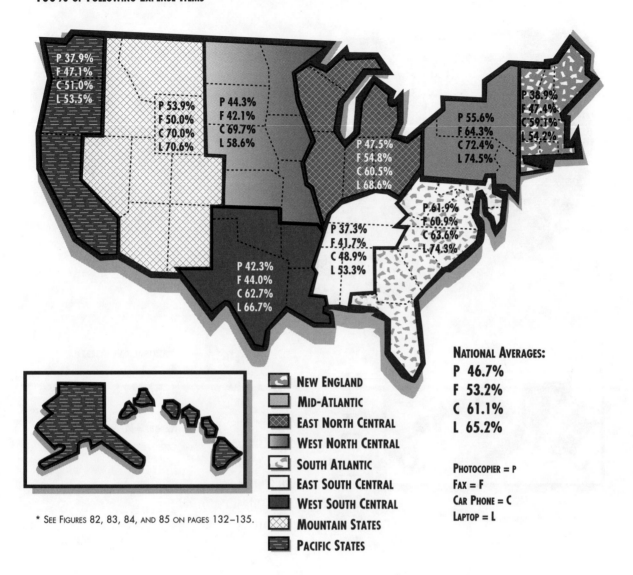

P 37.9%
F 47.1%
C 51.0%
L 53.5%

P 53.9%
F 50.0%
C 70.0%
L 70.6%

P 44.3%
F 42.1%
C 69.7%
L 58.6%

P 47.5%
F 54.8%
C 60.5%
L 68.6%

P 55.6%
F 64.3%
C 72.4%
L 74.5%

P 38.9%
F 47.4%
C 59.1%
L 54.2%

P 61.9%
F 60.9%
C 63.6%
L 74.3%

P 37.3%
F 41.7%
C 48.9%
L 53.3%

P 42.3%
F 44.0%
C 62.7%
L 66.7%

NEW ENGLAND
MID-ATLANTIC
EAST NORTH CENTRAL
WEST NORTH CENTRAL
SOUTH ATLANTIC
EAST SOUTH CENTRAL
WEST SOUTH CENTRAL
MOUNTAIN STATES
PACIFIC STATES

* SEE FIGURES 82, 83, 84, AND 85 ON PAGES 132–135.

NATIONAL AVERAGES:
P 46.7%
F 53.2%
C 61.1%
L 65.2%

PHOTOCOPIER = P
FAX = F
CAR PHONE = C
LAPTOP = L

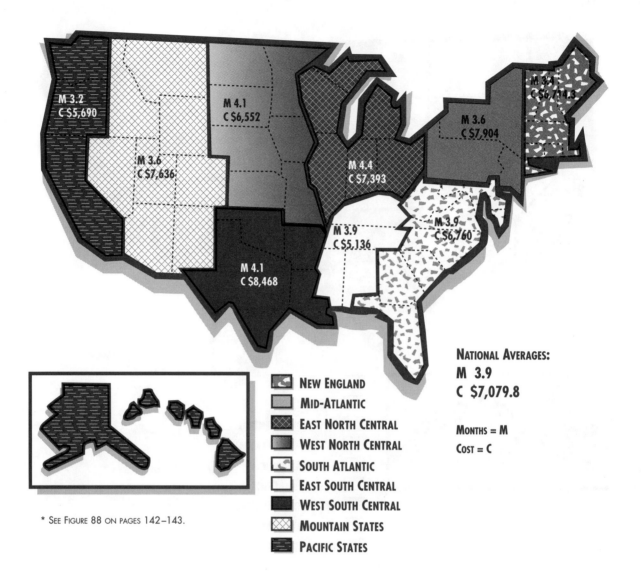

M 3.2
C $5,690

M 4.1
C $6,552

M 3.4
C $6,714.3

M 3.6
C $7,904

M 3.6
C $7,636

M 4.4
C $7,393

M 3.9
C $5,136

M 3.9
C $6,760

M 4.1
C $8,468

NATIONAL AVERAGES:
M 3.9
C $7,079.8

MONTHS = M
COST = C

NEW ENGLAND
MID-ATLANTIC
EAST NORTH CENTRAL
WEST NORTH CENTRAL
SOUTH ATLANTIC
EAST SOUTH CENTRAL
WEST SOUTH CENTRAL
MOUNTAIN STATES
PACIFIC STATES

* SEE FIGURE 88 ON PAGES 142–143.

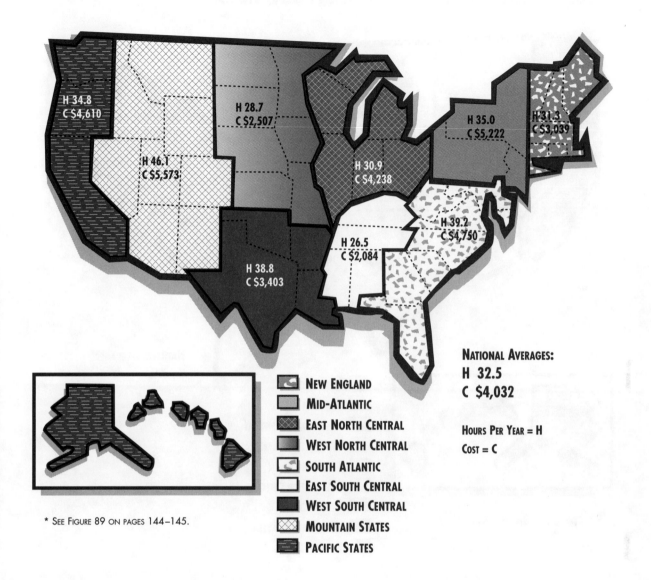

H 34.8
C $4,610

H 28.7
C $2,507

H 35.0
C $5,222

H 31.3
C $3,039

H 46.1
C $5,573

H 30.9
C $4,238

H 39.2
C $4,750

H 26.5
C $2,084

H 38.8
C $3,403

NATIONAL AVERAGES:
H 32.5
C $4,032

HOURS PER YEAR = H
COST = C

NEW ENGLAND
MID-ATLANTIC
EAST NORTH CENTRAL
WEST NORTH CENTRAL
SOUTH ATLANTIC
EAST SOUTH CENTRAL
WEST SOUTH CENTRAL
MOUNTAIN STATES
PACIFIC STATES

* SEE FIGURE 89 ON PAGES 144–145.

REGIONAL BREAKOUT FOR FIGURE 96 — DEGREE OF SALES FORCE EFFECTIVENESS*
PERCENTAGE OF FIRMS INDICATING THEIR SALES FORCE IS EFFECTIVE IN PERFORMING TASKS RATED IMPORTANT

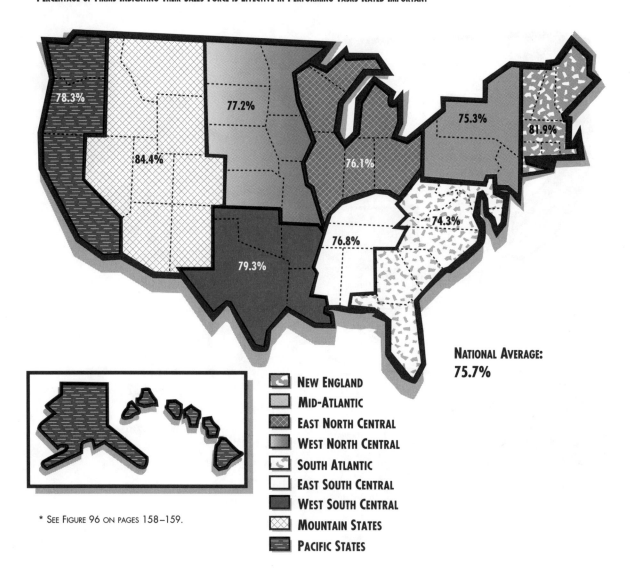

NATIONAL AVERAGE:
75.7%

🖻 NEW ENGLAND
□ MID-ATLANTIC
▨ EAST NORTH CENTRAL
▨ WEST NORTH CENTRAL
🖻 SOUTH ATLANTIC
□ EAST SOUTH CENTRAL
■ WEST SOUTH CENTRAL
▨ MOUNTAIN STATES
▨ PACIFIC STATES

* SEE FIGURE 96 ON PAGES 158–159.

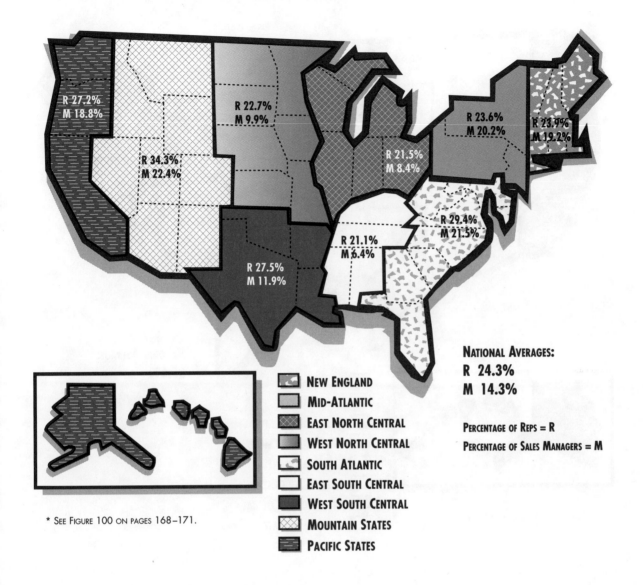

R 27.2%
M 18.8%

R 22.7%
M 9.9%

R 23.6%
M 20.2%

R 23.9%
M 19.2%

R 34.3%
M 22.4%

R 21.5%
M 8.4%

R 29.4%
M 21.5%

R 21.1%
M 6.4%

R 27.5%
M 11.9%

NATIONAL AVERAGES:
R 24.3%
M 14.3%

PERCENTAGE OF REPS = R
PERCENTAGE OF SALES MANAGERS = M

NEW ENGLAND
MID-ATLANTIC
EAST NORTH CENTRAL
WEST NORTH CENTRAL
SOUTH ATLANTIC
EAST SOUTH CENTRAL
WEST SOUTH CENTRAL
MOUNTAIN STATES
PACIFIC STATES

* SEE FIGURE 100 ON PAGES 168–171.

REGIONAL BREAKOUT FOR FIGURE 101 — EDUCATION LEVEL: PERCENTAGE OF SALESPEOPLE WHO HAVE A COLLEGE DEGREE*

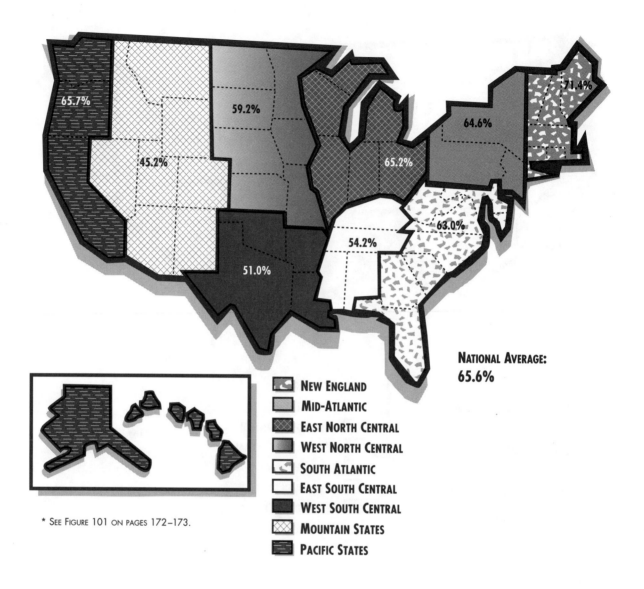

NATIONAL AVERAGE:
65.6%

- NEW ENGLAND
- MID-ATLANTIC
- EAST NORTH CENTRAL
- WEST NORTH CENTRAL
- SOUTH ATLANTIC
- EAST SOUTH CENTRAL
- WEST SOUTH CENTRAL
- MOUNTAIN STATES
- PACIFIC STATES

* SEE FIGURE 101 ON PAGES 172–173.

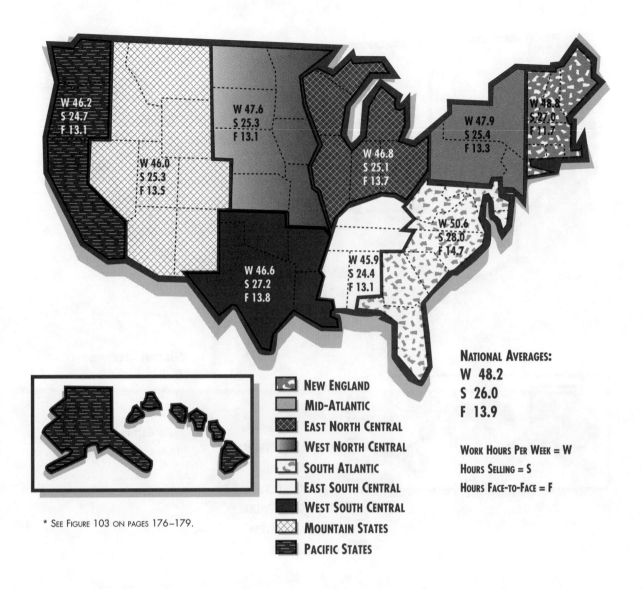

W 46.2
S 24.7
F 13.1

W 46.0
S 25.3
F 13.5

W 47.6
S 25.3
F 13.1

W 46.8
S 25.1
F 13.7

W 47.9
S 25.4
F 13.3

W 48.8
S 27.0
F 11.7

W 50.6
S 28.0
F 14.7

W 46.6
S 27.2
F 13.8

W 45.9
S 24.4
F 13.1

NATIONAL AVERAGES:
W 48.2
S 26.0
F 13.9

WORK HOURS PER WEEK = W
HOURS SELLING = S
HOURS FACE-TO-FACE = F

- NEW ENGLAND
- MID-ATLANTIC
- EAST NORTH CENTRAL
- WEST NORTH CENTRAL
- SOUTH ATLANTIC
- EAST SOUTH CENTRAL
- WEST SOUTH CENTRAL
- MOUNTAIN STATES
- PACIFIC STATES

* SEE FIGURE 103 ON PAGES 176–179.

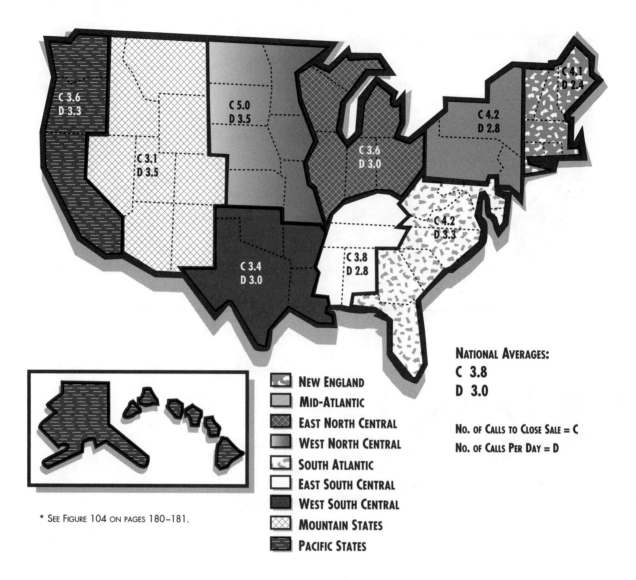

C 3.6
D 3.3

C 5.0
D 3.5

C 4.2
D 2.8

C 4.1
D 2.4

C 3.6
D 3.0

C 3.1
D 3.5

C 4.2
D 3.3

C 3.4
D 3.0

C 3.8
D 2.8

NATIONAL AVERAGES:
C 3.8
D 3.0

NO. OF CALLS TO CLOSE SALE = C
NO. OF CALLS PER DAY = D

NEW ENGLAND
MID-ATLANTIC
EAST NORTH CENTRAL
WEST NORTH CENTRAL
SOUTH ATLANTIC
EAST SOUTH CENTRAL
WEST SOUTH CENTRAL
MOUNTAIN STATES
PACIFIC STATES

* SEE FIGURE 104 ON PAGES 180–181.

REGIONAL BREAKOUT FOR FIGURE 105 — SALES FORCE SIZE*

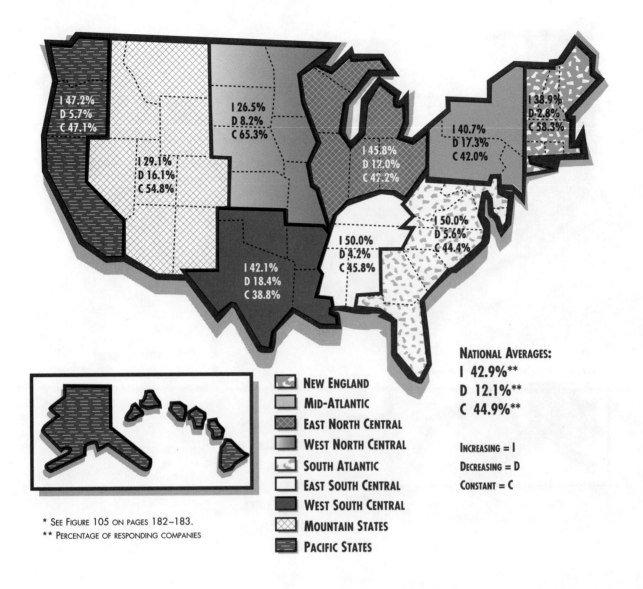

I 47.2%
D 5.7%
C 47.1%

I 26.5%
D 8.2%
C 65.3%

I 29.1%
D 16.1%
C 54.8%

I 45.8%
D 12.0%
C 42.2%

I 40.7%
D 17.3%
C 42.0%

I 38.9%
D 2.8%
C 58.3%

I 42.1%
D 18.4%
C 38.8%

I 50.0%
D 4.2%
C 45.8%

I 50.0%
D 5.6%
C 44.4%

NEW ENGLAND
MID-ATLANTIC
EAST NORTH CENTRAL
WEST NORTH CENTRAL
SOUTH ATLANTIC
EAST SOUTH CENTRAL
WEST SOUTH CENTRAL
MOUNTAIN STATES
PACIFIC STATES

NATIONAL AVERAGES:
I 42.9%**
D 12.1%**
C 44.9%**

INCREASING = I
DECREASING = D
CONSTANT = C

* SEE FIGURE 105 ON PAGES 182–183.
** PERCENTAGE OF RESPONDING COMPANIES

REGIONAL BREAKOUT FOR FIGURE 106 — SALES FORCE TURNOVER*

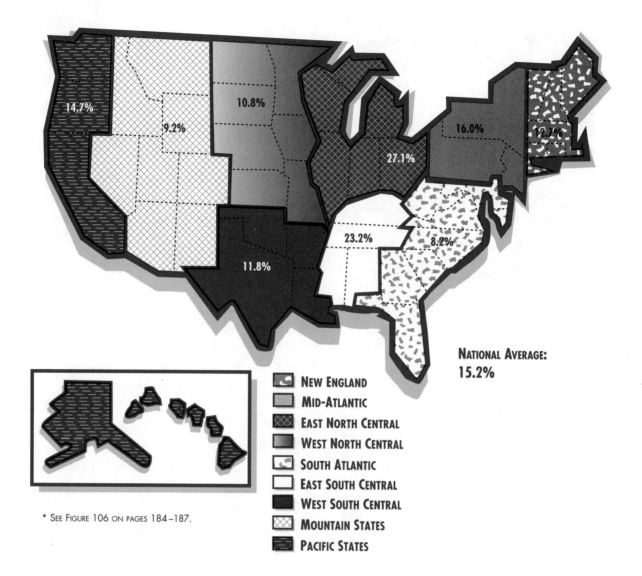

14.7%

10.8%

9.2%

16.0%

12.7%

27.1%

23.2%

8.2%

11.8%

NATIONAL AVERAGE:
15.2%

* SEE FIGURE 106 ON PAGES 184–187.

- **NEW ENGLAND**
- **MID-ATLANTIC**
- **EAST NORTH CENTRAL**
- **WEST NORTH CENTRAL**
- **SOUTH ATLANTIC**
- **EAST SOUTH CENTRAL**
- **WEST SOUTH CENTRAL**
- **MOUNTAIN STATES**
- **PACIFIC STATES**

PART THREE — WRAP-UP

A LOOK AHEAD

A new world of selling is upon us. Certainly, technology is having a profound impact — not only on how salespeople sell, but also on how buyers buy. Another powerful factor is the realization by most salespeople that relationship building is much more successful than strong-arm sales tactics. Today, there is a renewed emphasis on improving basic communication skills, becoming a resource to customers, and trying to treat each customer as an individual.

What does tomorrow look like for today's salespeople? Throughout this survey, we have focused on the "sales management" side of the selling equation. In this section, we give salespeople a chance to speak and tell us what's on their minds. You'll find that what they have to tell us is informative, enlightening, and instructive.

To gather the data for this section, The Dartnell Corporation stepped up its traditional survey efforts. Over the past year and a half, we surveyed thousands of salespeople in a wide variety of industries. We gathered their candid comments and observations on a dozen pertinent sales issues. Some of the areas we explored are places we'd visited in the past. In those cases, we present our previous data along with our current findings. Other topics are new and, to the best of our knowledge, have not been previously explored in-depth. What we found was thought-provoking and, in many cases, surprising.

Here are the questions we posed:

1. ARE YOU USING THE INTERNET IN ANY WAY AS A SALES TOOL?
2. HAS TECHNOLOGY *SIMPLIFIED* OR *COMPLICATED* YOUR WORK?
3. WAS YOUR SALES VOLUME HIGHER IN 1997 THAN IN 1996? HOW MUCH HIGHER — OR LOWER?
4. ON AVERAGE, HOW MANY HOURS DO YOU WORK A WEEK? HOW MANY OF THESE HOURS ARE SPENT FACE-TO-FACE WITH PROSPECTS OR CUSTOMERS?
5. DO YOU REGULARLY ACHIEVE YOUR YEARLY QUOTA?
6. DO YOU THINK YOUR COMPENSATION PLAN IS FAIR?
7. AT THE PRESENT TIME, DO YOU FEEL YOU ARE PAID FAIRLY, UNDERPAID, OR OVERPAID?
8. WOULD MORE COMPENSATION MAKE YOU MORE PRODUCTIVE?
9. HOW WOULD YOU RANK THE FOLLOWING NONFINANCIAL INCENTIVES IN TERMS OF EFFECTIVENESS: FACE-TO-FACE RECOGNITION; AWARDS/PLAQUES; MENTION IN COMPANY NEWSLETTER; ENTERTAINMENT/DINNER/SPORTS TICKETS; TRIPS; MERCHANDISE?
10. IN YOUR OPINION, IS SELLING GETTING TOUGHER — OR EASIER?
11. HAVE YOU SEEN DISHONESTY IN THE FIELD?
12. HOW DO YOU RESPOND WHEN A COMPETITOR USES DISHONEST TACTICS TO SELL?
13. WHAT TYPES OF DISHONESTY DO YOU SEE IN YOUR BUSINESS LIFE?

1. ARE SALESPEOPLE USING THE INTERNET IN ANY WAY AS A SALES TOOL?

Salespeople's use of the Internet is exploding! Two years ago, just 18.8 percent of salespeople said they were using the Internet as a sales tool. In a just-completed follow-up survey, a whopping 61.3 percent of salespeople say they are now "connected." This is a 226 percent increase in a relatively short time.

Although this growth is dramatic, it is hardly surprising. As we noted in our 1996 survey: "As more and more companies make Internet access available to their salespeople, we can expect to see the number of salespeople using this technology to increase rapidly. Based on the candid comments of respondents, explosive growth in this area can be expected."

What are reps using the Internet for? The biggest draw is still e-mail. But reps are becoming more familiar with this technology and adding Internet skills to their selling repertoire.

The most sophisticated reps are using the Internet to:
- Gather background information on prospects and competition to aid in pre- and post-call planning.
- Keep track of the competition by monitoring their websites.
- Research industries and specific companies in target markets.
- Read about sales and marketing issues.
- Exchange technical information through newsgroups and forums.

SALESPEOPLE USING THE INTERNET

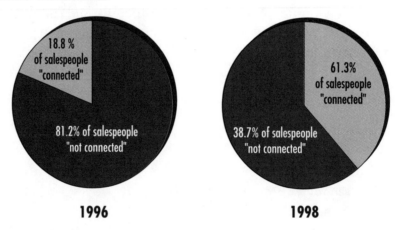

1996   1998

SOURCE: DARTNELL RESEARCH

2. HAS TECHNOLOGY *SIMPLIFIED* OR *COMPLICATED* THE SALES JOB?

Three out of four salespeople (75.3%) say technology has simplified their work. A major reason: Technology enables reps to accomplish more in less time. Our new data is consistent with survey results collected two years ago, when 81.4 percent of reps gave technology a big "thumbs-up."

Technology has **simplified** *selling.*

Salespeople who say technology has simplified selling tell us it is freeing them from nonselling activities. This means they have more time to spend in front of prospects and customers. Written comments from our survey respondents indicate that salespeople:
- **Feel more organized.** Computers store all pertinent information in one central location. Answers to customer inquiries are more readily available. Not as much information has to be committed to memory.
- **Have less paperwork to do.** Computers speed up repetitive tasks formerly done manually. They take the drudgery out of writing call reports, placing orders, billing customers, entering and transferring data, and compiling facts and figures.

- **Communicate better.** Computers help reps write better-sounding, more customized sales letters and create more effective mailings. Sophisticated promotional materials and ads can be designed on the computer. E-mail, fax machines, beepers, and cellular phones put reps in constant contact with customers.
- **Feel more confident.** Because computers make everything from price quotes to billing statements more accurate, sales reps feel more confident in their work. Says one respondent: "It's more efficient and faster. I can get more done in less time and know that my work is correct."
- **Make better decisions.** Better, more complete information leads to decisions that are more informed, timely, and creative. Says one respondent: "Our company databases give me much more detailed information much faster. Standard procedures require less time. Versatility aids problem solving."
- **Find new customers more effectively.** Technology makes it easier to track sales and identify what market segments they come from, and also to track hot prospects. Computers narrow prospect lists and help reps target certain potential customers, thus minimizing time wasted on low-potential prospecting. Because less time is spent writing orders and making price quotes, reps can spend more time prospecting and planning sales strategies. Says one rep: "I use e-mail for faster communications, access computerized databases, and use the Internet for prospecting. I also use broadcast faxing."
- **Are more successful on sales calls.** With laptop computers, reps can "take their office with them" and have instant access to information and computer programs that help them make the sale. Examples: product catalogs with easy-to-find information on product offerings, options, and accessories; polished, easy-to-modify sales presentations shown via desktop projectors; and up-to-the-minute inventory information.

Technology has **complicated** *selling.*

Salespeople who say technology has complicated selling are frustrated by a variety of problems. Written comments indicate that our respondents:

- **Have trouble coping with malfunctioning equipment.** Respondents say buggy software, problematic integration of equipment, and the use of equipment and software that aren't well-matched create additional stress.

HOW SALESPEOPLE SAY TECHNOLOGY AFFECTS THEIR WORK

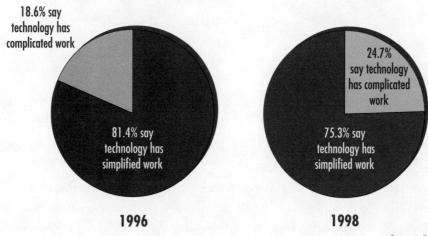

18.6% say technology has complicated work

81.4% say technology has simplified work

1996

24.7% say technology has complicated work

75.3% say technology has simplified work

1998

SOURCE: DARTNELL RESEARCH

- **Find the learning curve steep.** Says one salesperson: "It takes hours, days, weeks, and sometimes months to get a computer program up and running." Says another: "I spend selling time trying to learn software programs."
- **See a negative impact on the selling process.** Some sample remarks: "File cabinets never 'went down'"; "Simple tasks should be done simply"; "Some chores are now easier, but more chores get created. And, because of downtime, program error, etc., the equation shifts to technology making things more complicated."

But most respondents agree that whether you love the new technology or hate it, you have to live with it. As one respondent says: "Anything new is complicated until it is thoroughly understood. At that point, it usually simplifies work."

3. Did salespeople sell more or less in 1997 than in 1996? How much more — and how much less?

There's good news on the sales productivity front! According to our latest data, 91.8 percent of salespeople say they sold more in 1997 than they sold in 1996. Just 8.2 percent say they sold less. The median increase in sales volume: 25.6 percent. The median decrease: 16.2 percent.

In a similar survey two years ago, 81.6 percent of respondents told us they sold more in 1995 than in 1994. Just 18.4 percent said they sold less over that time period. The median increase in sales volume: 15 percent. The median decrease: 10 percent.

The trend is clear: More salespeople are cashing in on the economic boom and selling significantly more than they were just a few short years ago.

Salespeople Reporting Productivity Gains

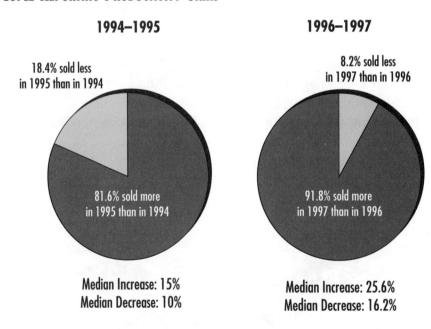

1994–1995

18.4% sold less
in 1995 than in 1994

81.6% sold more
in 1995 than in 1994

Median Increase: 15%
Median Decrease: 10%

1996–1997

8.2% sold less
in 1997 than in 1996

91.8% sold more
in 1997 than in 1996

Median Increase: 25.6%
Median Decrease: 16.2%

Source: Dartnell Research

4. On average, how many hours do salespeople work a week? How many of those hours are spent face-to-face with prospects or customers?

Our major survey asks sales managers these questions about their reps (see Figure 103 in Section 10). We thought it only fair to ask salespeople the same questions. If you think salespeople are working longer, you're right. But they're also spending less time in front of prospects and customers. Here's the data: Salespeople say they work

55.5 hours a week and spend 15.4 of those hours (about 27.7%) in front of prospects and customers.

Two years ago, salespeople said they worked 50.9 hours a week and spent 17.3 percent of those hours (about 34%) in front of prospects and customers. The bottom line: Salespeople are putting in 9 percent more time on the job, yet spending 15 percent less time in front of buyers.

One explanation: Technology is enabling reps to "work at a distance" and service their customer bases efficiently in lieu of face-to-face calls. If this is the case, one caution is in order: Reps should be careful not to neglect the personal touch. Although technology may make it easier and more efficient to serve customers at a distance, it is no substitute for face-to-face calls when it comes to assessing a customer's changing needs.

THE NUMBER OF HOURS SALESPEOPLE SAY THEY WORK PER WEEK

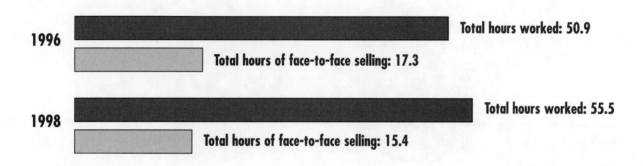

1996 Total hours worked: 50.9
Total hours of face-to-face selling: 17.3

1998 Total hours worked: 55.5
Total hours of face-to-face selling: 15.4

SOURCE: DARTNELL RESEARCH

5. HOW REGULARLY DO SALESPEOPLE ACHIEVE THEIR YEARLY QUOTA?

The vast majority of salespeople responding to our survey say they always (39.3%) or almost always (55.6%) meet quota. Just 5.1 percent of salespeople say they seldom meet quota.

SALESPEOPLE WHO ALWAYS, ALMOST ALWAYS, AND SELDOM MEET QUOTA

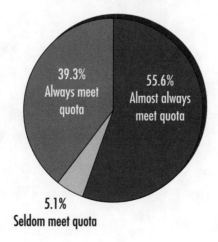

39.3%
Always meet quota

55.6%
Almost always meet quota

5.1%
Seldom meet quota

SOURCE: DARTNELL RESEARCH

6. Do salespeople think their sales compensation plan is fair?

Nearly 80 percent of salespeople say their compensation plan is fair. That's the good news. The bad news: Almost 41 percent of saleswomen report their plan is unfair compared with 21.5 percent of the men responding to our survey.

We also took at look at the perceived fairness of compensation plans by type. The surprising finding? A large percentage of sales reps surveyed perceive a commission-only compensation plan to be the most fair. Coming out on the bottom are salary-only plans. A key finding: Significantly more women than men are on a salary-only plan. This helps explain why more women than men thought their compensation plan was unfair. The graphics below tell the story.

How Salesmen and Saleswomen Rate Their Compensation Plan

Source: Dartnell Research

The Perceived Fairness of 3 Basic Compensation Plans

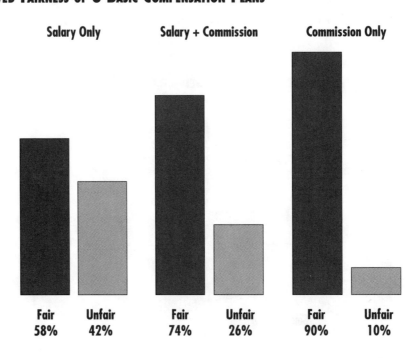

Source: Dartnell Research

7. Do salespeople feel they are paid fairly, underpaid, or overpaid?

The answer may surprise you. A little background: Two years ago, we asked if salespeople were satisfied or dissatisfied with their earnings. The results: 52.7 percent said they were *dissatisfied* with their earnings. However, on close analysis of what these reps said, it became clear that satisfaction meant complacency. These reps made it clear that, although their earnings may currently be satisfactory, they expected to earn more in the future. So, although we received strong evidence that money is a yardstick by which success, career growth, personal growth, and self-esteem are all measured, we didn't answer the question we intended. Which brings us to this year's question of fair pay.

If you think the majority of salespeople believe they're underpaid, you're wrong! In our latest survey, 62.8 percent of responding reps say they're paid fairly. Less than 40 percent (36.1%) of reps say they're underpaid. Only 1.1 percent of the reps admit they're overpaid.

Here's the key to understanding this data: Comp plans that do a good job of linking pay to performance are likely to be perceived as fair by reps. Conversely, comp plans that appear arbitrary and do not clearly link pay to performance are likely to be perceived as unfair by reps.

The following typical comments from survey respondents help make this clear:

Reps who say they are paid fairly:

- "I determine my own pay. The more I sell, the more I make."
- "I'm happy with my steady growth and performance."
- "The more productive I am, the more I am compensated."
- "My compensation is based on what I do."
- "My pay is based on production."

Reps who say they are underpaid:

- "For the job I have, and all the responsibilities I take care of, I should be compensated more."
- "A different compensation package based on what is accomplished would be much better."
- "Recent changes in sales commission reduce the reward for long hours of hard work and effort."
- "Being paid in relation to what I do would improve my attitude."
- "The current compensation plan distracts me from my work."

SALESPEOPLE WHO SAY THEY ARE PAID FAIRLY, UNDERPAID, OR OVERPAID

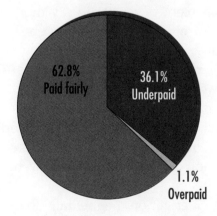

62.8%
Paid fairly

36.1%
Underpaid

1.1%
Overpaid

SOURCE: DARTNELL RESEARCH

Does your sales compensation plan create a strong link between pay and performance? If it doesn't, your reps may regard your plan as unfair and believe they're underpaid. In looking at the data in Question No. 6, the commission-only plan clearly links pay to performance and is regarded as the fairest plan by the reps in our survey. The message is clear: How you design and administer the incentive portion of your compensation plan can mean the difference between satisfied and disgruntled salespeople, regardless of pay level.

8. DO SALESPEOPLE THINK MORE COMPENSATION WOULD MAKE THEM MORE PRODUCTIVE?

Our respondents are almost evenly split on this issue. More than half (52.5%) of the salespeople responding to our survey say more compensation would not make them more productive. The prevailing reason: Salespeople say they are already working at top capacity and are unable to do more, regardless of an increase in pay.

Reps who say they wouldn't be more productive:
- "I can't work any harder."
- "I work as hard as I can, regardless of pay."
- "You can only do so much every day."
- "I try to be as productive as I can, compensation or not."
- "I am working to the best of my ability now. When the company shows significant profit, I will ask for a bonus."
- "I am a self-motivated person, doing the best I can."
- "I love what I do and give 110 percent always."

This is good news for sales managers: Many of your reps are satisfied, self-motivated, hardworking individuals. But they're working at top capacity. If that's the case, where are increases in sales volume going to come from? Here are the areas to take a look at: better targeting of high-volume accounts, better time management, and better working habits of existing salespeople. And let's not forget about increasing the sales staff as another possible option.

A key finding here is that the majority of salespeople already have enough — or too much — on their plates. Adding more to an already heavy load could result in demoralization and a deterioration in current productivity levels. Remember: Pay isn't always the answer to increasing productivity. As one rep says: "More pay probably wouldn't make me more productive, but it would make me happier."

Certainly, having happy reps is important. But it's also important that our compensation plan helps achieve the goals of the company. (See Section 13 for a discussion of how to align your sales compensation plan with your business plan.)

But what about the 47.5 percent of reps who say more compensation *would* make them more productive? Here are some of their comments:

Reps who say they would be more productive:
- "If compensation were paid for stretch goals — going above projected revenues — I would work harder."
- "I could spend less time on money-related problems."
- "The more money I get, the harder I feel I should work."
- "It would help settle a lot of cash problems. I could concentrate more on work."
- "A different compensation package with added incentives would definitely make me more productive."
- "I think it would make it easier on me mentally to justify the hours and stress. I think I would accomplish more."

Our respondents fall into two categories: Those who believe they are underpaid and those who say they would respond to a better incentive program. Sales managers who think their salespeople are holding back should ask themselves two questions: (1) "Are my salespeople being paid fairly compared with other salespeople in my industry?" (2) "Does my sales compensation plan provide the opportunity for salespeople to *earn* substantially more for *doing* substantially more?"

You can use the data in this survey to help you answer the first question. A careful look at your compensation plan, in conjunction with candid discussions with your salespeople, will help you answer the second question.

SALESPEOPLE WHO SAY MORE COMPENSATION WOULD OR WOULD NOT MAKE THEM MORE PRODUCTIVE

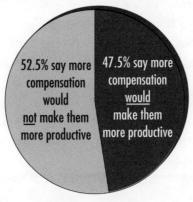

52.5% say more compensation would **not** make them more productive

47.5% say more compensation **would** make them more productive

SOURCE: DARTNELL RESEARCH

9. HOW DO SALESPEOPLE RANK THE FOLLOWING NONFINANCIAL INCENTIVES IN TERMS OF EFFECTIVENESS: FACE-TO-FACE RECOGNITION; AWARDS/PLAQUES; MENTION IN COMPANY NEWSLETTER; ENTERTAINMENT/DINNER/SPORTS TICKETS; TRIPS; MERCHANDISE?

We asked reps to rank a variety of popular nonfinancial incentives according to what would motivate them to do more. How do their choices compare with what you're offering your reps?

Here's how reps ranked six popular nonfinancial incentives:

1. Trips
2. Face-to-face recognition
3. Entertainment/dinner/sports tickets
4. Merchandise
5. Awards/plaques
6. Mention in company newsletter

The point is this: If your nonfinancial incentives focus on giving your reps awards and mentioning their accomplishments in the company newsletter, you may not be giving them the incentives they respond to best.

10. DO SALESPEOPLE THINK SELLING IS GETTING TOUGHER — OR EASIER?

We thought there might be a chance, given the strides in technology, that salespeople would tell us selling was actually getting easier. No way! Nearly 80 percent (79.7%) of salespeople responding to our survey say selling is definitely getting tougher.

The top two reasons: competition and better-educated buyers. Somewhat surprisingly, many reps told us technology was actually making selling tougher in some instances. Here's what the reps had to say:

Increased competition:
- "If we develop a new advantage, our competition is soon to follow."
- "More competition, more options for the customer."
- "The competition is getting as smart as we are."
- "Increased competition causing price wars."
- "Foreign competition; ease of transportation from one part of the world to another."
- "More competition. We need to add value."
- "More and better competition is driving prices down."
- "Everyone is making similar products, so you must promote value-added extras."

More knowledgeable buyers:
- "Customers are becoming better educated and even taking on my service as their own!"
- "Purchasing people are much more astute."
- "Customers are wiser and sometimes not eager."
- "Purchasing managers have become much smarter."
- "Customer standards are higher, and they want it at the lowest price."
- "More sophisticated customers who have little loyalty."

Technology adding to difficulty:
- "More and more customers are using voice mail to screen calls."
- "Ease of communication makes gathering information easier. Sales reps are not the resource they were in the past."
- "Technology has increased competition from remote sources and increased price competition."
- "Technology has given the customer more information and more sources of prices."
- "Telemarketing has changed our ability to get in front of customers."
- "Internet pricing has made it much more difficult in our industry. Buyers are getting too much info on cost and too little info on product."
- "Technology has given everyone access to the same information. This has taken away some competitive advantage."

Although all indications are that selling will continue to get tougher, one in five of the salespeople responding to our survey say selling is getting easier. Here are selected comments that are typical of this group:
- "I'm learning better selling tactics."
- "The more I sell, the better I get. The better I get, the easier selling is."
- "I feel it's getting easier, probably because I'm learning."
- "I'm new and learning, so it's easier as I learn the ropes."
- "As I age, I have more confidence and better contacts."
- "Learning 'the ropes' makes it smoother."

These salespeople present a strong case for continued training and personal development. Stronger competition, the increasing numbers of knowledgeable buyers, and the influx of technology are factors largely beyond our control. But we can give our salespeople the knowledge and experience they need to compete effectively in the 21st century. Sales managers who want to increase the effectiveness of their sales forces should make increased training a top priority.

SALESPEOPLE WHO SAY SELLING IS GETTING TOUGHER

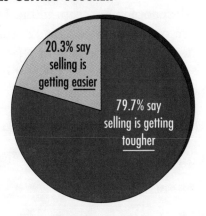

20.3% say selling is getting <u>easier</u>

79.7% say selling is getting <u>tougher</u>

SOURCE: DARTNELL RESEARCH

11. DO SALESPEOPLE SEE DISHONESTY IN THE FIELD?

Although the salespeople responding to our survey say that they themselves are completely honest, 95 percent of these respondents admit that they have seen dishonesty in the field.

SALESPEOPLE WHO SAY THEY HAVE SEEN UNETHICAL BEHAVIOR IN THE FIELD

5% say they do not see unethical behavior in the field

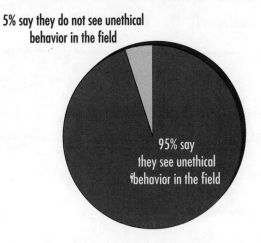

95% say they see unethical behavior in the field

SOURCE: DARTNELL RESEARCH

12. How do salespeople respond when a competitor uses dishonest tactics to sell?

Nearly half (40.1%) of the salespeople who see unethical behavior in the field discuss the situation with the customer. Another 30 percent (29.3%) discuss the situation with their manager and the customer. But just 2 percent of reps say they confront or discuss the matter with the offending salesperson. And 8 percent of the reps do nothing.

How Salespeople Respond When They See Dishonesty in the Field

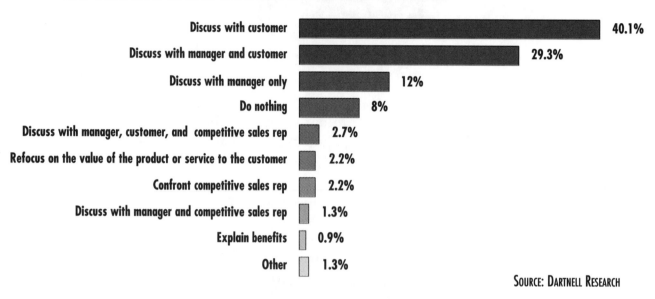

Discuss with customer	40.1%
Discuss with manager and customer	29.3%
Discuss with manager only	12%
Do nothing	8%
Discuss with manager, customer, and competitive sales rep	2.7%
Refocus on the value of the product or service to the customer	2.2%
Confront competitive sales rep	2.2%
Discuss with manager and competitive sales rep	1.3%
Explain benefits	0.9%
Other	1.3%

SOURCE: DARTNELL RESEARCH

13. What types of dishonesty do salespeople see in the business world?

The salespeople in our study say the dishonest tactics they see are varied and range from dishonesty in competitors to dishonesty in customers.

Here's a random sampling of the dishonest tactics reported:

Dishonest tactics of competitive reps:
- "False claims, unrealistic end results."
- "Misquoting of prices."
- "Spreading rumors about our company."
- "Promising what can't be delivered."
- "Product misrepresentation."
- "Price gouging."
- "Misrepresenting standard delivery times."
- "Not disclosing all charges."
- "Illegal discounts as determined by law."
- "Use of used parts."
- "Cutting corners to drive price down."

Dishonest tactics of customers:

Competitive salespeople aren't the only source of dishonesty. Customers are dishonest, too, reps tell us. Some of these unethical practices include:
- "Customers not paying their bills."
- "Customers writing 'insufficient funds' checks."
- "Buyers giving away pricing to get lower prices from competition."
- "Customers lying on credit applications."
- "Customers not living up to their agreements."

- "Customers returning items damaged by them but saying otherwise."

If your salespeople have been disturbed by the dishonest tactics of competitors, suggest that they:

1. Keep an eye on selected accounts for signs of trouble, such as missed deliveries, shipment of partial orders, or delivery of defective goods. Unhappy customers are often an excellent source of this information.
2. Keep up-to-date on the changing needs and requirements of the account.
3. Be ready to step in with a solution when the competitive rep falls into disfavor. Broken promises result in broken relationships. Your reps should position themselves as an alternative supplier by keeping the buyer fully informed of your company's capabilities.

Impress upon your salespeople that dishonesty will not lead to establishing long-term business relationships with their customers. And it is only by establishing long-term business relationships that they will achieve long-term success.

RELATIONSHIP BUILDING

The importance reps place on relationship building was highlighted in the previous edition of the survey. Two years ago, we asked more than 1,000 salespeople what they thought was the biggest new trend in selling.

"Customer-focused strategies" and "technology issues" were the two hot spots that emerged. Nearly 40 percent (36.4%) of reps told us that "customer-focused strategies" were the newest trend. Included in that category were the following subcategories, followed by the percentage of reps identifying it: customer service / service (11.2%); value-added selling (4.2%); consultative selling (4%); partnering (3.6%); solution selling (3.1%); relationship selling (3%); relationship building (2.7%); follow-up / follow-through (2.4%); and honesty (2.2%).

More than one-fourth (26.9%) told us "technology" was the trend worth watching. All responses were nonprompted. Follow-up research for this edition makes it clear that relationship building and technology are still the hot issues and will undoubtedly continue to dominate the world of selling.

OTHER TRENDS

As noted, new technologies will continue to improve sales force productivity. But there will be increasing reliance on individual effort, too. Companies will continue to become more selective in hiring only the best-qualified applicants. (See Figure 99, Section 9, for hard data that supports this trend.)

Those individuals just entering the selling profession will have to come up to speed quickly. Companies, more than ever before, realize that they can no longer afford to keep marginal salespeople on the payroll. Inadequate sales representation in any territory can no longer be tolerated as competitive pressures to maximize territory penetration mount.

For sales veterans and those just entering the selling profession, the future presents many challenges — and opportunities. Those who are able to meet those challenges head-on will prosper in the years ahead.

A Look to the Future

The basics will still be important. Salespeople will need to be highly proficient in planning, prospecting, qualifying, presenting, demonstrating, getting agreement, negotiating, closing, and following up.

But these skills alone will not be enough. As mentioned in previous editions of this survey, true top performers will have to know how to be able to:

• **Gather information.** Buyers are increasingly unreceptive to salespeople who say things like, "Tell me something about your business." Buyers expect salespeople to have done prior research on their companies in preparation for presenting solutions to problems. Buyers have no time to waste on salespeople who haven't thoroughly prepared for the sales call. The Internet is already helping reps gather the information they need to conduct this research.

• **Explore customer problems.** There are often many solutions to a problem. Salespeople who offer the first solution they think of without understanding the problem thoroughly will miss the boat. Often a particular customer problem is the outward manifestation of a more serious problem lurking just beneath the surface. Salespeople who uncover the entire picture will be in a position to offer a total solution — not just a stopgap remedy.

• **Build rapport.** The best product at the best price used to be a winning combination. Today's buyers, faced with the increasing complexity of their businesses, now put equal, if not more, weight on the honesty and integrity of the salesperson and the company he or she represents. All things being equal, buyers will more readily do business with salespeople they like and trust. Salespeople who want to succeed in the years ahead will have to add people skills to their arsenal of selling skills and product knowledge.

• **Build customer relationships.** Salespeople will need to spend more time developing relationships with buyers. This will require being in touch on a regular basis — even when there is no likelihood of a sale being made. Salespeople who only call on buyers in order to sell them something will, more often than not, find the door closed. Salespeople who develop true consultative relationships with their customers, on the other hand, will find these customers eager to see them — and eager to accept their solutions to problems. Again, reps will need to be careful that technology does not get in the way of establishing personal one-on-one relationships.

• **Get the customer to participate in the sales presentation.** The most successful salespeople in the years ahead will be those who actively involve their customers in the selling process. The sales presentation will become a two-way dialogue, with the salesperson and the buyer working together to find a solution to a particular problem. Buyers who participate in solving their own problems are more likely to accept the solutions.

Are today's salespeople up to the challenge? Based on the encouraging results presented in this survey, we can only conclude that the future looks very bright, indeed.

ALIGNING YOUR COMPENSATION PLAN WITH YOUR BUSINESS PLAN

All too often, we regard the sales compensation plan as an *expense item to be justified*. Enlightened managers regard the sales compensation plan as a *tool to increase profits*. These managers understand that a well-designed compensation plan can spell the difference between spectacular and so-so company performance.

In this section, we'll take a look at some of the basics of business planning and compensation-plan design so that you, too, can get the most out of your compensation plan in the future.

First, a little background: We at Dartnell often receive phone calls from excited sales executives who want to know what's wrong with their compensation plans — and how to fix them. A typical scenario: Due to declining margins and market share, management has cut base salaries, reduced the commission structure, eliminated bonuses, or taken some other action that has demoralized the sales force.

Faced with serious morale and productivity problems, management is now looking for a quick fix. A one-time quarterly bonus is sometimes seen as a stopgap solution. But how much should the bonus be? Five percent? Ten percent? Fifteen percent? Who knows? And who really knows if this is the route the company should take? The point is: One can't make reasonable compensation suggestions without taking a long look at a company's business plan and financial performance.

Let's hope you avoid the grim scenario of our hypothetical company above. One way to do that is to work through a chart similar to the one on the following page. The chart for your company will differ from ours in some respects, but the basic principles will remain the same. This chart puts the variables you're responsible for in front of you:

ANALYZE AND ASK WHY

The chart enables you to look at all the variables that will affect your results. It gives you perspective on what you might change to optimize volume growth, market share, and total profit for your company.

Here's an important point: Only when you have all the variables in front of you will you be able to ask why profit margins are so low for a particular product in particular territories. When you fill out the chart, you'll notice that some salespeople with very similar territories and sales environments are selling much more or much less of the same product than their peers. You'll also notice the same products bring different margins in different territories.

From a sales production standpoint, your analysis will enable you to put different amounts of sales pressure on different combinations of products and sales territories. This will enable you to focus more sales expense dollars and effort on those product and territory combinations that provide the most attractive combination of sales growth and profit growth.

By performing this analysis, you should be able to notice profit problems and be able to work on sales practices that affect margins. These sales practices could include such things as selling the wrong products to the wrong customer segment, granting

PRODUCT A

	LAST YEAR			NEXT YEAR			LAST YEAR	NEXT YEAR	LAST YEAR	NEXT YEAR
	Gross Profit Per Unit	No. of Units	Total Profit	Gross Profit Per Unit	No. of Units	Total Profit	Sales Expense	Sales Expense	Advertising, Promotion, and Expenses	Advertising, Promotion, and Expenses
Territory No. 1										
Territory No. 2										
Territory No. 3										
Territory No. 4										

PRODUCT B

	LAST YEAR			NEXT YEAR			LAST YEAR	NEXT YEAR	LAST YEAR	NEXT YEAR
	Gross Profit Per Unit	No. of Units	Total Profit	Gross Profit Per Unit	No. of Units	Total Profit	Sales Expense	Sales Expense	Advertising, Promotion, and Expenses	Advertising, Promotion, and Expenses
Territory No. 1										
Territory No. 2										
Territory No. 3										
Territory No. 4										

PRODUCT C

	LAST YEAR			NEXT YEAR			LAST YEAR	NEXT YEAR	LAST YEAR	NEXT YEAR
	Gross Profit Per Unit	No. of Units	Total Profit	Gross Profit Per Unit	No. of Units	Total Profit	Sales Expense	Sales Expense	Advertising, Promotion, and Expenses	Advertising, Promotion, and Expenses
Territory No. 1										
Territory No. 2										
Territory No. 3										
Territory No. 4										

PRODUCT D

	LAST YEAR			NEXT YEAR			LAST YEAR	NEXT YEAR	LAST YEAR	NEXT YEAR
	Gross Profit Per Unit	No. of Units	Total Profit	Gross Profit Per Unit	No. of Units	Total Profit	Sales Expense	Sales Expense	Advertising, Promotion, and Expenses	Advertising, Promotion, and Expenses
Territory No. 1										
Territory No. 2										
Territory No. 3										
Territory No. 4										
Grand Total	N/A	___	___	N/A	___	___	___	___	___	___

discounts rather than selling added value, and giving customers other extras. The aim is to increase gross profit margins on previously low-profit products.

A Different Perspective

Now, let's look at the process from a different perspective. For the moment, pretend you're the sales manager of a hypothetical company that realistically expects to make about $12 million in sales and make a gross profit of approximately $3.5 million in the coming year.

Although the company has a detailed version of the business plan, the short version looks something like this:

CORPORATE BUSINESS PLAN
(SHORT VERSION)

	PRODUCT A			PRODUCT B			PRODUCT C		
	No. of UNITS	REVENUE	GROSS PROFIT %	No. of UNITS	REVENUE	GROSS PROFIT %	No. of UNITS	REVENUE	GROSS PROFIT %
SEGMENT I	300,000	$3 MILLION	50%	500,000	$3 MILLION	30%	700,000	$2.8 MILLION	20%
SEGMENT II	100,000	$800,000	40%	200,000	$1 MILLION	20%	400,000	$1.2 MILLION	10%
SEGMENT III	20,000	$140,000	30%	40,000	$120,000	10%	50,000	$100,000	5%

The short form of the business plan for any company is really a chart showing:
- The product line of the company;
- The various classes of customers or market segments they serve;
- The number of units of each product they anticipate selling to each segment;
- The amount of revenue to be produced; and
- The amount of gross profit produced by each of the combinations of segments and products.

The company's accountant or vice president of finance looks most closely at the revenue and gross profit produced by customer and product combinations in the business plan. He or she focuses on the following kind of detail in the corporate business plan:

CUSTOMER/PRODUCT COMBINATION	REVENUE	GROSS PROFIT
SEGMENT I, PRODUCT A	$3 MILLION	$1.5 MILLION
SEGMENT II, PRODUCT A	$800,000	$320,000
SEGMENT III, PRODUCT A	$140,000	$ 42,000
SEGMENT I, PRODUCT B	$3 MILLION	$900,000
SEGMENT II, PRODUCT B	$1 MILLION	$200,000
SEGMENT III, PRODUCT B	$120,000	$ 12,000
SEGMENT I, PRODUCT C	$2.8 MILLION	$400,000
SEGMENT II, PRODUCT C	$1.2 MILLION	$120,000
SEGMENT III, PRODUCT C	$100,000	$5,000
TOTALS:	**$12,160,000**	**$ 3,499,000**

Now, what happens if the sales force produces only $1 million in sales through the combination of Product A being sold to Segment I? Instead of the planned $3 million in revenue and $1.5 million in gross profit, the company receives $1 million in revenue and $500,000 in profit. We just went from being a $12 million-volume company making $3.5 million in profit to a company with $10 million in sales and a $2.5 million profit.

SALES MANAGEMENT'S ROLE

Sales management has the responsibility to not accept merely total revenue and gross profit figures as their "quota" for the year. Neither should sales management accept a quota only in terms of the number of units or amount of revenue without understanding how it fits into the corporate business plan or financial plan.

Sales management must work back and forth with general management and financial management to determine realistic revenue and unit sales goals. And, they must determine the combination of customer segments and products that will produce a chart like the one on the previous page — a chart that makes clear where the volume and profit come from to achieve the overall corporate plan.

Often, when the sales force does not achieve the corporate business plan, general management discovers that the sales force was selling more Product C to Segment III than was expected. The sales force also sold much less Product A to Segment I than was expected.

If you look at the incentives for sales management and the sales force in these situations, you usually discover a critical error: The desirability of certain types of customers and certain products has not been recognized in the incentive plan for sales production. In other words, the corporate business plan and the sales plan were not aligned.

In our hypothetical company, the business plan calls for $12,160,000 in annual sales, producing $3,499,000 in profit, or an average gross profit of 29 percent. In this case, the sales manager should have been an active participant in producing the corporate business plan. He or she should have looked at the combination of customer segments and products, making certain that it was realistic to sell 300,000 units of Product A in Segment I, for example.

An incentive plan designed to pay sales management for making the corporate business plan come true might look something like this:

SALES MANAGEMENT INCENTIVE

GROSS MARGIN

		5%	10%	20%	25%	30%	35%	40%
VOLUME	1%	0	$500	$1,000	$1,500	$2,000	$2,500	$3,000
INCREASE	3%	$500	$1,000	$1,500	$2,000	$2,500	$3,000	$3,500
OVER	5%	$1,000	$1,500	$2,000	$2,500	$3,000	$3,500	$4,000
LAST	8%	$2,000	$2,500	$3,500	$4,500	$5,500	$6,500	$7,500
YEAR	12%	$3,000	$5,000	$7,000	$9,000	$11,000	$13,000	$15,000
	16%	$4,000	$7,000	$10,000	$12,000	$15,000	$17,000	$20,000
	20%	$5,000	$9,000	$12,000	$15,000	$18,000	$20,000	$25,000
	25%	$6,000	$12,000	$15,000	$18,000	$20,000	$25,000	$30,000
	30%	$7,000	$14,000	$18,000	$20,000	$25,000	$30,000	$35,000
	35%	$8,000	$16,000	$21,000	$25,000	$32,000	$37,000	$42,000
	40%	$9,000	$18,000	$22,000	$30,000	$34,000	$45,000	$50,000
	50%	$1,000	$20,000	$27,000	$32,000	$37,000	$50,000	$60,000

If our hypothetical company is in a growing industry and has been experiencing good growth, the $12 million revenue and $3.5 million profit are probably necessary just to maintain last year's market share.

Let's assume that's the case and that it would take a 30 or 35 percent increase in volume over the previous year to substantially increase the market share of this company in its industry. Let's also say that the "going rate" for sales managers in this industry is in the range of $50,000 to $60,000 base and $75,000 to $80,000 total earnings. You should be satisfied that you're getting a fair shake from the corporation if you attain a 20 percent volume increase and a 30 percent profit for the company. This would add $18,000 in incentive bonus to our $60,000 base salary to make the corporate business plan of $12 million in sales and $3.5 million in profit come true.

You also should be motivated by this plan to increase volume over the previous year by 30 to 35 percent and increase the average profit margin to 35 to 40 percent by exceeding quota in the most profitable product and customer segment combinations.

THE SALES FORCE

Most companies pay the sales force too much commission for the sale of low-profit products to low-margin customer segments and not enough commission for the sale of high-profit products to the high-margin customer segments. Sales management must fine-tune the commission and bonus schedule to make the corporate business plan a reality. Of course, quotas set by customer and product combination, rather than just total dollar volume, are necessary.

In order for sales management to make or exceed quota and maximize their own income, they would adjust the incentive plan for the sales force to look something like the chart below:

SALES FORCE INCENTIVE

CUSTOMER CLASSIFICATION

PRODUCT	SEGMENT I	SEGMENT II	SEGMENT III
A	150%	120%	70%
PRODUCT B	120%	100%	50%
PRODUCT C	75%	50%	25%

These charts are provided as examples only. But you can use these concepts to look at your own situation and align the efforts of each member of your sales force with the business objectives and financial plan of the corporation.

COMPENSATION PAY BASICS

CEOs of start-up companies or individuals thinking about hiring their first salesperson will want to pay particular attention to the following discussion. It's critical for you to have a clear idea of what sales representation you can and can't afford. We'll work through the math one step at a time.

Let's say that right now you're making a net profit of $180,000 on $600,000 in sales. If you were to hire a salesperson who cost you $50,000 a year in compensation and expenses, and there was no increase in sales volume, you would reduce your net profit to $130,000. What you need to do, of course, is increase sales volume to more than cover your risk — the risk of committing the extra expense of hiring a salesperson.

Here's how to look at the problem: If you need to sell 100,000 units at $6 each to net $180,000, then your margin is 30 percent. That is, you make 30 cents on each dollar of total revenue. (Thirty percent of $600,000 in revenue equals $180,000.)

Now, how many more units do you need to sell "to break even," or cover your additional expense ($50,000) of hiring a salesperson? To break even on your risk, you'll need to make a new net profit of $230,000 (your original net profit of $180,000 plus the $50,000 cost of hiring a salesperson).

Here's the math: At 30 percent margin, you need $166,667 more in sales for a new total sales volume of $766,667. (Thirty percent of $166,667 equals $50,000 — the amount of new revenue needed to generate an additional $50,000 in profit.) This translates into 27,778 more units that you need to sell ($166,667 in new revenue needed divided by a unit cost of $6 equals 27,778 units). Therefore, if you add $50,000 in additional expenses, you need to sell a new total of 127,778 units, or nearly 28 percent more (old unit volume of 100,000 plus 27,778 new units to be sold). This means you need a sales volume increase of nearly 28 percent just to break even or generate the same amount of net profit.

Now consider this: If your $50,000 salesperson can generate a 50 percent increase in sales to $900,000, or 150,000 units at $6 each and 30 percent profit per unit, net profit climbs to $220,000 — approximately a 22 percent increase in profit.

Now that you understand this concept, work on it with your accountant. Remember to also recognize any other expenses that increase with volume to get to the real new net profit. As you review your compensation plan, keep in mind these principles that your plan should address.

PRINCIPAL OBJECTIVES OF A SALES COMPENSATION PLAN

1. To be consistent with marketing objectives
2. To increase sales
3. To increase gross profit
4. To have sales expenses decline as a percent of sales and gross profit dollars as sales volume increases
5. To have company salespeople's total compensation relatively consistent with competition's total compensation (Use the survey data in this book to help you determine this)
6. To minimize turnover of salespeople
7. To alleviate seasonal influences on salespeople's income flow
8. To alleviate cyclical influences on salespeople's income flow
9. To maintain the relationship between the income of the salespeople and other company personnel
10. To provide equal treatment (not necessarily the same compensation levels) of all salespeople in various markets, territories, and/or branches
11. To provide continuous motivation for salespeople to:
    - Maximize sales with existing accounts
    - Maximize gross margin with existing accounts

- Open new accounts
12. To make it easy for management to:
    - Understand the plan
    - Hire salespeople
    - Add and/or subtract products from the line
    - Realign existing territories and create new ones
    - Reassign accounts
    - Control salespeople's cost in relation to sales and gross profit
    - Control travel and entertainment expenses
    - Calculate compensation levels and administer
13. To make it easy for salespeople to:
    - Understand the plan
    - Estimate incentive earnings per order, month, etc.
    - Maintain a positive attitude toward increasing sales in their territories
    - Maintain a positive attitude toward increasing gross profit in their territories
    - Maintain a positive attitude toward the company
14. To maintain existing compensation levels at existing sales and gross profit levels
15. To provide a mathematical formula for calculating incentive payments
16. To have incentive payments include a commission
17. To have incentive payments include a bonus
18. To have salespeople sell a "balanced line"
19. To generally have the salespeople increase their market penetration in order to earn more money

In a nutshell, you want your compensation plan to:
- Support your business plan
- Attain company goals
- Motivate salespeople
- Retain top performers
- Attract top performers

Is this too tall an order for most companies? Far from it, according to data from the previous edition of this survey. Two years ago, we asked more than 200 companies of all sizes how well their compensation plans supported these criteria. Here are the results of that survey:

SUPPORTS BUSINESS PLAN

RESPONSES	PERCENT OF RESPONSES
COMPENSATION PLAN SUPPORTS BUSINESS PLAN	73.4%
COMPENSATION PLAN DOES NOT SUPPORT BUSINESS PLAN	26.6
TOTAL	100%

ATTAINS COMPANY GOALS

RESPONSES	PERCENT OF RESPONSES
VERY EFFECTIVE	20.8%
EFFECTIVE	46.5
SOMEWHAT EFFECTIVE	25.0
NOT EFFECTIVE	4.9
NOT SURE	0.7
NO ANSWER	2.1
TOTAL	100%

MOTIVATES SALESPEOPLE

RESPONSES	PERCENT OF RESPONSES
VERY EFFECTIVE	22.2%
EFFECTIVE	47.9
SOMEWHAT EFFECTIVE	22.2
NOT EFFECTIVE	4.2
NOT SURE	1.4
NO ANSWER	2.1
TOTAL	100%

RETAINS TOP PERFORMERS

RESPONSES	PERCENT OF RESPONSES
VERY EFFECTIVE	31.9%
EFFECTIVE	36.1
SOMEWHAT EFFECTIVE	22.9
NOT EFFECTIVE	6.3
NOT SURE	0.7
NO ANSWER	2.1
TOTAL	100%

ATTRACTS QUALIFIED SALESPEOPLE

RESPONSES	PERCENT OF RESPONSES
VERY EFFECTIVE	15.3%
EFFECTIVE	35.4
SOMEWHAT EFFECTIVE	36.8
NOT EFFECTIVE	8.3
NOT SURE	0.7
NO ANSWER	3.5
TOTAL	100%

When you combine the totals for "very effective" and "effective," it is easy to see how well these companies are meeting the challenge of designing effective compensation plans. Does your plan stack up as well?

Now that you understand some of the mechanics, we'll take a look at how some forward-thinking companies are using their comp plans to boost profits. Section 14 presents selected case histories to help you see how modifications to the comp plan can make a big difference in company performance.

TRENDS IN SALES COMPENSATION: WHAT ENLIGHTENED COMPANIES ARE DOING TO BOOST PERFORMANCE

A s we noted earlier, there is no one right way to design a compensation plan. And we'll go one step further: It is impossible to design a perfect compensation plan. The best you can hope for is a plan that works well under a specific set of conditions. As those conditions change, so should your compensation plan.

To help you see how compensation plans boost performance, we've included 12 case histories. They will give you ideas for adjusting your pay plan to make it more effective.

CASE HISTORY NO. 1: BLUE CROSS & BLUE SHIELD OF MASSACHUSETTS, BOSTON

Overview: *How a comp plan redesign, with a new emphasis on incentives, boosted company revenue.*

Blue Cross & Blue Shield of Massachusetts (Boston) had operated somewhat traditionally in its marketplace. "We were not particularly aggressive when it came to acquiring new sales," says Patrick Hughes, senior vice president of sales and marketing. The sales comp plan reflected this traditional approach: It was approximately 60 percent base and 40 percent incentive, and in some instances was 70 percent base and 30 percent incentive.

As growth began to suffer, management realized it needed to become more aggressive in its sales activity. One of the key elements of the new strategy was a redesign of the sales comp plan. "We considered a number of things in designing the new plan," says Hughes. Three of the most important sources of information were the sales executives themselves, other companies, and the salespeople.

"In designing the plan, we remembered what made us run as salespeople," says Hughes. "I 'carried a bag' and came up through the ranks, and I remembered what I liked and didn't like about certain compensation plans." The team also surveyed and talked with executives at other service companies to see what worked and what didn't for them in their sales comp plans. "We also held focus groups with the salespeople to get input from them and get their ideas for the new plan," Hughes adds.

The resulting plan shifted compensation from 60 percent base and 40 percent incentive to 40 percent base and 60 percent incentive. It also added quarterly "kickers" (additional incentive compensation if a salesperson exceeded the goal in any given quarter, even if he or she missed the goal in any one of the months of the quarter). "This way, salespeople who hit two out of three months but missed the third could still qualify for the quarterly incentive if their total for the quarter exceeded the goal," he says.

At first, a number of salespeople felt the plan represented a "serious takeaway," but such attitudes did not last long for the majority of salespeople. "We scheduled a number of pre-position meetings before rolling the program out to explain how it would work and some of the benefits it would offer," says Hughes. "Most salespeople who 'did the math' quickly saw that there was significantly more upside potential to this plan than to the old one."

In addition, the salespeople also began to feel a sense of ownership of the plan. They saw some of their ideas actually being put to use, such as the quarterly "kicker" feature. "They saw it as everyone's plan, not management's plan," says Hughes.

Has the plan achieved its goal? It's definitely headed in the right direction. "In 1996, we lost $100 million," says Hughes. "In 1997, the year we implemented the new plan, we turned that around completely and earned $12 million. We still have a way to go, but we are definitely headed in the right direction."

CASE HISTORY NO. 2: ENTERGY SERVICES, INC., BEAUMONT, TEXAS

Overview: *How a fresh look at incentives gave this sales force a new desire to succeed.*

Before you create any sales incentive or bonus program, you have to know what it is you actually want to accomplish. "Whatever you incent, salespeople will do, so be sure you incent what you want them to accomplish. This may seem like a no-brainer, but you can't look back in six months and wonder why salespeople focused on certain things and why you ended up with the results you did," says David Morrison, director of business accounts for Entergy Services, Inc., in Beaumont, Texas.

To be successful with the sales incentive program, you need to provide salespeople with six elements:

1. Tell them *what* you want to accomplish.
2. Explain to them *why* you want to accomplish this. (This adds meaning to what the salespeople are doing.)
3. Announce what the incentive will be for accomplishing the goal.
4. Provide them with the appropriate work environment that will allow them to accomplish the goals.
5. Give them the tools and resources they need to meet the goals.
6. Issue feedback along the way to let them know how they're performing in relation to the goal.

Entergy schedules quarterly and annual incentive contests. The prize might be something like a $3,000 trip to Cancún, Mexico. "It's not a lot of money, but the recognition the salesperson receives for winning often means a lot more than the cost of the vacation itself," Morrison says.

The idea of changing the goal every quarter helps keep the salespeople fresh. An added plus: As the sales people begin performing the activities that achieve success in one area, they tend to develop them into long-term good habits, which then accumulate over time.

Waiting until the last minute to announce a new contest is another way to encourage salespeople to use all of their good habits. "Salespeople really can't all of a sudden shift gears one day and hope to be successful for a three-month contest," says Morrison. "They have to be off to a running start by the time the contest begins. They know that they have to be doing all of the right things all of the time." Announcing a contest at the last minute also discourages salespeople from "holding back" sales until contests are announced, because they won't know whether such sales will necessarily help them in the next contest.

Examples of some of the quarterly goals Entergy has set recently for its salespeople:
- Most sales volume
- Most profit margin

- Most market share increase
- Teamwork
- Customer satisfaction (Entergy uses a third-party firm to survey customers on their level of satisfaction with the company, including the role that salespeople play.)

You can use incentive compensation to increase sales and sales performance in other ways, too. For example: Don't forget nonsales employees. A few years ago, Entergy created the Employee Selling Program. It encouraged employees from all departments to look for sales opportunities and either make the sales themselves or refer them to the sales department. Participating employees received cash bonuses or points that could be used to purchase products from a catalog.

One engineer became so enthusiastic about the program, he began working evenings to look for sales opportunities. He earned more than $7,000 in bonus compensation the first year and eventually transferred to the sales department. "He has been selling for us now for seven years and has been very successful," says Morrison.

Case History No. 3: International Data Corporation, Iselin, New Jersey

Overview: *How a traditional pay plan was changed to accommodate rapid growth.*

International Data Corporation (Iselin, New Jersey) used a sales compensation program for approximately a decade. The plan paid salespeople on a percentage of the business they brought in: 3 percent for the company's mainline subscription service product and 2 percent for everything else.

The program has become outmoded for a number of reasons:

- **Rapid growth.** "When the program was introduced, we were a $40 million company," says Don Best, group vice president of sales. "Two years ago, we were at $70 million, and we are now a $120 million company."
- **A shift in the company's marketing strategy.** "We wanted to enter new markets," continues Best. "This would involve shifting from geographic-based sales teams to industry-based sales teams."
- **A change in strategy.** The company wanted to move some of its best salespeople to new sales markets. "Most of the revenue we received was from the annual subscription services," says Best. "The longer the salespeople held onto these accounts, the more annuities they received each year. They were making very good money off the installed base without having to generate any new sales. Because we wanted to move these really talented people to new sales markets without any 'legacy accounts' or installed base, we needed to find a way to compensate them for making this move."

The company set a new strategy, one that would require a restructuring of the sales comp program: "We wanted to control spiraling sales compensation costs that were not getting us any new incremental business," says Best.

There are several components to the new plan:

- **Professional "levels" or "bands" were created within the sales department.** "We had different sales titles, but these really didn't mean much," he says. "The new levels we created were actually 'compensation bands.'" There are five bands, based primarily on years of experience, but also on competencies in selling and overall value to the organization.
- **The company uncoupled the idea of having compensation tied to revenue.** Instead, it designed compensation around the bands. For example: The company might set a goal for salespeople in a certain band to have a target compensation

of $100,000, which was the average amount they were already making. "Whether they had $1 million or $10 million in installed base, the compensation changed from the percentage of dollars booked to a percentage of the new plan accomplished," notes Best. If salespeople reached 10 percent of their total plan in a month, they received 10 percent of their total annual incentive compensation ($10,000). "Again, it doesn't matter if they are in a new market with a $2 million quota or a legacy market with a $5 million quota," he says. "They still receive the same percentage and amount for equivalent performance."

In short, the program now compensates salespeople on what they do, not on how long they have been with the company. "This has helped to retain our good people *and* attract new good people," Best states.

- **The company leveled the playing field for "individual contributors."** Under the old program, salespeople who moved into management positions received part of their compensation based on the performance of the salespeople reporting to them. "This penalized the top-performing salespeople," he says. "It also led to some salespeople seeking managerial positions for the wrong reason — compensation only."

The new structure offers a dual career track with comparable compensation, whether one chooses to move into management or remain in direct sales.

- **The company added an "end-of-year accelerator."** "For every 1 percent a salesperson achieves over 100 percent of plan, there is a 2 percent incentive," says Best. For example, if a salesperson reaches 120 percent of goal, he or she receives 140 percent of original targeted compensation.

- **Compensation periods were shifted from quarters to trimesters.** Under the old program, salespeople who reached their first quarter goals received a special bonus. This presented a problem because the first quarter extended from October 1 through December 31. Even though many customers began their holiday vacations around the middle of December, salespeople often called them at home or at vacation lodges to generate the extra sales required to meet the December 31 quarter end.

To solve this problem, the company created trimesters, with the first trimester ending January 31.

The results: Most of these changes were implemented in late 1996. "To date, we have seen increased bookings of about 20 percent," says Best. "We have also seen a voluntary retention of salespeople of about 90 percent, which indicates that the salespeople consider the new plan to be fair and competitive. In fact, we continue to be able to recruit successfully from our competitors."

CASE HISTORY No. 4: AMERICAN SPEEDY PRINTING CENTERS, INC., TROY, MICHIGAN

Overview: *How a focus on base salary and incentive keeps this sales force focused on long-term sales.*

Until recent years, American Speedy Printing Centers, Inc. (Troy, Michigan) focused its efforts on recruiting and hiring salespeople who already had experience in the printing industry. "Our salespeople would work much the same way as other salespeople in the industry did," says Steve White, director of sales and marketing. "They would go 'up and down the street' and ask prospects for the opportunity to quote and bid."

All that has changed. "Our goal now is to change the way printing is sold in the industry," states White. "We want our salespeople to build long-term relationships with clients. We want them to do more consultative selling."

When hiring salespeople, White now looks for people who have a conviction about the sales profession and are interested in building long-term relationships. "If they seem to be transaction-oriented, and if all of their stories are about how they persuaded customers to make purchases, even though they weren't in the customers' best interests, it raises a red flag," he says.

What is the best way to compensate a sales force like this? "We provide a mix of base salary and commission," replies White. "Each franchise has the ability to 'tweak' the mix locally, based on what works best in its market."

The majority of the compensation comes from the business the salespeople have with their existing accounts. "Because we want to focus on building solid, long-term relationships, we don't want to offer straight commission," he says. "In addition, because it takes awhile to build business with accounts—especially larger accounts—salespeople need the salary to tide them over for a period of time."

This isn't to say that the company completely ignores incentives. "We do occasionally have some incentive contests, but our focus is on base salary and commission," White concludes.

CASE HISTORY NO. 5: STATES INDUSTRIES, INC., EUGENE, OREGON

Overview: *How a comp plan was redesigned to reflect a commitment to partnerships.*

For years, the sales compensation plan at States Industries, Inc., in Eugene, Oregon, had focused on volume. "It didn't matter what you sold, just as long as you sold a lot of it," says Rick Montoya, sales manager. "We paid quarterly incentives based on volume numbers and volume increases."

In 1997, the company shifted its overall strategy from being just a company that sold wood to a specialty company designed to meet the specific needs of certain types of customers. "We redesigned the compensation plan to support this goal," says Montoya. "We began to incentivize salespeople based on sales in three specialty product areas."

Now, Montoya is considering another shift in the plan—one that will support the company's commitment to developing long-term partnershiplike arrangements with major customers. Rather than paying on "today's results," the new plan will focus on paying for today's activities that will lead to tomorrow's results. "We want to incent salespeople not so much on sales volume, but on the activities they engage in to help build and manage customer relationships," he says.

The plan is designed to get salespeople thinking a different way—long-term. "In order to reach volume goals, salespeople tend to take the path of least resistance," he says. "There is a tendency to abandon good practices that are designed to reach long-term goals. Salespeople tend to fall back on the 'dial-and-smile' approach, then lower price as much as they have to to make a sale."

The new program will be designed to reward behaviors that lead to long-term results, as well as some immediate results. The current program rewards immediate results. "The plan will encourage salespeople to engage in strategic planning, stay on top of customers, go the extra mile with these customers, develop new relationships within customer organizations, and so on," Montoya says. "For example, the plan might encourage a salesperson to take the time to schedule an extra product knowledge seminar for customers."

The expected results? "If salespeople engage in the right activities, they should eventually get the best results," says Montoya. "Then, when things get tough in the marketplace, we will be the ones to maintain our market share, rather than our competitors."

Case History No. 6: American Cyanamid Agricultural Products, Parsippany, New Jersey

Overview: *How veteran salespeople are rewarded and encouraged to continue to develop as professionals.*

American Cyanamid Agricultural Products (Parsippany, New Jersey) has a number of successful, productive veteran salespeople. "We have always been committed to helping them continue to develop as professionals and continually challenge them beyond their routine sales functions," says Nick Ariemma, director of sales training. The company wants to find ways to provide these exceptional long-term professionals with appropriate compensation, new professional development opportunities, and recognition for their continuous cycle of success.

One way to compensate and recognize successful veterans is to move them into sales management. However, not all successful salespeople want to move into management. Second, often the best salespeople make the worst sales managers.

American Cyanamid bestows a special honor on its most successful senior sales representatives — the status of Master Rep. Only about 10 percent of the company's 400 salespeople achieve that level at any one time. "Criteria for Master Rep status are very stringent," says Ariemma. "These are veteran salespeople who have shown consistent success over the years and have received strong performance appraisals. They are, in fact, some of the highest-performing people in the industry." Each year, management selects no more than two or three new Master Reps.

Master Reps receive a salary increase upon being selected for the honor. It is based on a six-level salary scale:

- Sales Rep (two salary levels)
- Senior Rep (two salary levels)
- Master Rep (two salary levels)

In addition, Master Reps have the opportunity to:

- Attend a special three-day annual meeting. This meeting has a focus on professional development and leadership. Each meeting has a different theme and includes a presentation by an expert in that area. For example:
  - **Communication improvement.** This includes strategies for on-the-job use, as well as strategies to use in one's personal life.
  - **Financial consultation.** This includes information on how to manage sales bonuses and stock options, plan for retirement, fund a college education, manage tax issues, and so on.
- **Training in mentoring skills.** "We then pair them up with sales trainees," continues Ariemma. The increased salaries Master Reps receive include payment for their responsibilities as mentors.
- **Leadership opportunities.** Master Reps attend a two-day training program that outlines leadership roles they can assume in the sales department without being directly involved in management. Again, the leadership functions they assume are compensated through their increased salaries.

"In an industry where sales turnover is rampant, and where a lot of companies are rightsizing and downsizing, we are able to continue to grow with our most talented and experienced salespeople," observes Ariemma. "Our Master Reps have a lot of 'tribal elder' knowledge that is invaluable to the rest of our sales force."

Without the Master Rep status and the compensation and other benefits that go with it, the company would likely lose some of its most successful long-term reps who are, obviously, among the company's greatest assets.

CASE HISTORY NO. 7: SONITROL CORPORATION, ALEXANDRIA, VIRGINIA

Overview: *How restructuring both the sales force and the compensation plan helped this company better serve new and existing customers.*

Sonitrol Corporation in Alexandria, Virginia, a franchiser of security alarm systems, found its growth stifled by a traditional sales force structure. To solve the problem, the company not only restructured the sales force but also the compensation package to get the "biggest bang for the buck."

"In looking at our business growth and studying where our new business was coming from, we found that we were going back to existing customers for the majority of our new business," says William Meares, chief operating officer of Sonitrol. Management realized that to take full advantage of growth opportunities in the marketplace, the company would need to continue doing as much business as possible with existing customers, as well as make organized and assertive efforts to do more business with new customers.

The sales force was not in a position to achieve both goals. Salespeople spent part of their time serving existing customers and part of their time looking for new customers, an approach that was not working well. "We found that our salespeople had different skill sets," says Meares. Some were natural "hunters," who enjoyed going out and finding new business but felt constrained by having to nurture their existing customer base. Others were natural "nurturers," who were uncomfortable cold calling for new business but thrived on serving existing customers.

To eliminate these structural roadblocks, management elected to make some significant changes in the sales force. First, the department "divided," so that it could better "conquer" the marketplace. A number of salespeople, now called "account managers," were targeted to specialize in seeking new business. The rest of the salespeople, now called "client salespeople," were designated to serve the needs of existing customers and to look for new business opportunities within this established customer base.

To compensate appropriately for the new structure, the company revised its compensation system from a traditional combination of salary and commission to the following:

- Account managers, who spend their time seeking new business, receive a small salary and a strong commission plan.
- Client salespeople, who spend their time with existing customers, receive a larger base salary and a smaller commission plan.

Although the company already had a comprehensive training program, it improved the training by offering advanced courses in generating new business (for the account managers) and in customer service (for the client salespeople). "We are constantly tailoring our training to the needs of our people," says Doreen Levins, vice president of marketing.

The results: The company, which owns about 25 percent of its franchises, has implemented the new program in them. Many of the independent franchises also have adopted the program. When it was introduced, a few salespeople felt uncomfortable with the proposed compensation structure and left the company. "However, many of these people have come back to us," says Levins.

Overall, sales have increased over the last year, thanks in large part to the new structure. "Our franchisees who have implemented the program tell us that they couldn't run their businesses today without it," concludes Meares.

Case History No. 8: Automobile Protection Corporation, Atlanta

Overview: *How a unique incentive program keeps a sales force motivated.*

"To continually motivate salespeople, you need to appeal to several of their instincts," says Larry Dorfman, president and CEO of Automobile Protection Corporation in Atlanta. "On one level, salespeople want immediate gratification. They realize that reaching long-term goals is important, but achieving short-term goals brings quicker results. A compensation program that provides a payout 12 months from now will get some salespeople involved, but not most." For this reason, Dorfman continually looks for ways to motivate salespeople for the short term.

On what does he base motivation compensation? He focuses on a variety of things, but one of the most important is customer service. "We sell extended vehicle warranty service contracts to automobile dealers around the nation," he says. "These dealers then offer the coverage to their customers. Dealers need to develop a great deal of confidence in our ability to process claims if customers' vehicles break down."

As a way to motivate the salespeople to provide top-notch service to the dealers to whom they sell the contracts, Dorfman offers cash bonuses for letters of recommendation from the dealers.

Three months before each of the semiannual sales meetings, he announces the contest and encourages the salespeople to get busy. During those three months, the salespeople ask the dealers with whom they do business to write letters to Dorfman detailing the type of service they have been receiving. Salespeople wait a minimum of six months before asking new dealers to write letters, which gives the dealers a chance to assess the level of service they're receiving from the salespeople.

The winners are announced at the semiannual sales meetings. Each salesperson receives $100 for each letter that one of his or her dealers sends to Dorfman. The salesperson with the best letter receives $500. The salesperson with the most letters also receives $500.

The letter campaign provides three benefits:
1. It encourages the salespeople to do the very best work they can for their customers.
2. It gives Dorfman a good idea of which salespeople are providing the best service and which ones may need some additional training in customer service.
3. The letters provide excellent third-party references for the salespeople to use when meeting with new prospects.

Case History No. 9: Oracle Corporation, Herndon, Virginia

Overview: *How knowing what motivates different people can help you communicate with them in a way that gets results.*

Greg Christensen, branch manager for Oracle Corporation's Herndon, Virginia, office, has been motivated by compensation for most of his career, both in the field as a salesperson and now as a branch manager. "I just assumed that everyone else was motivated by money, including all of my salespeople," he says.

He focused virtually all of his motivational strategies on compensation. He dangled the "dollar carrot" in front of his salespeople, and most of his discussions with them — individually and in groups — focused on compensation as the major motivator.

It wasn't until Christensen took a sales management course that things began to change. "As part of the course, the instructor surveyed us on what motivated us," he says. The results surprised Christensen. Although he listed compensation at the top of his list, he found that a number of other managers listed different top motivators, such as accomplishment, advancement, challenge, and recognition.

"I quickly realized that it would be very beneficial for me to survey my own salespeople," he continues. He did, and the results were similar: Although some salespeople cited compensation as their No. 1 motivator, most listed other motivators. "In fact, each of the five motivators — compensation, accomplishment, advancement, challenge, and recognition — was listed as either No. 1 or No. 2 by at least one salesperson," says Christensen.

The implications? Christensen did not attempt to change the branch's compensation system. It is still a balanced and successful combination of base salary, commission, and bonus. What is different is the way in which he communicates with his salespeople — what he emphasizes when he talks with them and what he offers them as incentives.

"We have structured our sales contests differently," he says. "Although they used to be exclusively based on compensation, we now offer other motivators." These include pictures of salespeople displayed prominently in the sales office, a special parking space for the "Rep of the Month," and so on.

When Christensen talks with his salespeople as a group, he now emphasizes all five motivators, rather than just compensation. And when he talks with salespeople individually, he remembers what their No. 1 and No. 2 motivators are and focuses on these during their discussions.

Christensen is also aware that motivators can change over time, based on sales experience, the aging process, changing philosophies, and different needs in life. A few salespeople have shifted from one major motivator to another, but Christensen has not spotted any one trend. He does note, however, a shift in importance to compensation from other motivators when salespeople are in the market to purchase either a home or a vehicle.

This all sounds good on paper, but does it work in the real world? "Yes," replies Christensen. "We have seen improvements in sales performance as a result of expanding the elements of motivation." In many sales contests, for example, he has seen 30 percent improvements in sales performance over what was expected. "In addition, morale has improved overall," he adds.

A final recommendation: "It is important to remember that what motivates you may be completely different from what motivates your salespeople," Christensen says. "It's easy to assume they are motivated the same way you are. If you want to get the most out of your people, don't make this assumption."

CASE HISTORY NO. 10: BT MILLER BUSINESS SYSTEMS, ARLINGTON, TEXAS

Overview: *How to compensate your superstars so they stay productive.*

For a number of years, Jim Miller, now retired chairman of the board of BT Miller Business Systems (Arlington, Texas) found himself quite impressed with the office manager of one of his company's largest customers. In the back of his mind, he always thought she would make a wonderful salesperson. Eventually, the woman left the company and did, indeed, begin working as a salesperson for another company.

"I continued to keep track of her and, as I expected, she was experiencing great success in sales," he says. Miller had discussions with her on occasion to see if she might be interested in coming to work for his company. The first few conversations, although cordial, were unproductive. She was quite happy where she was.

Miller persisted, though, and, one day at lunch, was able to convince the woman to go to work for his company. What had happened? "The company had changed the sales compensation plan, and the superstars ended up making less money," he replies. "This disenchanted her enough to leave and come work for us." The woman not only became a sales superstar at BT Miller, she eventually became general manager of one of the company's branch offices and continued her superstar performance.

Although much of the conventional wisdom suggests that you should change your sales compensation plan every year or two (or at least tweak it on occasion), Miller disagrees with that thinking. He sums up his philosophy of sales compensation in two concise sentences: Create a system that allows your superstars to make a lot of money. Then, don't change the system.

While Miller was with the company, the 100-plus sales force experienced turnover of only 5 percent a year. Most of these were women whose husbands were transferred to different cities. "Very few salespeople ever left our company because they were unhappy," he states.

Miller, author of *The Corporate Coach* (HarperCollins, 1994) and *Best Boss, Worst Boss* (Summit, 1996), frequently talks with sales executives who question the wisdom of large compensation packages for top salespeople. They rationalize their beliefs with statements such as:

- "They couldn't be making this kind of money if we weren't giving them all these great opportunities."
- "They have these large blue-ribbon accounts, so it's easy to sell a lot."

Whether true or not, Miller disagrees with the belief that compensation should therefore be diminished as a result. "Superstars respond to high-stakes compensation," he says. "Marginal performers do not."

If you removed your superstars from their "cushy accounts" and replaced them with average performers, sales would not continue at their existing levels. They would decrease — possibly dramatically. "As long as you are making a lot of money on superstar sales accounts, there is no reason the salespeople themselves shouldn't also be making a lot of money," emphasizes Miller.

In fact, when you consider the profits you make, most sales compensation is paltry in comparison. Before Miller retired, he had a special incentive plan: He awarded four "dream vacations" to Hawaii each year to top salespeople, based on volume sales in four different categories. "We were doing $150 million in sales at the time," he says. "Each trip was worth $6,000, all expenses paid, including ocean-front condos." The total expenditure: $24,000. "You better believe it was worth it!" exclaims Miller.

He also disagrees with executives who like to change comp plans frequently. "Companies that change their compensation plans because certain salespeople are making too much money are making a mistake," he says. "You should never cut back on a sales comp program as long as you continue to make money on the effort." When you do, according to Miller, your poor performers stay and most of your average performers stay. These are the two groups least affected by the cut in top-level compensation. But the very people you want to keep — your top performers — will bail out in no time.

Another problem: "Anytime you play with the sales comp program, the distrust factor goes up," he says. "Even if you just tweak it every once in a while, your top performers become restless. Many of them start looking elsewhere for employment."

Finally, don't forget nonfinancial compensation. It can have just as meaningful an impact on top performers as the "big bucks." When Miller was a salesperson years ago, his boss would offer "Tiger of the Month" awards. The winning salesperson would receive a small toy tiger to display on his or her desk. "I'm sure those things didn't cost my boss more than 49 cents each at Woolworth's," he says, "but I wanted more tigers than anyone else, and I worked hard to get them!"

CASE HISTORY NO. 11: PHOENIX TECHNOLOGIES LTD., SAN JOSE, CALIFORNIA

Overview: *How one company restructured its comp plan to reflect its transformation into a global enterprise.*

For years, the way Phoenix Technologies Ltd. (San Jose, California) organized its sales regions and compensated its sales force made sense. Gradually, as the computer industry and market changed, the company realized it made sense to restructure its compensation program. "Some new dynamics in the computer industry no longer matched up with the way our regions were laid out," notes David Everett, vice president of Worldwide Field Operations. "While we were still arranged regionally, the computer industry had become a global village. Most customers were requiring multiple-region and even multiple-continent development cycles, which required multiregional sales and marketing coordination."

The problem: Customers with operations in many regions were requiring coordinated efforts from Phoenix, rather than making individual purchases at each of their facilities. The mismatch was causing unhealthy internal competition and less-than-efficient selling activity and customer responsiveness. "In the past, incentive compensation was driven by regional revenue, so it was important to each salesperson that revenue be consummated in his or her territory," says Everett. "If it wasn't, the salesperson would receive zero commission for that sale, even though he or she had assisted in the overall sale."

Management elected to identify a compensation program that would turn the negative situation into a positive one — a program that would take full advantage of the evolving marketplace. "We wanted a program that would help us energize ourselves," says Everett. He says the new compensation program has three elements:

1. **Individual revenue.** The company still has a number of customers who have single locations, or multiple locations within a single region, in which sales take place completely within that sales region.
2. **Teamed revenue.** This component of the incentive compensation is based on the teamwork that takes place among salespeople in two or more regions working together with a customer who has locations in two or more regions.
3. **Stated individual objectives.** This component covers compensation for individual objectives, such as number of prospects turned into customers.

The results: The new system, selected in July 1996 and implemented three months later, has been an overwhelming success. "It has led to a lot more communication among salespeople and a major increase in cooperation," states Everett.

The success of the program has even resulted in a strategic improvement. "The program helped us realize the value of reassessing our overall regional sales concept," he says. "We have since realigned some regions." For example, after realizing that many of its large original equipment manufacturer customers in the United States are dependent on design and supply from Taiwan, Phoenix combined its North American and Taiwan regions, creating a seamless selling effort in these areas.

Overview: *How varying incentive programs can motivate your team.*

Sales compensation at Premenos Corporation in Concord, California, is based on a 50-50 split between base and commission. Beyond base and commission, it's all up in the air, and it's meant to be that way. "Our incentives are never the same, and there are some good reasons for it being this way," says Gary Ludlow, vice president of North American sales.

Incentives vary in terms of what is measured, the details of the current program, and the time of year the program will be introduced. Everything is always a surprise, and this helps to ensure that the salespeople are always working to the best of their abilities and not wasting time trying to plan for certain programs or "sandbagging" until a program comes into play.

The company sets its sales incentive program goals based on overall company strategic goals. "What gets measured gets done," says Ludlow. Once the corporate goals are established and communicated, the incentive program is determined. "The most common incentive program goal relates to revenue, because this is always one of our strategic goals," he adds.

However, salespeople can't always assume this will be the only measurement. At times, an incentive program will be set up to reward something else, such as the number of sales completed in a certain period of time.

Even the way the programs are handled can differ. For example, during one recent contest, each salesperson was able to draw a slip of paper from a hat for each new account signed during the quarter. "Each slip of paper represented incentives of different prizes and values," says Ludlow. "These included prizes such as $5 to $50 in cash, CDs, cameras, TVs, or weekend trips. These incentives change every once in a while to help add energy and make the programs more interesting and fun."

The timing of incentive programs varies, and salespeople can't be absolutely positive when a particular program will run. This keeps them guessing — and on their toes. "They know that they always need to be performing, and it prevents them from 'sandbagging,'" notes Ludlow. In fact, it's not uncommon for Premenos to announce a monthlong sales incentive program being measured in the middle of the month! These "retroactive" programs have value for two reasons:

- The salespeople are always working hard all year long, never knowing when they are being measured.
- If they find themselves a bit behind when the program is announced, they still have the second half of the allotted time to achieve the required goals.

For example: The company sets annual quotas for its salespeople. However, it expects them to be on track all year long, rather than slide the first part of the year and then try to catch up near the end. As a way to encourage this consistency, the company may announce a surprise one-month incentive program at midyear, with rewards based on being "on track" with year-to-date goals. "Most of the salespeople will already be on track when we announce the contest," says Ludlow. "Those who are not still have time before the end of the month to get back on track."

If your salespeople need an extra boost, you might want to try varying the incentive programs at your company. It could add just the amount of excitement your team has been lacking.

PARTICIPATING COMPANIES BY STANDARD INDUSTRIAL CLASSIFICATION (SIC) CODE — 4 DIGIT LISTINGS

To help users of this survey select relevant comparator groups when comparing their company's data with data in this survey, we have again expanded our SIC reporting method to include four digits. Our previous three-digit listing immediately follows our expanded listing. The following types of companies are represented in this edition of *Dartnell's Sales Force Compensation Survey*:

Agriculture, Forestry, and Fishing
Agricultural Production — Crops
0191   Farms

Agricultural Production/Livestock
0211   Livestock Feeding

Fishing, Hunting, and Trapping
0921   Fish Hatcheries

Mining and Quarrying-Nonmetallic Minerals
1429   Stone-Crushed

Construction
Building Construction — General Contractors — Home Builders
1521   Garage Builders
1523   General Contractors
1541   Designers Industrial
1542   Buildings — Precut, Prefabricated, and Modular

Construction — Special Trade Contractors
1711   Heating/Air-Conditioning Contractors
1731   Electric Contractors

Manufacturing
Food and Kindred Products
2011   Meat Packing Plants
2041   Flour and Other Grain Mill Products
2051   Bread and Other Bakery Products
2052   Potato Chips, Corn Chips/Similar Snacks
2099   Food Preparations, Not Elsewhere Classified

Textile Mill Products Manufacturers
2211   Fabrics Manufacturing
2269   Finishers of Textiles, Not Elsewhere Classified

Apparel and Other Finished Products Manufacturers
2339   Womens Misses and Juniors Outerwear, Not Elsewhere Classified
2389   Apparel and Accessories, Not Elsewhere Classified
2399   Fabricated Textile Products, Not Elsewhere Classified

Lumber and Wood Products, Except Furniture
2448   Wood Pallets and Skids
2452   Prefab Wood Buildings and Components

Furniture and Fixtures Manufacturers
2522   Office Furniture, Except Wood
2542   Office and Store Fixtures, Except Wood
2599   Furniture and Fixtures, Not Elsewhere Classified

Paper and Allied Products Manufacturers
2621   Paper Mills
2653   Corrugated and Solid Fiber Boxes
2656   Sanitary Food Containers, Except Folding
2678   Stationery Tablets and Related Products
2679   Converted Paper and Paperboard Products, Not Elsewhere Classified

Printing, Publishing, and Allied Industries
2711   Newspapers, Publishing and Printing
2721   Periodicals, Publishing and Printing
2731   Books, Publishing and Printing
2732   Book Printing
2741   Miscellaneous Publishing
2752   Commercial Printing — Lithographic
2759   Commercial Printing, Not Elsewhere Classified
2771   Greeting Cards
2796   Platemaking and Related Services

Chemicals and Allied Products
2819   Industrial Inorganic Chemicals, Not Elsewhere Classified
2833   Medicinal Chemicals and Botanical Products
2834   Pharmaceutical Preparations
2836   Biological Products — Except Diagnostic
2844   Perfumes, Cosmetics and Other Toilet Preps
2851   Paints, Varnishes, Lacquers, and Enamels
2869   Industrial Organic Chemicals, Not Elsewhere Classified
2875   Fertilizers — Mixing Only
2879   Pesticides and Agricultural Chemicals, Not Elsewhere Classified
2891   Adhesives and Sealants
2895   Carbon Black
2899   Chemicals and Chemical Preparations, Not Elsewhere Classified

Petroleum Refining and Related Industries
2911   Petroleum Refining
2992   Lubricating Oils and Greases

Rubber and Miscellaneous Plastic Manufacturers
3061   Molded Extruded/Lathe-Cut Rubber Goods
3069   Fabricated Rubber Products, Not Elsewhere Classified
3089   Plastic Products, Not Elsewhere Classified

Leather and Leather Products Manufacturers
3149   Footwear — Except Rubber, Not Elsewhere Classified

Stone, Clay, Glass, and Concrete Products Manufacturers
3229   Pressed and Blown Glass and Glassware, Not Elsewhere Classified
3231   Glass Products Made of Purchased Glass
3273   Ready-Mixed Concrete

Primary Metal Industries Manufacturers
3312   Steel Works and Blast Furnaces
3365   Aluminum Foundries
3398   Metal Heating and Treating

Fabricated Metal Products Manufacturers
3411   Metal Cans
3423   Hand and Edge Tools
3429   Hardware, Not Elsewhere Classified
3432   Plumbing Fixtures, Fittings and Trim
3433   Heating Equipment
3441   Fabricated Structural Metal
3444   Sheet Metalwork
3446   Architectural and Ornamental Metalwork
3449   Miscellaneous Structural Metalwork
3465   Automotive Stampings
3466   Crowns and Closures
3469   Metal Stampings, Not Elsewhere Classified
3471   Electroplating and Polishing
3479   Coating, Engraving, and Allied Services, Not Elsewhere Classified
3491   Industrial Valves
3492   Fluid Power Valves and Hose Fittings
3495   Wire Springs
3496   Miscellaneous Fabricated Wire Products
3499   Fabricated Metal Products, Not Elsewhere Classified

Industrial and Commercial Machinery Manufacturers
3511   Steam, Gas, and Hydraulic Turbines
3542   Machine Tools — Metals Forming Types
3545   Cutting Tools and Machine Tool Access
3548   Electric and Gas Welding and Soldering Equipment

3549	Metalworking Machinery, Not Elsewhere Classified
3555	Printing Trades Machinery and Equipment
3556	Food Products Machinery
3559	Special Industry Machinery, Not Elsewhere Classified
3561	Pumps and Pumping Equipment
3562	Ball and Roller Bearings
3563	Air and Gas Compressors
3564	Industrial and Commerical Fans and Blowers
3569	General Industrial Machinery, Not Elsewhere Classified
3571	Electronic Computers
3575	Computer Terminals
3577	Computer Peripheral Equipment, Not Elsewhere Classified
3579	Office Machines, Not Elsewhere Classified
3581	Automatic Vending Machines
3589	Service Industry Machinery, Not Elsewhere Classified
3596	Scales and Balances — Except Laboratory
3599	Industrial and Commerical Machinery, Not Elsewhere Classified

Electronic and Other Electrical Equipment and Components, Except Computer Equipment

33612	Power and Distribution Transformers
3621	Motors and Generators
3629	Electrical Industrial Apparatus, Not Elsewhere Classified
3643	Current-Carrying Wire Devices
3648	Lighting Equipment, Not Elsewhere Classified
3661	Telephone and Telegraph Apparatus
3669	Communications Equipment, Not Elsewhere Classified
3672	Printed Circuit Boards
3674	Semiconductors and Related Devices
3677	Electronic Coils and Transformers
3678	Electronic Connectors
3679	Electronic Components, Not Elsewhere Classified
3694	Electrical Equipment for Internal Combustion Engines
3699	Electrical Machinery Equipment and Supplies, Not Elsewhere Classified

Transportation Equipment Manufacturers

3711	Motor Vehicles and Passenger Car Bodies
3713	Truck and Bus Bodies
3714	Motor Vehicles Parts and Accessories
3715	Truck Trailers
3724	Aircraft Engines and Engine Parts
3743	Railroad Equipment

Measuring, Analyzing, and Controlling Instruments; Photographic, Medical, and Optical Goods; Watches and Clocks

3822	Auto Controls — Regulating Environments
3823	Industrial Instruments for Measurements
3825	Instruments for Measuring Electricity
3826	Laboratory Analytical Instruments
3829	Measuring and Controlling Devices, Not Elsewhere Classified
3841	Surgical Medical Instruments/Apparatus

Miscellaneous Manufacturing Industries

3911   Jewelry — Precious Metal

3949   Sporting and Athletic Goods, Not Elsewhere Classified

3953   Marking Devices

3993   Signs and Advertising Specialties

3999   Manufacturing Industries

Transportation, Communications, Electric, Gas, and Sanitary Service

Railroad Transportation

4011   Railroads

Motor Freight Transportation and Warehousing

4213   Truck, Heavy Hauling

4222   Warehousing — Cold Storage

4225   Warehouses

United States Post Office

4311   Post Offices

Transportation by Air

4512   Airline Companies

4581   Aircraft Servicing and Maintenance

Transportation Services

4724   Travel Agencies and Bureaus

Communications

4812   Cellular Telephones (Services)

4813   Long-Distance Telephone Service

4833   Television Stations and Broadcasting Companies

4841   Television-Cable and CATV

4899   Communications Services — Common Carriers

Electric, Gas, and Sanitary Services

4911   Electric Companies

4924   Gas — Natural

4925   Gas Companies

4941   Water Supply System

4953   Wastes Disposal — Hazardous

Wholesale Trade

Wholesale Trade — Durable Goods

5013   Automobile Parts and Supplies — Wholesale

5021   Office Furniture and Equipment — Wholesale

5023   Floor Materials — Wholesale

5032   Tiles, Ceramic Distributors

5044   Copying and Duplicating Machines and Supplies

5047   Hospital Equipment and Supplies — Wholesale

5063	Power Transmission Equipment — Wholesale
5063	Electronic Equipment and Supplies — Wholesale
5072	Hardware — Wholesale
5074	Plumbing — Fixtures and Supplies — Wholesale
5075	Heating Equipment and Systems — Wholesale
5078	Water Coolers and Filters
5082	Safety Equipment and Clothing — Wholesale
5084	Welding Equipment and Supplies — Wholesale
5085	Valves — Wholesale
5087	Vacuum Equipment and Systems
5099	Distribution Centers

Wholesale Trade — Nondurable Goods

5113	Packaging Materials — Wholesale
5149	Food Service Distributors
5169	Chemical and Allied Products, Not Elsewhere Classified
5172	Fuel Dealers — Wholesale
5193	Plants — Wholesale
5199	Wholesale

Retail Trade

Building Materials, Hardware, Garden Supplies

5211	Roofing Materials
5211	Wood Windows
5211	Building Materials
5261	Fertilizers — Retail

Food Stores

5411	Convenience Stores
5499	Health and Diet Foods — Retail

Automotive Dealers and Gasoline Service Stations

5511	Automobile Dealers — New Cars
5531	Automobile Parts and Supplies — Retail-New
5551	Marine Equipment and Supplies
5561	Trailers — Equipment and Parts

Apparel and Accessory Stores

5699	Sportswear — Retail

Home Furniture, Furnishings, and Equipment Stores

5712	Futons
5713	Floor Materials
5722	Appliances — Household-Small Dealers
5731	Electronic Equipment and Supplies
5734	Computer Software
5736	Musical Instruments — Supplies and Accessories

Miscellaneous Retail

5941	Pool Table Equipment and Supplies
5941	Sporting Goods — Retail
5943	Rubber and Plastic Stamps
5943	Office Supplies
5944	Jewelry Designers
5945	Games and Games Supplies
5947	Novelties — Retail
5999	Cellular Telephones — Equipment and Supplies

Finance, Insurance, and Real Estate

Depository Institutions

6021	Banks
6035	Savings and Loan Associations
6061	Credit Unions
6099	Money Transfer Service

Nondepository Credit Institutions

6162	Real Estate Loans

Security and Commodity Brokers

6282	Investment Management

Insurance Carriers

6311	Life Insurance (Underwriters)
6324	Health Plans
6331	Insurance — Property and Casualty
6351	Bonds — Surety and Fidelity
6371	Employee Benefit and Compensation Plans

Insurance Agents, Brokers, and Service

6411	Insurance Agents, Brokers, and Service

Real Estate

6513	Apartments
6531	Real Estate Investments

Holding and Other Investment Offices

6719	Holding Companies (Nonbank)
6799	Venture Capital Companies

Services

Hotels and Other Lodging Places

7011	Hotels and Motels

Personal Services

7261	Funeral Services, Cemetery Property, and Merchandise
7299	Massage

Business Services

7311   Advertising — Agencies and Counselors
7313   Advertising, Not Elsewhere Classified
7217   Carpet and Rug Cleaners
7319   Advertising — Promotional
7322   Collection Agencies
7331   Advertising — Direct Mail
7342   Pest Control
7349   Janitor Service
7359   Office Equipment and Furniture — Renting
7361   Employment Agencies and Opportunities
7363   Employment Contractors — Temporary Help
7371   Computer Services
7372   Prepackaged Software
7374   Data Processing Service
7378   Computers — Service and Repair
7379   Computer Networking
7381   Security Guard and Patrol Services
7382   Burglar Alarm Systems
7389   Business Services, Not Elsewhere Classified

Automotive Repair, Services, and Parking

7513   Truck Renting and Leasing
7514   Automobile Renting and Leasing

Miscellaneous Repair Services

7699   Repair Shops and Related Services

Motion Pictures

7812   Audiovisual Product Service

Amusement and Recreation Services

7922   Theatrical Managers and Producers
7997   Recreation Centers

Health Services

8021   Dentists
8051   Health Care Facilities
8059   Homes and Institutions
8071   Laboratories — Medical
8099   Health Services

Legal Services

8111   Attorneys

Educational Services

8211   Schools
8243   Computer Training
8249   Schools — Industrial, Technical, and Trade
8299   Training Programs and Services

Social Services

8361   Residential Care Homes

Membership Organizations

8611   Associations

8641   Fraternal Organizations

Engineering, Accounting, and Management Services

8711   Engineers — Consulting

8712   Architects

8721   Payroll Preparation Service

8732   Market Research and Analysis

8734   Air Pollution Measuring Service

8742   Business Management Consultants

8748   Training Consultants

STANDARD INDUSTRIAL CLASSIFICATION (SIC) CODES

Code   Industrial Classification

Agriculture, Forestry, and Fishing
010	Agricultural Production—Crops
020	Agricultural Production—Livestock
070	Agricultural Services
090	Hunting, Fishing, and Trapping

Construction
150	General Building Contractors
160	Heavy Construction Contractors
170	Special Trade Contractors

Manufacturing
200	Food and Kindred Products
210	Tobacco Manufacturers
220	Textile Mill Products
230	Apparel and Other Textile Products
240	Lumber and Wood Products
250	Furniture and Fixtures
260	Paper and Allied Products
270	Printing and Publishing
280	Chemicals and Allied Products
290	Petroleum and Coal Products
300	Rubber and Miscellaneous Plastics Products
320	Stone, Clay, and Glass Products
330	Primary Metal Industries
340	Fabricated Metal Products
350	Machinery, Except Electric
360	Electric and Electronic Equipment
370	Transportation Equipment
380	Instruments and Related Products
390	Miscellaneous Manufacturing Industries

Transportation and Public Utilities
420	Trucking and Warehousing
450	Transportation by Air
470	Transportation Services
480	Communication
490	Electric, Gas, and Sanitary Services

Wholesale Trade (Consumer Goods)
500	Wholesale Trade—Durable Goods

Wholesale Trade (Industrial Goods)
510	Wholesale Trade—Nondurable Goods

Retail Trade
520	Retail—Building Materials and Garden Supplies
530	General Merchandise Stores

540	Food Stores
550	Automotive Dealer and Service Stations
570	Furniture and Home Furnishings Store
590	Miscellaneous Retail Stores

Finance, Insurance, and Real Estate

600	Banking
610	Credit Agencies, Other Than Banks
630	Insurance
640	Insurance Agents, Brokers, and Services
650	Real Estate
670	Holding and Other Investment Offices

Services

700	Hotels and Other Lodging Places
730	Business Services
750	Auto Repair, Services, and Garages
760	Miscellaneous Repair Services
780	Motion Pictures
790	Amusement and Recreation Services
800	Health Services
820	Educational Services
860	Membership Organizations
870	Engineering and Management Services
890	Miscellaneous Services

Descriptions of Job Positions Used in This Survey Edition

1. **Top Marketing Exec** — Typical title: Vice President of Marketing. Directs marketing functions and may oversee international operations, as well as field marketing support and field service. Reports to CEO, President, or Division President.

2. **Top Sales Exec** — Typical title: Vice President of Sales. Directs U.S. sales, has minimal marketing responsibilities, and may oversee field service. Reports to CEO, President, Division President, or Top Marketing Executive.

3. **Regional Sales Manager** — Manages specific region, industry, product or distributor sales. Reports to Top Sales Executive.

4. **District Sales Manager** — Manages a more limited region, industry, or product segment. Reports to Regional Sales Manager.

5. **Senior Sales Rep** — A salesperson with three or more years of sales experience.

6. **Intermediate Sales Rep** — A salesperson with one to three years of sales experience.

7. **Entry-Level Sales Rep** — A salesperson with less than one year of sales experience.

8. **National or Major Account Sales Manager** — Segments accounts and develops account strategies. Manages only National or Major (Key) Account Reps. Reports to Top Sales Executive.

9. **National Account Rep** — Sells to national customers. Typically requires at least seven years of industry-specific experience. Reports to National Account Sales Manager.

10. **Major (Key) Account Rep** — Sells to major (key) accounts with a central purchasing point. Reports to National Account Sales Manager.

This concludes the 30th edition of *Dartnell's Sales Force Compensation Survey*. Readers wishing to share their comments or observations regarding this survey or wanting to become participants in future Dartnell surveys should contact Christen P. Heide, Executive Editor, The Dartnell Corporation, 4660 N. Ravenswood Ave., Chicago, IL 60640-4595; telephone: (800) 621-5463; fax: (800) 327-8635; e-mail: cheide@dartnellcorp.com

NOTES

NOTES

NOTES

NOTES

NOTES

NOTES